AF663849

SOIL ENVIRONMENT AND CONSERVATION

ENV BOOKS SERIES

SOIL ENVIRONMENT AND CONSERVATION

Editors

Dr. Ashok K. Rathoure
Director
Biohm Consultare Pvt. Ltd.,
Surat - 395 007 (Gujarat)
(India)

Dr. Pawan Kumar 'Bharti'
Society for Environment, Health Awareness of Nutrition & Toxicology (SEHAT)
B-225/5D, Top Floor, Subhash Gali, Road No. 7, Block B
Ashok Nagar, Shahdara, Delhi - 110 093
(India)

&

Dr. Alka Chauhan
Society for Environment, Health Awareness of Nutrition & Toxicology (SEHAT)
B-225/5D, Top Floor, Subhash Gali, Road No. 7, Block B
Ashok Nagar, Shahdara, Delhi - 110 093

DPH

DISCOVERY PUBLISHING HOUSE PVT. LTD.
INDIA

Published by:
Namit Wasan
DISCOVERY PUBLISHING HOUSE PVT. LTD.
4383/4B, Ansari Road, Darya Ganj
New Delhi-110 002 (India)
Phone : +91-11-23279245; 23253475; 43596065
E-mail : discoverybooksindia@gmail.com
discoverypublishinghouse@gmail.com
namitwasan9@gmail.com
web : www.discoverypublishinggroup.com

***First Edition:* 2019**

ISBN: 978-93-88854-10-8

Soil Environment and Conservation

© Editors

All rights reserved. No part of this publication should be reproduced, stored in a retrieval system, or transmitted in any form or by any means: electronic, mechanical, photocopying, recording or otherwise, without the prior written permission of the author and the publisher.

This book has been published in good faith that the material provided by authors/editors is original. Every effort is made to ensure accuracy of material, but the publisher and printer will not be held responsible for any inadvertent error(s). In case of any dispute, all legal matters are to be settled under Delhi jurisdiction only.

Printed at:
Infinity Imaging Systems
Delhi

PREFACE

Developmental activities carry with them the seeds of environmental damage, assisted and abetted by both needs and greed of man. Activities such as manufacturing, processing, transportation and consumption not only deplete the stock of natural resources but also add stress to the environmental system by accumulating the stock of wastes. The productivity of the economic system, however, depends on the supply and quality of natural and environmental resources. While water, soil, air, forest and fisheries resources are productive assets, the pollution of water, air, atmosphere and noise are the by-products of economic development.

Nutrient cycling, water regulation and other soil functions are normal processes occurring in all ecosystems. From these functions come many benefits to humans, such as food production, water quality and flood control, which have value economically or in improved quality of life. People can increase or decrease the value of soil benefits because land-management choices affect soil functions. Thus, it is important to understand what benefits we derive from soil and their value so we can appreciate the importance of managing land in a way that maintains soil functions. People tend to emphasize benefits with the most direct, private economic value.

The present book updates the subject content of soil quality characteristics, soil analysis, edaphic ecosystem, soil amendment techniques and soil conservation.

Thanks are due to publisher and contributors from various institutions and universities.

The book will be helpful for the researchers, academia working in the field of soil quality characteristics, soil analysis, edaphic ecosystem, soil amendment techniques and soil conservation.

Editors
(envbooks@gmail.com)

PREFACE

CONTENTS

Soil Environment and Conservation **Pages 1-11**
Edited by: **Dr. Ashok K. Rathoure; Dr. Pawan Kumar 'Bharti' and Dr. Alka Chauhan**
ISBN: 978-93-88854-10-8
Edition: **2019**
Published by: **Discovery Publishing House Pvt. Ltd., New Delhi (India)**

1

Soil Quality and Soil Sustainability

[1]Dr. Ashok K. Rathoure

ABSTRACT

Soil is an important and complex part of our environment. The agro-ecosystem is made up of many interacting components with multiple goals. Soil quality is one important part of sustainable agro-ecosystem management, analogous to water and air quality. Assessing soil quality may help managers identify practices that could be adapted to become more sustainable. Soil quality is the ability of a soil to perform functions that are essential to people and the environment. Soil quality is not limited to agricultural soils, although most soil quality work has been done in agricultural systems. Soil quality definitions emphasize several features. Dynamic properties include organic matter, soil structure, infiltration rate, bulk density, and water and nutrient holding capacity. Changes in dynamic properties depend both on land management practices and the inherent properties of the soil.

Introduction

Soil is an important and complex part of our environment. As per Miller and Wali, (1995) sustainability lies in the dynamic nature of its fundamental components: ecological (spatial and temporal relations, diversity, stability and resilience; economic (resource distribution and allocation); and social (equity, access, stewardship and institutions). The agro-ecosystem is made up of many interacting components with multiple goals. Soil quality is one important part of sustainable agro-ecosystem management, analogous to water and air quality. Assessing soil quality may help managers identify practices that could be adapted to become more sustainable. Soil quality is one aspect of sustainable agro-ecosystem management. Soil quality is the ability of a soil to perform functions that are essential to people and the environment. Soil quality is not limited to agricultural soils, although most soil quality work has been done in agricultural systems.

[1] Independent Researcher, India, Eco Chem Sales & Services Surat

Background

Soil quality assessments focus on the dynamic, or management-affected, properties of soil, such as nutrient status, salinity and water-holding capacity. These properties are assessed in the context of the inherent capability of a particular soil. Soils support plant growth, recycle dead material, regulate and filter water flows, support buildings and roads and provide habitat for many plants and animals. Depending on the land use, many of these functions occur simultaneously. Soil quality assessments go beyond measuring degradation (erosion, compaction or contamination) to focus on these soil functions and the processes that create them. Soil functions provide private benefits such as crop production or structural support for buildings (Karlen, 2001). Simultaneously, the same soil may provide societal benefits such as carbon sequestration, water quality protection, or preservation of soil productivity for future generations. Evaluating soil quality requires that we identify and prioritize these benefits and pay attention to the interactions and trade offs among them. The ability to continue providing essential services in the face of disturbance, whether natural or human induced, is essential to maintain or improve soil quality over time. A soil is not considered healthy if it is managed for short term productivity at the expense of future degradation (Doran *et al.*, 1994).

Soil quality cannot be measured directly because it is a broad, integrative, context-dependent concept. Indicators of soil quality may include characteristics of soil solids, soil solutions, soil atmospheres, vegetation and other soil biota and possibly even economic analyses of land-uses or ecosystem services. Although the quantity and quality of data may differ, the process of soil quality evaluation follows the same basic steps regardless of the method used: identification of soil use issues followed by indicator selection and interpretation. More specifically, in order to select appropriate indicators, one must first determine the land-use objectives and then indicators must be proposed, measured and assessed across a representative set of lands and management practices.

Intrinsic and Vigorous Properties of Soil

The quality of a soil is a combination of intrinsic and vigorous soil properties. The focus of most soil quality work is vigorous soil properties and how they change in relation to the intrinsic features of the soil. Inherent or use-invariant properties change little, if at all, with land use or management practices. They may include soil texture, depth to bedrock, type of clay, CEC and drainage class. These properties were established as soil formed over millennia. The soil form depends on the five soil-forming factors (Jenny, 1941):

- Climate (precipitation and temperature),
- Topography (shape of the land),
- Biota (native vegetation, animals and microbes),

- Parent material (geologic and organic precursors to the soil),
- Time (time that parent material is subject to soil formation processes).

Dynamic properties or use-dependent properties can change over the course of months and years in response to land use or management practice changes. Dynamic properties include organic matter, soil structure, infiltration rate, bulk density and water and nutrient holding capacity. Changes in dynamic properties depend both on land management practices and the inherent properties of the soil. For example, the organic matter levels in soil depend on tillage practices and the types of plants growing (management), but the total amount of organic matter is constrained by soil texture and climate (inherent features).

Value of Soil

Nutrient cycling, water regulation and other soil functions are normal processes occurring in all ecosystems. From these functions come many benefits to humans, such as food production, water quality and flood control, which have value economically or in improved quality of life. People can increase or decrease the value of soil benefits because land-management choices affect soil functions. Thus, it is important to understand what benefits we derive from soil and their value so we can appreciate the importance of managing land in a way that maintains soil functions. People tend to emphasize benefits with the most direct, private economic value. In rural areas, this is usually plant growth especially as crops and rangeland, but also as recreation areas. In urban/suburban areas, the most direct economic benefits of soil relate to structural support for buildings, roads and parking. Landscaping, gardening and park lands may also be valued economically. Those are all on-site, short-term benefits. That is, the landowner who decides how to manage the soil also reaps the benefits of those management decisions. In contrast, many important benefits are long-term or go beyond the land being managed.

Aggregate Stability

Soil aggregates are groups of soil particles that bind to each other more strongly than to adjacent particles. Aggregate stability refers to the ability of soil aggregates to resist disintegration when disruptive forces associated with tillage and water or wind erosion are applied. Wet aggregate stability suggests how well a soil can resist raindrop impact and water erosion, while size distribution of dry aggregates can be used to predict resistance to abrasion and wind erosion.

Changes in aggregate stability may serve as early indicators of recovery or degradation of soils. Aggregate stability is an indicator of organic matter content, biological activity and nutrient cycling in soil. Generally, the particles in small aggregates (< 0.25 mm) are bound by older and more stable forms of organic matter. Microbial decomposition of fresh organic matter releases products that bind small aggregates into large aggregates (> 2-5 mm). These large aggregates are more sensitive to management effects on organic matter, serving as a better indicator of changes in soil quality. Greater amounts of stable aggregates suggest better soil quality. When the proportion of large to small aggregates increases, soil quality generally increases. Stable aggregates can also provide a large range in pore space, including small pores within and large pores between aggregates. Pore space is essential for air and water entry into soil and for air, water, nutrient and biota movement within soil. Large pores associated with large, stable aggregates favor high infiltration rates and appropriate aeration for plant growth. Pore space also provides zones of weakness for root growth and penetration. Surface crusts and filled pores occur in weakly aggregated soils. Surface crusts prevent infiltration and promote erosion; filled pores lower water-holding and air-exchange capacity and increase bulk density, diminishing the conditions for root growth. Aggregate stability is critical for infiltration, root growth and resistance to water and wind erosion. Unstable aggregates disintegrate during rainstorms. Dispersed soil particles fill surface pores and a hard physical crust can develop when the soil dries. Infiltration is reduced, which can result in increased runoff and water erosion and reduced water available in the soil for plant growth. A physical crust can also restrict seedling emergence. Wind normally detaches only loosely held particles on the soil surface, but as blowing soil particles are accelerated by the wind they hit bare soil with sufficient energy to break additional particles loose from weakly aggregated soil.

Practices that lead to poor aggregate stability include:

- Tillage methods and soil disturbance activities that breakdown plant organic matter, prevent accumulation of soil organic matter and disrupt existing aggregates,
- Cropping, grazing, or other production systems that leave soil bare and expose it to the physical impact of raindrops or wind-blown soil particles,
- Removing sources of organic matter and surface roughness by burning, harvesting or otherwise removing crop residues,
- Using pesticides harmful to beneficial soil microorganisms.

Conservation practices resulting in aggregate stability favorable to soil function include:

- Conservation Crop Rotation,
- Cover Crop,
- Pest Management,
- Prescribed Grazing,
- Residue and Tillage Management,

- Salinity and Sodic Soil Management,
- Surface Roughening.

Loss of Organic Matter

The plow is a potent tool of agriculture for the same reason that it has degraded productivity. Plowing turns over soil, mixes it with air and stimulates the decomposition of organic matter. The rapid decomposition of organic matter releases a flush of nutrients that stimulates crop growth. But over time, plowing diminishes the supply of soil organic matter and associated soil properties, including water holding capacity, nutrient holding capacity, mellow tilth, resistance to erosion and a diverse biological community. After several decades of farming using intense tillage and much lower inputs of new organic matter, much of that land lost up to half of its original organic matter. Sandy lands that once contained 2% organic matter are now below 1%. Rich prairie loam that carried 8% or more is now at 4%. The initial rise in atmospheric CO_2 levels can be explained largely by the conversion of soil organic matter into CO_2 and by the conversion of forests to other land uses. Soil organic matter in some regions began to stabilize or rise slightly as farmers began to use higher yielding varieties, apply fertilizers and remove less straw at harvest (Cole *et al.*, 1990). Improved yields have been important in improving soil organic matter levels over the past few decades (Allmaras *et al.*, 1998, 2000).

Soil Enzymes

Soil enzymes increase the reaction rate at which plant residues decompose and release plant available nutrients. The substance acted upon by a soil enzyme is called the substrate. For example, glucosidase (soil enzyme) cleaves glucose from glucoside (substrate), a compound common in plants. Enzymes are specific to a substrate and have active sites that bind with the substrate to form a temporary complex. The enzymatic reaction releases a product, which can be a nutrient contained in the substrate. Sources of soil enzymes include living and dead microbes, plant roots and residues and soil animals. Enzymes stabilized in the soil matrix accumulate or form complexes with organic matter (humus), clay and humus-claycomplexes, but are no longer associated with viable cells. It is thought that 40 to 60% of enzyme activity can come from stabilized enzymes, so activity does not necessarily correlate highly with microbial biomass or respiration. Therefore, enzyme activity is the cumulative effect of long term microbial activity and activity of the viable population at sampling. However, an example of an enzyme that only reflects activity of viable cells is dehydrogenase, which in theory can only occur in viable cells and not in stabilized soil complexes. Enzymes respond to soil management changes long before other soil quality indicator changes are detectable. Soil enzymes play an important role in organic matter decomposition and nutrient cycling. Some enzymes only facilitate the breakdown of organic matter *e.g.*

hydrolase, glucosidase, while others are involved in nutrient mineralization *e.g.* amidase, urease, phosphatase, sulfates. With the exception of phosphatase activity, there is no strong evidence that directly relates enzyme activity to nutrient availability or crop production. The relationship may be indirect considering nutrient mineralization to plant available forms is accomplished with the contribution of enzyme activity. Absence or suppression of soil enzymes prevents or reduces processes that can affect plant nutrition. Poor enzyme activity *e.g.* pesticide degrading enzymes can result in an accumulation of chemicals that are harmful to the environment; some of these chemicals may further inhibit soil enzyme activity. Organic amendment applications, crop rotation and cover crops have been shown to enhance enzyme activity. The positive effect of pasture is associated with the input of animal manure and less soil disturbance. Agricultural methods that modify soil pH can also change enzyme activity.

Soil Structure and Macropores

Sand, silt and clay particles are the primary mineral building blocks of soil. Soil structure is the combination or arrangement of primary soil particles into aggregates. Using aggregate size, shape and distinctness as the basis for classes, types and grades, respectively, soil structure describes the manner in which soil particles are aggregated. Soil structure affects water and air movement through soil, greatly influencing soil's ability to sustain life and perform other vital soil functions. Soil pores exist between and within aggregates and are occupied by water and air. Macro-pores are large soil pores, usually between aggregates, that are generally greater than 0.08 mm in diameter. Macro-pores drain freely by gravity and allow easy movement of water and air. They provide habitat for soil organisms and plant roots can grow into them. With diameters less than 0.08 mm, micro-pores are small soil pores usually found within structural aggregates. Suction is required to remove water from micro-pores. Important soil functions related to soil structure are: sustaining biological productivity, regulating and partitioning water and solute flow and cycling and storing nutrients. Soil structure and macro-pores are vital to each of these functions based on their influence on water and air exchange, plant root exploration and habitat for soil organisms. Granular structure is typically associated with surface soils, particularly those with high organic matter. Granular structure is characterized by loosely packed, crumbly soil aggregates and an interconnected network of macro-pores that allow rapid infiltration and promote biological productivity. Structure and pore space of subsurface layers affects drainage, aeration and root penetration.

Clay soils with poor structure and reduced infiltration may experience runoff, erosion and surface crusting. On-site impacts include erosion-induced nutrient and soil loss and poor germination and seedling emergence due to crusted soil. Off-site impacts include reduced quality of receiving waters due to turbidity, sedimentation and nutrient enrichment. Water entry into a sandy soil can be rapid, but subsurface drainage of sandy soils with poor structure can also be rapid such that the soil cannot hold water needed for plant growth or biological habitat.

Practices that lead to poor soil structure include:

- Disturbance that exposes soil to the adverse effects of higher than normal soil drying, raindrop and rill erosion and wind erosion.
- Conventional tillage and soil disturbance that accelerates organic matter decomposition.
- Residue harvest, burning or other removal methods that prevent accumulation of soil organic matter.
- Overgrazing that weakens range and forage plants and leads to declining root systems, poor growth and bare soil.
- Equipment or livestock traffic on wet soils.
- Production and irrigation methods that lead to salt or sodium accumulation in surface soils.

Practices that provide soil cover, protect or result in accumulation of organic matter, maintain healthy plants and avoid compaction improve soil structure and increase macro-pores.Practices resulting in improved soil structure and greater occurrence of macro-pores favorable to soil function include:

- Cover Crop,
- Conservation Crop Rotation,
- Irrigation Water Management,
- Prescribed Grazing,
- Residue and Tillage Management,
- Salinity and Sodic Soil Management.

Total Organic Carbon

Total organic carbon (TOC) is the carbon (C) stored in soil organic matter (SOM). Organic carbon (OC) enters the soil through the decomposition of plant and animal residues, root exudates, living and dead microorganisms and soil biota. SOM is the organic fraction of soil exclusive of non-decomposed plant and animal residues. Nevertheless, most analytical methods do not distinguish between decomposed and non-decomposed residues. SOM is a heterogeneous, dynamic substance that varies in particle size, C content, decomposition rate and turnover time.

Soil Organic Carbon

Soil Organic Carbon (SOC) is the main source of energy for soil microorganisms. The ease and speed with which SOC becomes available is related to the SOM fraction in which it resides. In this respect, SOC can be partitioned into fractions based on the size and breakdown rates of the SOM in which it is contained. The first three fractions listed are part of the active pool of SOM. Carbon sources in the active pool are relatively easy to break down. SOM contains approximately 58% C; therefore, a factor of 1.72 can be used to convert OC to SOM. There is more inorganic C than TOC in calcareous soils. TOC is expressed as percent C per 100 g of soil. SOC is one of the most important constituents of the soil due to its capacity to affect plant growth as both a source of energy and a trigger for nutrient availability through mineralization. SOC fractions in the active pool, previously described, are the main source of energy and nutrients for soil microorganisms. Humus participates in aggregate stability and nutrient and water holding capacity. OC compounds, such as polysaccharides bind mineral particles together into micro-aggregates. Glomalin, a SOM substance that may account for 20% of soil carbon, glues aggregates together and stabilizes soil structure making soil resistant to erosion, but porous enough to allow air, water and plant roots to move through the soil. Organic acids *e.g.* oxalic acid, commonly released from decomposing organic residues and manures, prevents phosphorus fixation by clay minerals and improve its plant availability, especially in subtropical and tropical soils. An increase in SOM and therefore total C, leads to greater biological diversity in the soil, thus increasing biological control of plant diseases and pests. Data also reveals that interaction between dissolved OC released from manure with pesticides may increase or decrease pesticide movement through soil into groundwater. A direct effect of poor SOC is reduced microbial biomass, activity and nutrient mineralization due to a shortage of energy sources. In non-calcareous soils, aggregate stability, infiltration, drainage and airflow are reduced. Scarce SOC results in less diversity in soil biota with a risk of the food chain equilibrium being disrupted, which can cause disturbance in the soil environment.

Soil Quality Management

An important function of soil is to buffer and detoxify chemicals, but soil's capacity for detoxification is limited. Pesticides and chemical fertilizers have valuable benefits, but they also can harm non-target organisms and pollute water and air if they are mismanaged. Nutrients from organic sources also can pollute when misapplied or over-applied. Efficient pest and nutrient management means testing and monitoring soil and pests; applying only the necessary chemicals, at the right time and place to get the job done; and taking advantage of non-chemical approaches to pest and nutrient management such as crop rotations, cover crops and manure management. Regular additions of organic matter improve soil structure, enhance water and nutrient holding capacity, protect soil from erosion and compaction and support a healthy community of soil organisms (Lal *et al.*, 1998). Practices that increase organic matter include: leaving crop residues in the field, choosing crop rotations that include high residue plants, using optimal nutrient and water management practices to grow healthy plants with large amounts of roots and residue, growing cover crops, applying manure or compost, using low or no tillage systems, using sod-based rotations, growing perennial forage crops and mulching (Ditzler, 2002).

Compaction reduces the amount of air, water and space available to roots and soil organisms. Compaction is caused by repeated traffic, heavy traffic, or traveling on wet soil. Deep compaction by heavy equipment is difficult or impossible to remedy, so prevention is essential. Subsoil tillage is only effective on soils with a clearly defined root-restricting plow pan. In the absence of a plow pan, subsoil tillage to eliminate compaction can reduce yield. Prevention, not tillage, is the way to manage compaction (Moebius, 2007).

Bare soil is susceptible to wind and water erosion and to drying and crusting. Ground cover protects soil, provides habitats for larger soil organisms, such as insects and earthworms and can improve water availability. Ground can be covered by leaving crop residue on the surface or by planting cover crops. In addition to ground cover, living cover crops provide additional organic matter and continuous cover and food for soil organisms. Ground cover must be managed to prevent problems with delayed soil warming in spring, diseases and excessive build-up of phosphorus at the surface (Pankhurst, 1997).

Diversity is beneficial for several reasons. Each plant contributes a unique root structure and type of residue to the soil. A diversity of soil organisms can help control pest populations and a diversity of cultural practices can reduce weed and disease pressures. Diversity across the landscape can be increased by using buffer strips, small fields, or contour strip cropping. Diversity over time can be increased by using long crop rotations. Changing vegetation across the landscape or over time not only increases plant diversity, but also the types of insects, microorganisms and wildlife (Pankhurst *et al.*, 1997; Magdoff, 1992; Coleman and Crossley, 1996; Lal, 1998).

Conclusion

Both soil and water are crucial natural resources which are essential for life on earth. Because of the position soils occupy at the surface of the earth and the fact that they receive huge quantities of water which they then help to re-distribute, there is an important relationship between soils and water. The soil health is the capacity of soil to function as a vital living system, within ecosystem and land-use boundaries, to sustain plant and animal productivity, maintain or enhance water and air quality, and promote plant and animal health. Anthropogenic reductions in soil health, and of individual components of soil quality, are a pressing ecological concern. The soil can only be assessed for the particular purposes for which it is to be used, such as suitability of soils for a particular crop or a particular program. Properties of soils ideal for one use may not be the ones useful for another use. There are several fundamental properties of soils that influence soil quality. A well balanced healthy soil is one that is likely to be the most robust and capable of meeting the requirements for a wide range of uses. Some properties, such as texture, are static and cannot be changed readily. Others are more sensitive to change and it is these that we need to monitor carefully to maintain optimum levels. One of the most important is organic matter because it contributes to many functions, such as stability of soil structure, water holding capacity, nutrient-supplying power, and is the food for the huge numbers of organisms that live in the soil. Hence it is usually the number one selection in any monitoring of soils, now particularly because of it large potential impact on climate change. Soil acidity or pH, is another usually essential indicator to be monitored particularly because of the sensitivity of some plants to changes in pH. The agro-ecosystem is made up of many interacting components with multiple goals. Soil quality is one important part of sustainable agro-ecosystem management, analogous to water and air quality. Assessing soil quality may help agronomist to identify practices that could be adapted to become more sustainable.

REFERENCES

Allmaras, R.R., H.H. Schomberg, C.L. Douglas Jr. and T.H. Dao.(2000). Soil Organic Carbon Sequestration Potential of Adopting Conservation Tillage in U.S. Croplands. Journal of Soil and Water Conservation 55:365-373.

Allmaras, R.R., D.E. Wilkins, O.C. Burnside and J.D. Mulla.(1998). Agricultural Technology and Adoption of Conservation Practices. In: F.J. Pierce and W.W. Frye, eds. Advances in Soil and Water Conservation. Chelsea: Ann Arbor Press.

Cole, C.V., I.C. Burke, W.J. Parton, D.S. Schimel, D.S. Ojima and J.W.B. Stewart.(1990). Analysis of Historical Changes in Soil Fertility and Organic Matter Levels of the North American Great Plains. In: P.W. Unger, T.V. Sneed and R.W. Jensen, eds. Proc. International Conference on Dryland Farming, Amarillo, TX, 15-19 Aug. 1988. Texas A&M University, College Station, TX.

Coleman, D.C., and D.A. Crossley, Jr. (1996). Fundamentals of Soil Ecology. Academic Press, San Diego CA. http://www.academicpress.com.

Ditzler, C.A. and A.J. Tugel.(2002). Soil Quality Field Tools: Experiences of USDA-NRCS Soil Quality Institute. Agronomy Journal 94: 33-38.

Doran, J.W., D.C. Coleman, D.F. Bezdicek and B.A. Stewart.(1994). Defining Soil Quality for a Sustainable Environment. SSSA Spec. Publ. No. 35, Soil Sci. Soc. Am., Inc. and Am. Soc. Agron., Inc., Madison, WI.

Doran JW, Jones AJ, editors.Methods for Assessing Soil Quality. Madison, WI. p. 123-41.

Jenny, H. (1941). Factors of Soil Formation: A System of Quantitative Pedolog. Dover Pub., Mineola, N.Y.

Karlen, D.L., S.S., Andrews, and J.W. Doran. (2001). Soil Quality: Current Concepts and Applications. Advances in Agronomy, Vol. 74. pp. 1-39.

Lal, R. (Editor). (1998). Soil Quality and Soil Erosion. CRC Press, Boca Raton.

Lal, R., J.M. Kimble, R.F. Follet, and B.A. Stewart (Eds).(1998). Management of Carbon Sequestration in Soil. CRC Press, Boca Raton.

Miller, F.P. and M.K. Wali.(1995). Soils, Land Use and Sustainable Agriculture: A Review. Canadian Journal of Soil Science. 75 (4): 413-422.

Moebius, B.N., H.M. van Es, R.R. Schindelbeck, O.J. Idowu, J.E. Thies, and D.J. Clune.(2007). Evaluation of Laboratory-Measured Soil Properties as Indicators of Soil Physical Quality. Soil Science 172:895-912.

Magdoff, F. (1992).Building Soils for Better Crops: Organic Matter Management. University of Nebraska Press, Lincoln, NE. (1-800-755-1105) NRCS: Soil Biology Primer - available upon request.

Pankhurst, C.E., B.M. Doube, and V.V.S.R. Gupta (Eds).(1997). Biological Indicators of Soil Health. CAB International, New York. (1-800-528-4841).

Pankhurst, C.E., B.M. Doube, and V.V.S.R. Gupta (Eds).(1997). Biological Indicators of Soil Health. CAB International, New York. (1-800-528-4841).

Soil Environment and Conservation **Pages 12-33**
Edited by: Dr. Ashok K. Rathoure; Dr. Pawan Kumar 'Bharti' and Dr. Alka Chauhan
ISBN: 978-93-88854-10-8
Edition: 2019
Published by: Discovery Publishing House Pvt. Ltd., New Delhi (India)

2 Fertility Grouping of Vedavati River Basin Soils Based on Soil Characteristics in Plow Layer

A Case Study from Shidlaianakote Village, Karnataka, India

B.P. Bhaskar[1], S.C. Ramesh Kumar[1], M. Lalitha[1], B.P. Laxmikantha[2], Sunil Maske[1] and Rajendra Hegde[3]

ABSTRACT

The variability of soil chemical properties were assessed for better understanding of soil attributes in undulated granitic terrain supporting red and black soils cropped to ground nut and pigeon pea with coconut/arecanut plantations in vedavati river basin of Hirriyur tehsil, Karnataka. The soil-landform map at cadastral level (1:10000 scale) of Shidlaianakote village was used to test the significant difference of soil properties in relation to land units using routine soil chemical data. The results showed that the high degree of homogeneity for soil pH, organic carbon and DTPA extractable Mn in upper pediplains (UP) and high heterogeneity in case of Lower pediplains (LP) and stream Floors (SF) for all chemical properties except available phosphorus that negating the need for soil profiles. The grid data of 125 sites for 13 soil variables from georeferenced were used to characterize by means of cluster analysis and principal component analysis (PCA). Nine clusters were derived and assessed high organic carbon in cluster-6; high for available phosphorus in cluster 2, 3, 4, 6, 7, 8 and high available K in cluster 9 occurring on basin floors with low in available sulphur, boron and Zn status. Five principal components were derived having 76 per cent of total variance with strong positive association with pH (0.85) and negative effect of Elevation (–0.72). The results further suggested that landscape analysis at cadastral level will reduce the confounding effects of landscape elements on larger-scale spatial trends in soil attributes. The study suggested that soil classification systems are useful to organize soil variability groupings to promote effective land resource management and agro technology transfer.

Key words: Grid survey, Principal component analysis, Cluster analysis, Hiriyur, Northern dry zone.

1 ICAR-NBSS&LUP, Regional Centre, Hebbal, Bangalore-560024 , Karnataka, India
2 Karnataka State Remote Sensing Application Centre, Bangalore, India
3 ICAR NBSS&LUP, Amravati road, Nagpur-440033, Maharashtra, India

Introduction

Land surveys of soil attributes can provide valuable information on the geographic distribution of important soil attributes and summarize the levels found. Landscape position can have a major influence on soil attributes. Consideration of field landscape variables in selecting sampling locations and interpreting results, even in large-scale surveys, should help to reduce unexplained variability in many soil attributes (Frazen *et al.,* 2006). The variability of soils attributes at landscape level are major causes of spatial variability in crop yields (Kravchenko and Bullock, 2000; Li *et al.,* 2001; Bronson *et al.,* 2003) and soil water availability (Paz *et al.,* 1998; Li *et al.,* 2001). Hence, it is not surprising that yield variability is normally correlated with soil properties and terrain attributes (Kravchenko and Bullock, 2000; Fraisse *et al.,* 2001; Li *et al.,* 2001). This has prompted to group and manage soils in a similar way to optimize inputs and/or maximize profits for agronomic, economical, and environmental benefits (Plant, 2001; Fraisse *et al.,* 2001; Terra *et al.,* 2005).

However, in the last two decades, soil fertility has been widely reported declining. Consequently, farmers have been forced to intensify crop production on existing lands and expand cultivation into more marginal lands on rough terrain, steep slopes and subjected to varying degrees of land degradation. It is, therefore, important to understand the status and dynamics of soil nutrients in relation to land-use and landscape position. A comprehensive study by ICAR involving analysis of 2,51,547 soil samples across the country revealed deficiency of zinc in as many as 48 per cent of soil samples followed by boron (33%), molybdenum (13%) iron (12%) manganese (5%) and copper (3%) while a large number of farmers in India are aware of using chemical fertilizers involving major nutrients (N,P,K) but they are unaware of deficiencies of micronutrients in their individual farms. (Amrit Patel, 2016). In southern states, a recent general reduction in the yield of locally grown crops has drawn attention of stakeholders in the agricultural sector to this serious trend. Therefore, at present, the greatest challenge before dryland agriculture is to boost food production and productivity as well as sustainability of agriculture as a whole (FAO Handbook, 2004). There are problems that impose limits on these objectives or goals which raise serious concerns about national food security. These include deterioration of soil fertility, increase in cost of production, and low diversity of production systems (Rajendra Hegde, *et al.,* 2015). The frequent droughts in the region invariably leads to soil fertility depletion through continuous or intensive cropping along with short, unfertilized fallow system, Low fertility of red soils is the major constraint in achieving high productivity goals.

The eastern dry zone of Karnataka state in South India is considered as a bioresource-deficient zone for agricultural purposes (Ramachandran *et al.,* 2004), where almost 50% of rain falls during July to October. The soils are coarse textured, with a predominance of gravel. Management of soil fertility in the soils of the region is crucial to support good productivity under water stress., Hypothetical estimations suggested that the generalized soil mass based estimations(GSM method) would overestimate nutrient content for the degraded soils of this region and, therefore, the current practice of using this method needs to be modified (Nagaraja and Srinivasamurthy, 2016). It was reported that soil fertility status in a portion of Ghataprabha Left Bank canal (GLBC) command area in relation to different physiographic units and reported that the nutrient status did not follow any distinct trend with respect to physiographic units and crops grown (Binta *et al.*, 2009). Similar kind of soil fertility mapping was carriedout in a part of intensively cultivated with high yielding crops such as finger millet, maize, red gram and vegetables in Doddaballapur Taluk of Karnataka and reported that 42% of area is deficient in available nitrogen, 13% in available phosphorus and 47% low in available Potassium(Roopa *et al.*, 2014). The short comings of soil surveys and validitiy of soil maps is often linked with ignoring the relationship between landforms and soils (Chartres, 1982; Fagbami and Vega catalan, 1985) at mapping scale (1:10000). It is hypothesized that amount and distribution of a wide array of soil nutrients may vary among land-uses and landscape positions. The message is that management of variable soil landscapes requires a balanced approach—the causes of the variability must be managed as well as the effects. The objectives of this paper were therefore to (*i*) determine the distribution of different land-use/cover along the landscape (summit, upper backslope, footslope, and valley) and (*ii*) evaluate the nutrient status on small holder farms with respect to land-use class (perennials, annuals, and woodland) and slope position (upper, middle and lower) in the siddhalaihnakote village, Hiriyur tehsil, Karnataka.

Materials and Methods

Study Area

Sidlaiahnakote village in Hiriyur tehsil lies between 13°.95′N and 76°.62′E at an elevation of 520 to 630 m above mean sea level (Figure 2.1). Hiriyur is renowned for having the oldest dam vani vilas in Karnataka, built on the Vedavati river. The average rainfall is 562 mm ± 166 mm and coefficient of variation of 29 per cent. The seasonal distribution of rainfall shows that this tehsil receives 21% of annual rainfall during pre-monsoon, 49% during south west monsoon and 29% during north east monsoon. The coefficient of variation is 58 per cent for pre monsoon season, 43% for south-west monsoon and 52 per cent for north east monsoon. Coconut plantations can be seen in this part of Chitradurg district wherever water resources are available. During winter (November - February), the night temperature may come down to 18^0 C. The March and April are the hottest months of the year. The study area falls under agroecological region of southern Karnataka plateau with a length of growing period of 90 to 120 days (Velayutham *et al.*, 1999). This regional experiences seasonal droughts and incurred serious crop loss (Kannan *et al.*, 2013). The schematic diagram of water balance (Figure 2.2) summarizes the different steps and procedures followed to classify the climate of study area on on availability of WS and WD through water balance analysis. This region has a moisture index of –63.6 ($Im = Ih - Id$) to define climate as semiarid following the scheme of Thornthwaite and Mather (1955) with the following limits of Im %. Dry deciduous scrub type of forest is dominant with trees such as *Kamara, Sone or Swami-mara, Tharad or Kempu Khaira, Dindiga, Bevu, Honge, Hunase, Kakke, Sujjalu.*

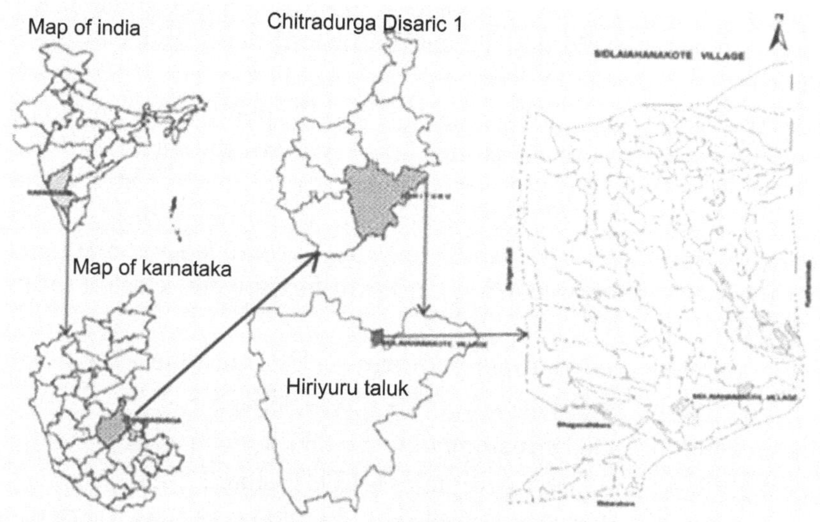

Fig. 2.1: Location map of study area

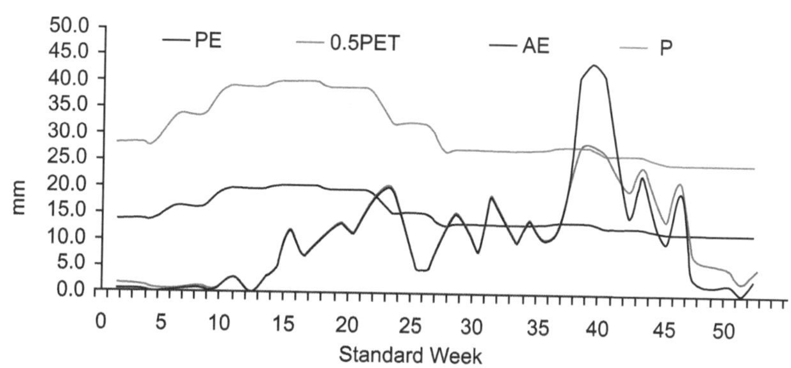

Fig. 2.2: Standard week wise waterbalance diagram of Hiriyur tehsil

Field Survey at Cadastral Level

The soil samples should be taken evenly over the study site. A completely regular sampling network, however, can be biased if it coincides with a regular pattern in the landscape. On the other hand, any kind of randomisation can lead to uneven distribution of the samples (Burrough and Mcdonnell, 1998). The dominant geology of study site is Archanes (Granitic terrain) is under the dryland agricultural system consisting of sorghum, ragi and pigeon pea as main crops and moreover is uniform and repeatable undulating landscapes with wide pediment surfaces and pediplains with varied soil categories, crop alteration, field size and orientation. For these reasons, it was not found necessary to conduct preliminary sampling for possible stratification or to select random samples in order to record hidden heterogeneity. A total of 126 soil surface samples were sampled at 325 × 325 m grid interval for these landform facets and recorded geographic coordinates and elevation from Global positioning system (GPS).

Grid soil samples should be taken at a specific point, either within the grid cell consisting of 8-10 cores per sample taken within a 10-foot. The 1:10000scale using IRS LISS - IV + Cartosat image plus cadastral map of Shidlaiahnakote village of Hiriyur tehsil, in the Central dry zone of Chitradurg district, Karnataka state were interpreted. Several landforms were recognized and mapped (Table 2.1) but the most widely occurring landform facets were selected for present study such as:

(*i*) moderately eroded upper pediplains – UP (212.98ha, 22%),
(*ii*) moderately eroded back slopes – BS (54.38ha, 5.6%),
(*iii*) severely dissected stream floors – SF (301.8ha, 31.4%),
(*iv*) slightly eroded lower pediplains – LP(115.4ha, 12%);
(*v*) slightly dissected upper pediments – UPED (138.35ha, 14.4%) and
(*vi*) slightly eroded barren summit s – SB (76.92ha, 8%).

Table 2.1: Extent of Landforms with Dominant Soil Series and their Image Characteristics

Image characteristics	Land forms	Soil series	Area	
			(ha)	(%)
Light greenish grey tone, coarse texture, spotty dark red tone, 15% surface stone cover, single cropped	Moderately eroded, Upper pediplains(UP)	Rangena halli/ Gudanoor halli	212.98	22.0
Dark gray, fine texture, single cropped, checkered pattern	Back slopes, moderately eroded, concave (UMP)	Bidarkere	54.36	5.6
Dark pink, coarse texture, >35% rockoutcrops whitish tinge	Severely dissected stream floors (upper), infested with Prosopis *juliflora* (SF)	Vedavati / Kanive Maramma	301.8	31.4

Dark red tones with rectangular patterns of coconut plantations, very gently sloping lands, slightly eroded	Lower pediplains, slightly eroded (LP)	Shidalaiahnakote	115.4	12.0
Light yellowish green, rectangular fields, cultivated, fine texture	Upper pediment, slightly dissected (UPD)	Ambalgere	138.35	14.4
Whitish tone with bluish tinge, rectangular pattern, broad	Barren lands, summits 1 to 3% slopes, slightly eroded (S B)	Thore obbanahalli	76.92	8.0

Laboratory Analysis

Soil samples were air-dried at room temperature (30 °C), then grinded and passed through 2 mm sieve for fine earth fraction before starting the analyses. Soil reaction was determined in 1:2.5 soil / water ratio using standard pH meter (Hanna instrument) and electrical conductivity using conductivity meter (Toshniwal insts. Mfg. Pvt. Ltd, TC 17). Soil organic carbon (OC) was estimated using the wet digestion method as described by Walkley and Black (1934) and expressed in percentage. About 0.5 g of soil sample was oxidised by 10 ml potassium dichromate 1N. The excess of the oxidant was titrated with an iron sulfate standard solution. The available phosphorus was determined by taking 1 gram of air-dried soil and 20 milliliters of 0.5 molar sodium bicarbonate ($NaHCO_3$) solution and was shaken for 30 minutes. Blue color in the filtered extract was developed with molybdate- ascorbic acid reagent and measured the intensity of blue colour using spectrophotometer at 660nm (Olsen, 1954 and Olsen and Sommers, 1982). The available potassium in 20g soil sample was extracted with a 1 M NH_4OAc solution at pH =7.00 (1:2 ratio). The soil solution was shaken for 5 minutes and the solution was separated from the solid by centrifugation. The concentrations of K, was subsequently analysed by Flame photometer (Black, 1965).The available sulphur was determined in the 20g soil using monocalcium phosphate extracting (500 mg/l) and was shaken for one hour to get clear filtrate. 10 ml of filtrate was taken in 25 ml volumetric flask and added 2.5ml of 25% HNO_3 and 2 ml of acetic phosphoric acid and then diluted to 22 mil. Added 0.5ml of $BaSO_4$ seed suspension (18 g in 44 ml of hot water and added 4 ml gum acacia). This solution was added and measured the intensity of colourat 440 nm (blue filter) using spectrophotometer (William and Steinberg, 1959). The available Boron in soils was estimated using 0.01 M $CaCl_2$ solution as extractant and used Azomethine – H to develop colour. Measured absorbance at 420 nm as described by Jhon *et al.*, (1975). The micronutrients such as Fe, Mn, Zn and Cu were determined in 12.5 g of soil mixed with 25 mil of 0.05 MDTPA extractant at pH 8.3. Shaked this mixture for 2 h at 70 to 80 oscillation per minute (Lindsay and Norvell,1978). The concentration micronutrients in the filtrate were determined using atomic absorption spectrophotometer.

Calculation

The nutrient index were computed and then classified as per the formulae proposed by Ramamoorthy and Bajaj (1969) and given as below:

$$\text{Nutrient index} = \frac{(1X \text{ number of samples in low category}) \times 2 \text{ (number of samples in medium category)} \times 3 \text{(lnumber of same)}}{\text{total number of sampples}}$$

Nutrient index	class	Symbol
<1.67	Low	
1.67- 2.33	Medium	
>2.33	High	

Rating of Soil Fertility

Fertility status of N, P, K and S were interpreted as low, medium and high and that of DTPA extractable zinc, iron, copper and manganese interpreted as deficient, sufficient and excess by following the criteria (Arora, 2002) and details were given in Table 2.2.

Table 2.2: Soil Fertility Ratings for Available Nutrients

Nutrients	Fertility rating		
	Low	Medium	High
Organic carbon (%)	<0.5	0.5-0.75	>0.75
Phosphorus (P_2O_5) (kg ha^{-1})	<22	22-55	>55
Potassium (K_2O) (kg ha^{-1})	<110	110-280	>280
Sulphur (mg kg^{-1})	<20	20-40	>40
Boron(mg kg^{-1})	<0.5	-	-
Micronitrients	**Deficient**	**Sufficient**	**Excess**
Copper (mg kg^{-1})	<0.2	0.2-5.0	>5.0
Iron (mg kg^{-1})	<2.5	2.5-4.5	>4.5
Zinc (mg kg^{-1})	<0.6	0.6-1.5	> 1.5
Manganese (mg kg^{-1})	<2.0	2-4	>4.0

Statistical Analysis

The 11 soil characteristics analysed in the laboratory were used to calculate the following statistics: mean, standard deviation, coefficient of variation using Microsoft excel and F test calculated using SPSS windows 15 version.

The variability within the landforms was measured by coefficient of variation expressed as per centage. For estimating the differences between landforms, 95% confidence intervals were calculated : simply by listing in descending order of mean value for each variable for comparision of facet mean diagrams. The significance of difference between any pair was determined by comparing the lower limit of higher mean with the upper limit of lower mean. There were 21 possible pairs for each variable for comparision in the matrix. Wilding (1985) described a classification scheme for identifying the extent of variability for soil properties based on their CV values, in which CV values of <15, 16-35 and > 36% indicate low (least), moderate and high variability, respectively.

Principal component analysis (PCA) technique was used to reduce the number of variables and eliminate the relations among input variables by developing a set of new variables that are linear functions of the original variables. This set was retained as the original ones, provided that the number of new variables should not exceed the original number. The number of variables m is chosen components to sufficiently explain the variation of the data (Jolliffe, 1986). The number of principal components that underwent interpretation was set on the basis of Kaiser's criterion, according to which those variables were chosen whose eigen values are greater than 1 (Stanisz, 2007).

The cluster analysis of soil properties for the computation of using the hierarchical cluster analysis (CA) which represents a quantitative independent approach of samples. CA was performed to identify analogous behaviour among soil fertility parameters. It was performed on the normalized data set by means of Ward's method using squared Euclidean distances as a measure of similarity between samples.

Results

Top Soil Properties and their Variability

The statistical summary of 125 top soil samples (Table 2.3) shows that these soils have a mean soil pH of 7.26(neutral) with deviation of 1.35 and variation of 18.65 per cent. In general the organic carbon is medium with a mean of 0.76 ± 0.48% and variation of 63.17 per cent). These soils have low salt concentration with mean EC of 0.24 ± 0.4 dSm^{-1} with CV of 167.62%. The mean of available P_2O_5 is high (mean 63.57 ± 45.55 kg/ha) with CV of 71.65% and medium status of available K_2O (mean of 222.17 ± 121.45 kg/ha) with CV of 54.66%. The available S and B contents are low with CV of 166.63% for S and 64.7% for B. Albeit DTPA extractable Zn with mean of 0.38 is below critical limit with CV of 211.48%. The mean DTPA extractable Cu, Fe and Mn are above critical limit with CV more than 45%.

Table 2.3: Descriptive Statistics for Soil Fertility Parameters

Statis-tical para-meters	pH	EC (dSm^{-1})	OC %	Available				DTPA extractable(mg/kg)			
				P_2O_5	K_2O	S	B	Cu	Fe	Mn	Zn
				kg/ha		mg/kg					
Mean	7.26	0.24	0.76	63.57	222.17	14.66	0.37	0.91	9.8	13.11	0.38
Minimum	5.14	0.03	0.08	2.29	13.26	0.83	0.08	0.12	2.8	3.6	0.06
Maximum	9.59	3.25	2.25	242.74	671.19	187.5	1.31	3.74	39.82	36.46	9.06
SD	1.35	0.4	0.48	45.55	121.45	24.43	0.24	0.66	4.8	6.03	0.81
CV	18.65	167.62	63.17	71.65	54.66	166.63	64.7	72.12	48.99	45.97	211.48

Variability of Soil Properties with Respect to Landforms

The mean, standard deviation and coefficient variation (CV) for 11 soil properties with respect to landforms are given in Table 2.3. Considering the variation of soil properties is homogeneous when CV is less than 33% (Fagbami andega Catalan, 1982). The eleven soil chemical variables were taken to workout variability. Except pH (CV <33%), all variables under study have high variability and vary considerably between landforms. This is attributed due to the fact that pH is on logarithamic scale but also relatively uniform within the landform. The variables having CV >33% in surface soil properties for all landforms include : Electrical conductivity (EC), organic carbon (OC), available phosphorus, potassium, sulphur, boron and DTPA extractable Fe, Cu, Zn and Mn. These results confirm earlier findings that chemical properties vary considerably and do not often result in high homogeneity with in the soil mapping units (Chartres, 1982; Sharma and Bhaskar, 2003). The results show that the level of homogeneity expected to map is approached by pH, organic carbon and DTPA extractable Mn in upper pediplains (UP) and high heterogeneity in case of Lower pediplains (LP) and stream Floors (SF) for all chemical properties except pH. It is clear that upper pediplains in the study area has been accurately mapped while other land units have high variability as unexpected at 1:10000 scale in semi arid regions of Chitradurga district. Although demarcated the recognizable and mappable land units with the use of cartosat data, still more detailed ground survey is needed to enhance precision and purity of map (consociation) as recorded for other units lacking better descriptions and micro relief features not clearly visible on satellite imageries.

Comparison of Facet Means

The comparision of means of soil properties among landforms were estimated by using 95% confidence interval. The results showed that there is no significant difference in DTPA extractable Fe, Mn, Zn and available B (except between stream floors and lower pediplains) indicating a very low potential for differentiating mapping unit within the study area. Only pH, EC, OC, available phosphorus showed significant difference among facets but regarded as good discriminants within the landforms. The pH is very useful for separating soils with high potential for rice / ragi cultivation at the distal end of stream floors. The mapping method successfully separates important landforms from the point of land use management but variability can be reduced with more ground survey especially in areas under coconut / arecanut / banana cultivation, so prevalent in upland regions. This analysis showed significant difference of top soil chemical properties (Figure 2.3; Table 2.4) among mapping units. This study suggests to include soil physical variables such as depth, slope, field capacity, bulk density, particle size and geochemical parameters to separate mapping units with least variability. The stream floors near vedavati river in the village is used for ragi/rice cultivation at the distal basin floors which is the best area and the proximal basin that has lower potential for rice is used for coconut / arecanut / banana or for arable crops like sorghum, groundnut and redgram. The production of these crops can be enhanced by supplemental irrigation with high repaying capacity.

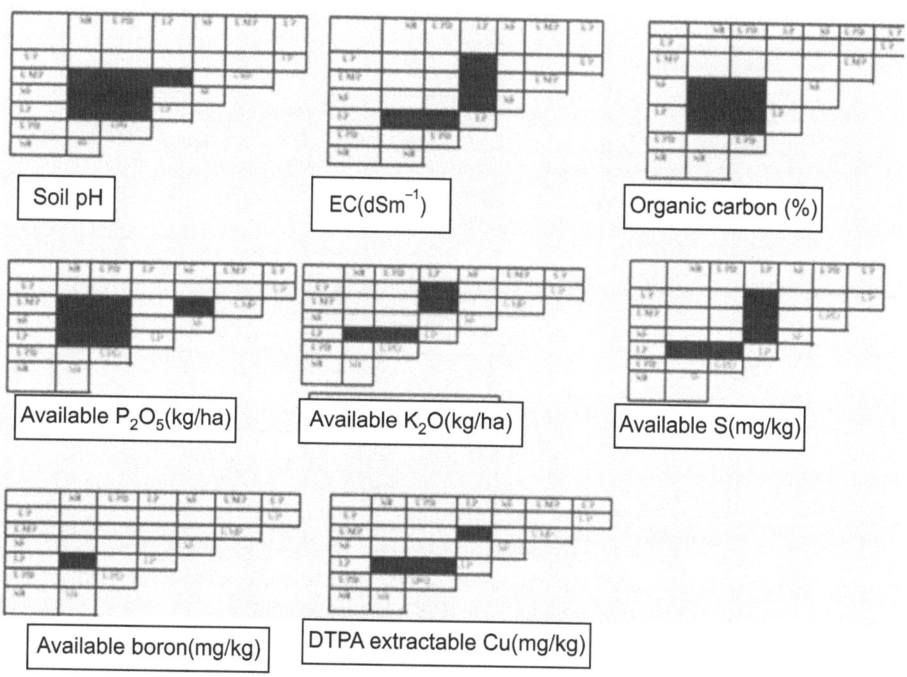

Fig. 2.3: Comparision of means of soil chemical properties

Table 2.4: Mean, Standard Deviation, Coefficient of Variation and F Test of Soil Variable with Respect to Landscape Positions

Soil facet	pH(1:2 soil water)			EC(dSm-1)			Organic carbon (%)			Available P_2O_5 ($kgha^{-1}$)			Available K_2O ($kgha^{-1}$)		
	Mean ± SD	CV	F	Mean ± SD	CV	F	Mean ± SD	CV	F	Mean ±SD	CV	F	Mean ± SD	CV	F
UP	6.89 ± 1.21	17.52	16.71 **	0.15 ± 0.14	91.5	9.96 **	0.83 ± 0.28	33.9	5.64 *	71.4 ± 41.0	57.4	7.73 *	188.2 ± 100.8	53.6	5.56 *
UMP	7.41 ± 1.19	16.04		0.17 ± 0.16	95.0		0.75 ± 0.40	53.3		58.3 ± 38.3	65.6		219.2 ± 132.1	60.3	
SF	8.27 ± 0.86	10.34		0.28 ± 0.31	110.2		1.05 ± 0.65	62.1		27.94 ± 20.7	74.1		251.1 ± 122.3	48.7	
LP	8.66 ± 0.84	9.75		0.80 ± 0.87	108.5		1.02 ± 0.58	57.1		42.4 ± 33.4	78.8		345.3 ± 136.4	39.5	
UPD	6.3 ± 0.96	15.19		0.12 ± 0.15	120.1		0.57 ± 0.32	55.6		90.8 ± 49.5	54.5		187.2 ± 84.8	45.3	
SB	6.27 ± 1.17	18.71		0.09 ± 0.04	46.9		0.46 ± 0.29	63.1		87.6 ± 50.2	57.4		167.1 ± 62.6	37.5	

	Available S (mg kg^{-1})			Available B (mg kg^{-1})			DTPA extactable Fe (mg kg^{-1})			DTPA extactable Cu (mg kg^{-1})			DTPA extactable Zn (mg kg^{-1})		
UP	8.5 ± 5.5	64.9	10.2 **	0.3 ± 0.2	66.2	2.3 *	11.25 ± 4.2	37.3	0.61	0.83 ± 0.53	63.51	3.97 *	0.35 ± 0.19	55.34	0.53
UMP	8.7 ± 8.2	94.4		0.34 ± 0.22	63.0		9.7 ± 4.2	43.3		0.94 ± 0.52	55.11		0.53 ± 1.48	280.9	
SF	13.3 ± 13.9	104.1		0.45 ± 0.35	77.5		8.4 ± 3.8	45.2		0.98 ± 0.67	68.91		0.43 ± 0.33	76.0	
LP	50 ± 56.0	110.8		0.51 ± 0.23	44.9		9.8 ± 8.6	87.2		1.49 ± 0.85	57.23		0.43 ± 0.28	63.8	
UPD	9.4 ± 8.2	87.11		0.34 ± 0.17	51.9		9.9 ± 2.9	29.2		0.63 ± 0.48	76.59		0.25 ± 0.14	55.8	
SB	9.6 ± 5.2	61.6		0.29 ± 0.19	64.2		10.5 ± 5.3	50.1		0.75 ± 0.73	97.4		0.22 ± 0.11	51.7	

DTPA Extactable Mn(mg kg^{-1})

UP	14.23 ± 5.5	38.3	0.22
UMP	13.04 ± 5.1	38.9	
SF	13.3 ± 7.3	55.2	
LP	12.9 ± 5.0	38.7	
UPD	13.5 ± 4.7	34.5	
SB	12.1 ± 8.7	71.8	

Note : UP =upper pediplains; UMP = upper middle pediplains with concave slopes; SF = stream floors; LP=Lower pediplains; UPD= upper pediments and SB = barren summits

Cluster Analysis

Using the 11 selected top soil variables, an agglomerative hierarchical cluster analysis based on Ward's grouping method and correlation matrix (Webster and Oliver, 1990) was conducted to group the 125 regional soil observations. All soils were used to arrange individuals together into larger and larger groups in such a way that individuals belong to small groups, the small groups belong to larger groups, and so on. It is based on dissimilarity matrix of Euclidean distances between individuals, the 125 soil samples for 13 soil variables are grouped into nine clusters and worked out descriptive statistics for each cluster (Table 2.5). Based on mean pH, the top soils are grouped as moderately acid (cluster 4 & 6), slightly acid (Cluster-3), neutral (Cluster-2 & 7), slightly alkaline (Cluster-1 & 5) and moderately alkaline (cluster 8 & 9). The coefficient of variation among cluster is varied from 9.54 per cent in Cluster-6 to 17.51 per cent in Cluster-7. There is striking differences in occurrence of moderately alkaline soils grouped under Cluster-9 at an elevation of 433.83 ± 121.03m with CV of 27.91 per cent where as moderately acid soils occurring at 605.29 ± 54,29 m with CV of 9.03 per cent. Even though, these soils have low salt content, high coefficient of variation is recorded in Cluster-3 (270.99%), Cluster-4 (140.16%), Cluster-6 (110.07%), Cluster-7 (134.73%) and Cluster-8 (115.91%). The Cluster-6 has low organic carbon (mean of 0.38 ± 0.23%, CV of 59.75%) where as high organic carbon in Cluster-8 (mean of 1.08 ± 0.71%, CV of 65.8%) and in remaining clusters have medium organic carbon. All clusters have high coefficient of variation for organic carbon (> 35%) expect Cluster-8 that has moderate variation of 26.59%. The mean available phosphorus is recorded high in Cluster 2,3,4,6 & 7, whereas moderate in Cluster-8, 5 & 1 and low in Cluster-9. The coefficient of variation is least for Cluster-2 (CV of 15.01%), moderate for Cluster-3, 4 but highly variable in other Clusters. Similarily , available K_2O content in Cluster-5 is low with mean of 102.62 ± 18.66 kg/ha with CV of 18.66 % but high available K in Cluster-7 (mean of 370.21 ± 29.87 kg/ha, CV of 8.07%) and Cluster - 9 (mean of 295.43 ± 21.45 kg/ ha, CV of 7.26%). All clusters have low available S and B contents with high coefficient of variation. Among micro nutrients, DTPA extractable Zn is below critical limit (< 0.6 mg/kg) in all clusters, except in Cluster-1 where the mean Zn content is 0.75 ± 2.14 mg/kg with CV of 18.7%.

Table 2.5: Clusterwise Descriptive Statistical Summary of Soil Properties

Soil variable Clusters	Eleva-tion (m)	pH	EC (dSm^{-1})	OC (%)	Available				DTPA extractable			
					P_2O_5	K_2O	S	B	Cu	Fe	Mn	Zn
					kg/ha	mg/kg	mg/kg					
1												
Mean	520.24	7.50	0.15	0.63	34.22	170.62	9.08	0.42	0.67	8.60	10.84	0.75
SD	83.14	1.19	0.13	0.26	21.14	10.21	7.58	0.19	0.42	3.64	3.97	0.14
CV(%)	15.98	15.90	84.09	41.23	61.77	5.98	83.57	45.00	62.75	42.30	36.66	
2												
Mean	547.57	6.86	0.12	0.58	63.79	211.05	11.54	0.31	1.44	11.41	17.45	0.34
SD	114.22	1.12	0.08	0.41	9.57	20.11	5.54	0.15	0.89	4.56	4.65	0.21
CV(%)	20.86	16.27	65.97	71.14	15.01	9.53	47.98	47.15	61.75	39.91	26.65	62.35

3												
Mean	553.23	6.51	0.32	0.69	87.72	181.68	18.04	0.35	0.77	8.85	13.54	0.31
SD	66.94	1.10	0.88	0.38	23.04	54.63	46.10	0.15	0.72	3.53	7.72	0.20
CV(%)	12.10	16.92	270.99	54.64	26.26	30.07	255.62	43.31	93.73	39.83	57.05	63.50
4												
Mean	536.22	6.04	0.21	0.56	62.85	127.60	8.81	0.33	0.67	12.27	14.26	0.19
SD	63.65	0.70	0.30	0.20	12.12	11.50	5.56	0.25	0.41	4.54	5.16	0.07
CV(%)	11.87	11.58	140.16	36.66	19.29	9.01	63.09	75.54	61.32	36.99	36.19	35.13
5												
Mean	522.79	7.69	0.13	0.68	33.14	102.62	7.23	0.29	0.86	9.07	11.38	0.21
SD	72.81	1.26	0.09	0.34	19.39	18.66	3.93	0.18	0.70	4.57	6.53	0.11
CV(%)	13.93	16.37	67.32	49.96	58.51	18.18	54.31	61.14	81.90	50.35	57.40	53.69
6												
Mean	605.29	5.86	0.11	0.39	128.08	152.35	9.23	0.24	0.87	10.88	15.91	0.27
SD	54.69	0.56	0.12	0.23	26.32	33.17	5.85	0.13	0.61	4.65	9.38	0.10
CV(%)	9.03	9.54	110.07	59.75	20.55	21.77	63.35	54.31	69.66	42.72	58.93	37.18
7												
Mean	537.67	7.12	0.36	0.86	88.29	370.21	19.16	0.47	0.94	9.40	11.66	0.57
SD	118.98	1.25	0.49	0.56	49.63	29.87	11.26	0.21	0.81	3.84	3.46	0.40
CV(%)	22.13	17.51	134.73	64.87	56.22	8.07	58.78	45.93	86.97	40.83	29.70	70.28
8												
Mean	522.47	7.95	0.32	1.08	43.64	251.92	17.50	0.45	0.81	8.76	12.85	0.37
SD	100.55	1.08	0.37	0.71	30.56	24.27	18.00	0.40	0.34	3.69	5.20	0.27
CV(%)	19.25	13.55	115.19	65.82	70.01	9.64	102.89	88.94	41.37	42.10	40.49	74.66
9												
Mean	433.83	**8.63**	0.22	0.77	18.32	295.43	16.11	0.28	0.95	7.95	10.60	0.35
SD	121.03	0.90	0.10	0.21	8.06	21.45	15.25	0.19	0.42	2.18	2.35	0.33
CV(%)	27.90	10.44	46.71	26.59	44.02	7.26	94.69	69.44	44.18	27.43	22.15	95.40

The cluster wise nutrient index categorization (Table 2.6) showed that organic carbon is high in Cluster-6 with low contents in Cluster-7 & 8 but medium in other clusters. The nutrient index is high for available phosphorus in Cluster 2, 3,4,6,7 & 8 but low in Cluster-9 and medium in Cluster-5 and 1. The available K is high in Cluster 9 on basin floors and 7 on upper pediplains but low in Cluster -5 on upper pediment surfaces. These soils have low available sulphur and boron and high content of DTPA extractable Fe and Mn but low in Zn.

Table 2.6: Categorization of Cluster Wise Nutrient Index

Soil variable → Cluster ↓	OC (%)	Available				DTPA extractable (mg/kg)			
		P_2O_5	K_2O	S	B	Cu	Fe	Mn	Zn
		kg/ha		mg/kg					
1									
2									

3									
4									
5									
6									
7									
8									
9									

Principal Component Analysis (PCA)

The PCA results show that the five principal components are derived from 125 cases of 13 soil variables explain 75.75% of cumulative variance where eigen values are more than one (Stanisz, 2007). The scree plot (Figure 2.4) shows the eigen values (>1) with respect to % principal component number. The loading factors for each component along with % of variance contributed by each PC is presented in Table 2.7 & 2.8. The first PC1 contributes 29.67 % of variance with strong positive association with pH (0.852) and negative effect of Elevation (–0.719) indicating that as elevation decreases the soil alkalinity increases in the study area that falls under northern dry zone with erratic rainfall and having subsodicity problem in the region. Similar kind of observations were reported in a part of Cauvery command area of Karnataka (Jena & Natarajan, 2013) and in Chitradurga district of Southern parts of Karnataka (Mohammad, 2010). It is in agreement with the reports of Eaton (1950) that the increase in soil pH beyond 8.5 was mainly because of sodiumization of soils. PC-2 contributes 18.08 % of variance but strongly associated with electrical conductivity (0.899) and available sulphur (0.938). Like wise, PC3 with 10.76 % of variance is

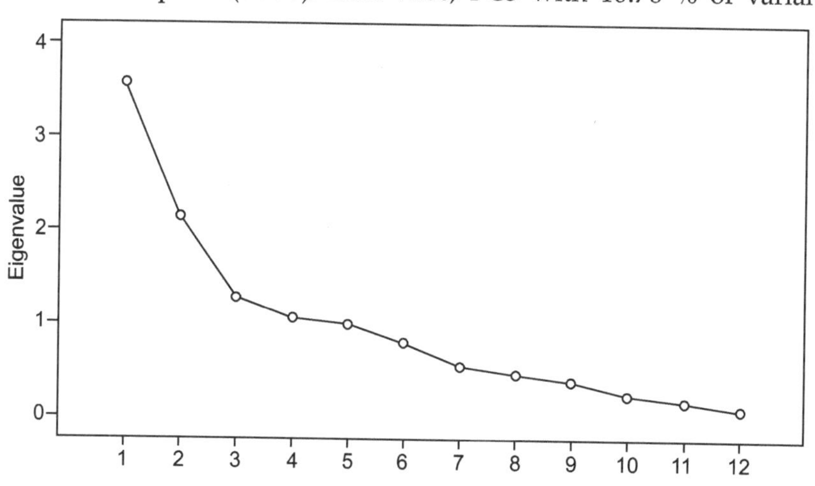

Fig. 2.4: Scree plot diagram showing eigen value and component number

strongly associated with DTPA extracted Mn (0.86), Fe (0.719) and Cu (0.712) and PC4 with available Boron (0.80), organic carbon (0.675) and available K_2O (0.523). The PC5 includes only DTPA Zn (0.934) showing high variability in all samples in the region.

Table 2.7: Total Variance Explained

Component	Initial Eigenvalues			Extraction Sums of Squared Loadings			Rotation Sums of Squared Loadings		
	Total	% of Variance	Cumu-lative %	Total	% of Variance	Cumu-lative %	Total	% of Variance	Cumu-lative %
1	3.561	29.674	29.674	3.561	29.674	29.674	2.479	20.662	20.662
2	2.170	18.084	47.758	2.170	18.084	47.758	2.149	17.912	38.574
3	1.292	10.767	58.525	1.292	10.767	58.525	1.923	16.021	54.595
4	1.079	8.988	67.513	1.079	8.988	67.513	1.498	12.482	67.077
5	1.013	8.444	75.957	1.013	8.444	75.957	1.066	8.880	75.957
6	.819	6.825	82.783						
7	.571	4.757	87.539						
8	.485	4.039	91.578						
9	.416	3.467	95.046						
10	.267	2.229	97.275						
11	.202	1.683	98.958						
12	.125	1.042	100.000						

Extraction Method: Principal Component Analysis.

Table 2.8: Rotated Component Matrix

Component number	Component				
Soil properties	**1**	**2**	**3**	**4**	**5**
pH	**.852**	.252	-.181	.139	-.020
EC	.154	**.899**	-.007	.178	.014
OC	.458	.032	.062	**.675**	.163
AvailP	**-.780**	.116	.209	-.031	.135
AvailK	.324	.228	.261	**.523**	.264
AvailS	.085	**.938**	.047	.139	.011
AvailB	-.072	.194	-.064	**.801**	-.223
DTPACu	.365	.392	.712	-.086	-.016
DTPAFe	-.313	-.245	.719	.120	.017
DTPAMn	-.212	.051	**.861**	.032	-.005
DTPAZn	-.024	.008	-.021	-.021	**.934**
elevation	**-.719**	-.280	-.054	-.179	-.166

Extraction Method: Principal Component Analysis.
Rotation Method: Varimax with Kaiser Normalization.
a Rotation converged in 8 iterations.

Discussion

The land resources inventory of Sidlaiahnakote village having area of 996 ha, Hiriyur Takuk of Chitradurga district was carried out on 1:10,000 scale using IRS +Cartostat image to prepare Landform map. The area is divided into visual interpretation of imagery as shown major landform representing three geological formations, Dhawar group capping over Granite and the alluvium of Vedavathi River. The granitic landform identified are further divided into summits, upper pediplain, pedesediment; Dhawar landform into moderately eroded upper pediment and lower pediment with dark gray tone fine gray textured with checked pattern mostly under rainfed condition. The alluvium of Vedavathi River includes striped basin floor with whitish tones and dark red tones (Table 2.1). The first order stream flowing from North to South and a broad valley portion towards South have dark red tones in a regular fashion representing land uses of coconut, arecanut and banana. This unit covers 301.8ha (31.4% of total area). The bright white tone represents severely eroded and salt affected of upper taresse in the basin floor. This area has an elevation of 605 m above MSL in the North and gradually decreases to 560 m above MSL toward South. The soil topo sequence model of granitic landforms of Shidlaianakote village describes the close relationship between the sequences of soils in different positions in the landscape just like a chain of soils linked by topography (Figure 2.1). This soil topo sequence model of 0.4km from North West to South East wards is providing the ability to present a variety of soil, regolith, water movement, and soil property changes in one diagram that can communicate complicated information in a form that assists land management decisions. These mental models that the original soil surveyor created to relate observable features and measurable soil properties to a landscape position are often only intuitively understood and rarely explicitly presented. A farmer's understanding of soil variation is also strongly influenced by terrain, to graphically convey information that can easily be understood and apply. It is observed that there is 2nd order polynomianal equation is derived between soil depth (Surface + subsurface, solum thickness) with Coefficient of determination ($R^2 = 0.443$) and F value of 9.07 significant at 5% level. More than 60% samples are in the depth range of 50 to 100cm. The Detailed soil survey was carried out with intensive field traverse for ground truth verification of field boundaries and the soils were collected, analyzed and classified. Based on the methodology given in the memorandum of soil correlation, the differentiating characteristics for each soil series are identified and grouped into twelve major soil series as 1. Rangenahalli series (Typic Haplustalfs), 2. Gudunoorhalli series (Lamellic Haplustalfs), 3. Bidarkere series (Typic Rhodustalfs), 4. Vedavathi series (Fluventic Haplustepts), 5. Kanive Maramma series (Typic Natrustalfs), 6.Shidalaiahnakote series (Typic Haplustepts), 7. Ambalgere series (Typic Rhodustalfs), 8. Thore obbanahalli series (Typic Haplustalfs),

9. Bhagavathikere (Sodic Haplusterts), 10. Hulikunte series (Typic Haplustepts), 11. Kandikere series (Typic Haplustalfs), 12. Shivganaga series (Typic Haplustalfs). These soils are low in available P, K and DTPA extractable Zn status (Table 2.3). The multiple linear regression equations were derive with notable physico-chemical properties as listed below:

- Available P (kg/ha) = 20.57 – 1.57(pH) + 4.553 (Organic Carbon g/kg) + 0.407($CaCO_3$ g/kg) + 0.039(CEC cmol/kg) + 0.304 (Ex.Mg cmol/kg) –0.245(Ex.Na cmol/kg)
  R^2 = 0.141, F =1.173
- Available K (kg/ha) = 83.95 + 3.107(Clay%) +120.079 (Organic Carbon g/kg) + 0.952(CEC cmol/kg) – 4.227($CaCO_3$ g/kg) – 4.998(Fine Silt %)
  R^2 = 0.229 F = 2.612
- Available boron(mg/kg) = –1.684 +0.282(pH) – 0.334 (Organic Carbon g/kg) – 0.001 (Clay%) +0.015(Total Silt %)+ 0.013(CEC, cmol/kg)
  R^2 = 0.238 F = 2.94
- DTPA extractable Cu (mg/kg) = 2.079 – 0.19(pH) + 0.89 (Organic Carbon g/kg) + 0.013(CEC cmol/kg) +0.003(Clay%) + 0.032(Silt %)
  R^2 = 0.279 F = 3.634

The soil map was derived from 12 soil series identified with 44 phases covering an area of 997 ha (Figure 2.5). The 12 soil series identified in Shidlaianakote, Villageare: Ranganahalli (RGH), Tore obbanahalli(TOB), Bidarkere (BDK), Bhagirathikere (BGK), Sivaganga (SGG), Ambalagere (ABG), Shidlaianakote (SDK), Gudoornahalli (GUH), Kandikere (KDK), Hulikunte (HKT), Kanvi maramma (KMR), Vedavati (VDA).The estimation of each mapping unit area is made and reported here as given in figure 2.8. The data shows that two soil series viz., bidarkere (BDK) and Shivganga (SGG) cover 372 ha out of 997 ha with per cent coverage of 37.24% of total area. Next to these two series, the soils on the basis of area are ranked as : Ambalagere (ABG) – 112ha (11.21%) > Tore obbanahalli (TOB)-105ha (10.45%) > Ranganahalli (RGH)-99 ha (10.04%) > 80ha (7.9%) but other soils cover less than 5% of total area.

The data shows that very high impact of water erosion is reported in 9 soil mapping units (SMU) covering 110 ha(I1% of total area) with high severity of current impact on crop yield of groundnut and pigeon pea under drylands and with low time frame of current impact. The soil condition can be improve with stone removal and land leveling with crop cover and forage cultivation. Next to this, high impact of water erosion is recorded in five SMU's covering 129ha (12.9%) with high severity and medium time frame of current impact on crop productivity. It is interesting to pointout here that the very high impact of sodicity in Kareve maramma and vedavathi units (41,42,43 & 44) covering 73ha(7.38%) in stream floors of sidhlaiahnkote village with severe structural decline and subsoil compaction with severe signs of degradation and high cost of reclamation through chemical amendments and agronomic methods. These soils on uplands have stoniness there by subsoil compaction and structural decline is mostly categorized as medium to low both its severity and time frame of current impacts. The area under each biophysical parameter shows that 59% of area is subjected to slight erosion under very gently sloping lands (76.43% of total area)having surface texture of loamy sand (26.28%) and sandy loam (49.85%). The soils under study are have moderately to strongly (76% of total area) with low to very low water holding capacity (60% of area). The soils in the village are gravelly covering 447ha (44.83% of total area) and very gravelly with 249ha (24.97%). Generally, the study area has brown , sandy loam to loamy sand surface texture and dark red to red, sandy clay loam to sand clay subsoils with slightly acid to neutral pH soils in uplands but its colour changed to dark grayish brown with sandy clay loam texture and strongly to very strongly alkaline soils in lowlands of vedavati river basin.

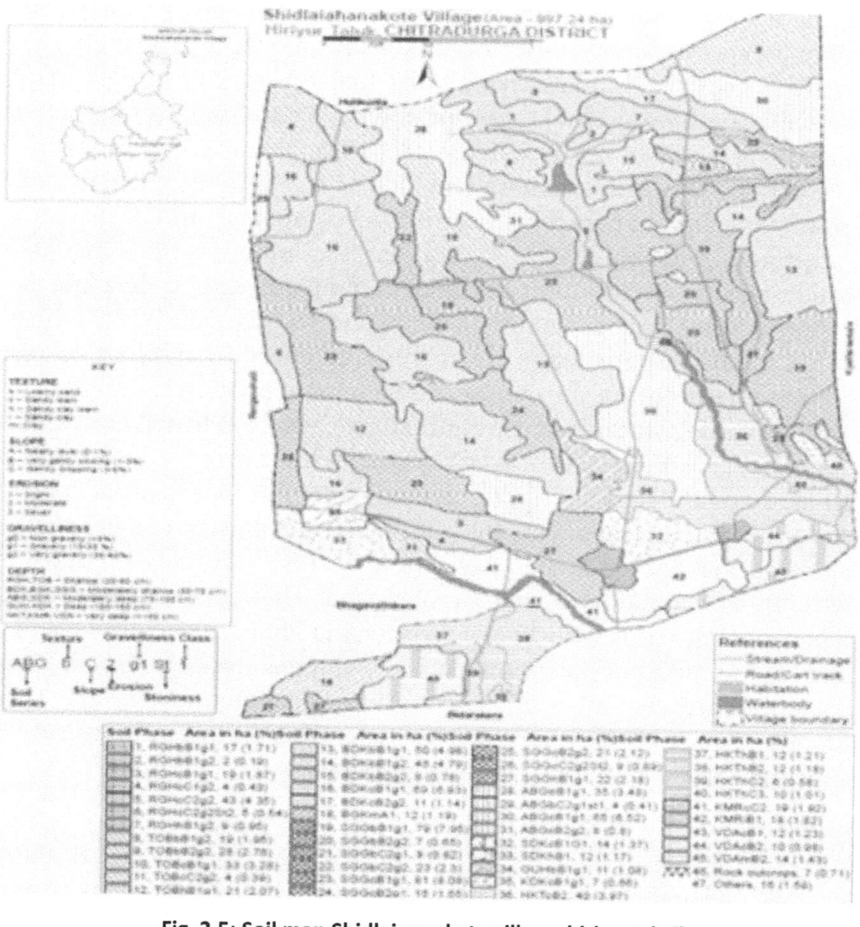

Fig. 2.5: Soil map Shidlaiannakote village, hiriyurtehsil

The area estimated in the study area regarding Soil pH showing that 22,69% of area is under slightly acid whereas 23% of area is under strongly to very strongly alkaline. The ten soil chemical variables were taken to workout variability. Except pH (CV <33%, Fagbami &Vega Catalan, 1982), all variables under study have high variability and vary considerably between landforms. The variables having CV >33% in surface soil properties for all landforms include (Figure 2.3 and Table 2.4) : Electrical conductivity (EC), organic carbon, available phosphorus, potassium, sulphur, boron and DTPA extractable Fe, Cu, Zn and Mn. These results confirm earlier findings that chemical properties vary considerably and donot often result in high homogeneity of soil mapping units (Chartres, 1982; Sharma & Bhaskar, 2003). The results show that the level of homogeneity expected to map is approached by pH, organic carbon and DTPA extractable Mn in upper pediplains (UP) and high heterogeneity in case of lower pediplains (LP) and stream floors (SF) for all chemical properties except pH. Nine clusters are derived and categorized nutrient index categorization (Table 2.6) showing high organic carbon in Cluster-6 with low contents in cluster-7 & 8 but medium in other clusters. The nutrient index is high for available phosphorus in cluster 2, 3,4,6,7 & 8, and available K in Cluster 9 and 7 on upper pediplains These soils have low available sulphur and boron and high content of DTPA extractable Fe and Mn but low in Zn. In principal component analysis, five main components which accounted for 76% of the variability of the data. It is interesting to pinpoint here that The principal component 1(PC1) includes pH, Elevation and Available P and are used as descriptors for inherent chemical potentiality of the soil to supply essential mineral nutrients to the plant as well as its nutrient retaining capability (Kyuma and Kawaguchi, 1973; Nolin *et al.*, 1989). As these soil parameters are greatly influenced by fertilization history and can be interpreted as the management factor in relation to elevation in the study area. The PC3 includes micro-nutrient such as Cu, Mn and Fe in sufficient amounts but DTPA-Zn is mostly below critical limit irrespective of soil types in the study area. The soil organic carbon is medium but doesnot contribute much to first three components indicating its contribution to CEC of soils. It is estimated that 85% of area is deficient in DTPA extractable Zn making Zn application as mandatory at rate of 12.5kg/ha. These soils have medium to high phosphorus status with 45% of soils having high organic carbon and 68% of area having medium potassium content. The results show that soil testing in groundnut growing areas of vedavati river basin of study site can be used as a tool to diagnose the soil fertility status and guide them in implementing management and fertilization recommendations.

Conclusion

The grid survey at 325m × 325m interval was carried out on 1:10000 scale covering 900 ha and collected 126 top soil samples (0-15 cm) over six dominant granitic landforms of Sidlaiahnakote village in Hiriyur tehsil. The laboratory analysis for twelve chemical parameters were considered as important in land evaluation and then nutrient management at watershed level. The results from the study showed that it is possible to attain high degree of homogeneity within land facet for mapping and variability of soil properties. Glimpses of data showed that there is a need to consider differentiating characteristics such as depth, surface configuration textural parameters and water retention characteristics to make satisfactory separation of mapping units in basin floors and lower pediplains. In the study, 9 clusters were identified and categorized nutrient indices to indicate deficiencies of available sulphur, boron and Zn. Five components were derived from principal component analysis indicating the relevance of soil elevational grouping in explaining the development of alkalinity in basin floors and related fertility constraints at landscape level

REFERENCES

Amrit Patel (2016): Addressing Soil Health Management Issues in India, International Journal of Research – Granthaalayah, 4(12): 110-123.

Arora, V.K. (2002): The Use of the Aridity Index to Assess Climate Change Effect on Annual Runoff, Jour. Hydrology, 265:164-177.

Binta, N.K., Dasog, G.S. and Patil, P.L.(2009): Soil Fertility Mapping in Ghataprabha Left Bank Canal Command Area of North Karnataka by Geographic Information System Technique, Karnataka J. Agric. Sci., 22(1) : (73-76).

Black, C.A.(1965):Methods of Soil Analysis, Part-1. Am.Soc.Agron.Inc.Publi., Madison, Wisconsin, USA.

Bronson, K.F., Keeling, J.W. , Booker, J.D,. Chua, T.T., Wheeler, T.A., Boman, R.K. and Lascano, R.J. (2003): Influence of Landscape Position, Soil Series, and Phosphorus Fertilizer on Cotton Lint Yield, Agron. J., 95:949–957.

Burrough, P. A. and McDonnell, R. A. (1998): Creating Continuous Surfaces from Point Data, In: Burrough, P.A., Goodchild, M.F., McDonnell, R.A., Switzer, P., Worboys, M. (Eds.), Principles of Geographic Information Systems. Oxford University Press, Oxford, UK.

Chartres, C.J.(1982): The Use of a Landform – Soil Association in Irrigation Soil Surveys in Northern Nigeria, Journ. Soil Sci., 33:317-318.

Fagbami, A. and Vega catalan, F. (1985): An Evaluation of the Physiographic Soil Map of the Benue Valley at Makurdi, ITC Journal, 4:268-274.

FAO. Handbook (2004) : Federal Department of Agricultural Land Resources in Collaboration with FAO on Soil Test-based Fertilizer Recommendations for Extension workers, pp. 6-19.

Fraisse, C.W., Sudduth, K.A. and Kitchen. N.R. (2001): Delineation of Site-specific Management Zones by Unsupervised Classification of Topographic Attributes and Soil Electrical Conductivity, Trans. ASAE, 44:155–166.

Franzen, D.W., Nanna, T. and Norvell, W. A. (2006) : A Survey of Soil Attributes in North Dakota by Landscape Position, Agron. J., 98:1015–1022.

Jena, J.K. and Natarajan, A.(2013): Assessment of Soil Sodicity Problem in Part of Cauvery Command Area of Karnataka, An Asian Journal of Soil Science, 8 (2): 339-341.

John, M.K., Chuah, H.H. and Neufld, J.H.(1975): Application of Improved Azomethine-H Method for the Determination of Boron in Soils and Plants, Anal.Lett., 8:559-568.

Jolliffe I.T. (1986): Principal Component Analysis, Springer-Verlag, New York.

Kannan, E., Kumar, P., Vishnu, K., and Abraham, H. (2013): Assessment of Pre and Post Harvest Losses of Rice and Redgram in Karnataka. Research Report:IX/ ADRTC / 153. pp.1-99.

Kravchenko, A.N., and Bullock, D.G. (2000): Correlation of Corn and Soybean Grain Yield with Topography and Soil Properties, Agron. J., 92:75–83.

Kyuma, K. and Kawaguchi, K. (1973): A Method of Fertility Evaluation for Paddy Soils I. First Approximation: Chemical Potentiality Grading, Soil Sci. Plant Nutr., 19: 1-9.

Li, H., Lascano, R.J. Booker, J. , Wilson, L.T. and Bronson, K.F. (2001): Cotton Lint Yield Variability in a Heterogeneous Soil at a Landscape Scale, Soil Tillage Res., 58:245–258.

Lindsay, W. L., Norvell, W. A., (1978): Development of a DTPA Soil Test for Zinc, Iron, Manganese and Copper, Soil Sci. Soc. Am. J., 42: 421-448.

Mohammad, F.2010. Soil Degradation Due to Salinity and Sodicity in Chitradurga District of Southern Karnataka.PhD Thesis. University of Agricultural Sciences, Bangalore.

Nagaraja, S.M., Bharadwaj, A.K., Prabhakara Reddy, G.V., Srinivasa Murthy, C.A. and Sandeep Kumar. (2016): Estimations of Soil Fertility in Physically Degraded Agricultural Soils Through Srlective Accounting of Fine Earth and Gravel Fractions, Solid Earth, 7 : 897–903.

Nolin, M. C., Wang, C. and Callier, M.J. (1989): Fertility Grouping of Montreal Low Lands Soil Mapping Units Based on Selected Soil Characteristics of the Plow Layer, Can. J. Soil Sci. 69: 525-541

Olsen, S. R., Cole, C. V., Watanabe, F. S. and Dean, L. A. (1954): Estimation of Available Phosphorus in Soils by Extraction with Sodium Bicarbonate, U. S. Department of Agriculture Circular No. 939. Banderis, A. D., Barter, D. H. and Anderson, K.. Agricultural and Advisor.

Olsen, S.R. and Sommers, L.E. (1982): Phosphorus. pp. 403-430. In: A.L. Page, R.H. Miller, and D.R. Keeney (eds.), Methods of Soil Analysis. 2nd ed. Agronomy Series No. 9, Part 2. Soil Science Society of America, Inc., Madison, WI.

Paz, J.O., Batchelor, W.D., Colvin, T.S., Logsdon, S.D., Kaspar, T.C. and. Karlen, D.L. (1998): Analysis of Water Stress Effects Causing Spatial Yield Variability in Soybeans. Trans. ASAE, 41:1527–1534.

Plant, R.E. (2001): Site Specific Management: The Application of Information Technology to Crop Production, Comput. Electron. Agric., 30:9–29.

Rajendra Hegde, Natarajan, A., Meena, R.S., Niranjana, K.V. and Singh, S.K.(2015): Status of Soil Degradation in an Irrigated Command Area in Chikkarasinakere Hobli, Mandya district, Karnataka, Current Science 108(8):1501-1511.

Ramachandra, T.V., Kamakshi , G. and Shruthi, B.V. (2004): Bioresource status in Karnataka, Renewable and Sustainable Energy Reviews, 8 : 1–47.

Ramamoorthy, B. and Bajaj, J. C. (1969) : Soil Fertility map of India, Fertilizer News, 14(8):25.

Roopa, V.M., Naveen, D.V. and Mamtha, B. (2014): Soil Fertility Maps of Villages as Assessment of Soil Fertility Status in Different Cropping Systems of Doddabelavangala Raitha Samparka Kendra(RSK), Doddaballapur Taluk of Karnataka, International Journal of Scientific Research, 3(1):1-2.

Sharma, J.P. and Bhaskar, B.P. (2003): Variability and Similarity of Soils in Rajkot District, Gujarat. Journal of the Indian Society of Soil Science,51(3):279-287.

Stanisz A. (2007): Przystêpny Kurs Statystyki z zastosowaniem Statistica PL.TATISTICA PL na przyk³adach z medycyny. T. 3. Analizy wielowymiarowe [Accessible Statistics

Course with the Use of Statistica PLTATISTICA PL on Medical Examples]. StatSoft Kraków [in Polish].

Terra, J.A., Shaw, J.N., Reeves, D. W., Raper, R. L. , van Santen, E., Schwab, E. B. and Mask, P. L. (2005): Soil Management and Landscape Variability Affects Field-Scale Cotton Productivity, Soil Sci. Soc. Am. J., 70:98–107

Thornthwaite, C.W. and Mather, J.R. (1955): Water Balance Publication in Climatology, Drexel Ins. of Tech., 8(1).

Velayutham, M,. Mandal, D. K., Mandal, C. and Sehgal, J. (1999): Agroecological Sub Regions of India for Planning and Development, NBSS & LUP, 35-372.

Walkley, A. and Black, I. A. (1934): An Examination of the Degtjareff Method for Determining Soil Organic Matter and a Proposed Modification of the Chromic Acid Titration Method, Soil Sci., 37 : 29-38.

Webster, R. and Oliver, M.A. (1990): Statistical Methods in Soil and Land Resource Survey. Spatial Information Systems. Oxford University Press, Wilding, L.P. 1985. Spatial Variability: Its Documentation, Accommodation and Implication to Soil Surveys, pp. 166-194. In D.R. Nielsen and J. Bouma (eds.). Soil Spatial Variability: Pudoc, Wageningen, Netherlands.

Williams, C. H. and Steinberg, A. (1959): Soil Sulphur Fractions as Chemical Indices of Available Sulphur in some Australian soils, Aust. J. Agric. Res., 10: 340-352.

Soil Environment and Conservation **Pages 34-71**
Edited by: **Dr. Ashok K. Rathoure; Dr. Pawan Kumar 'Bharti' and Dr. Alka Chauhan**
ISBN: 978-93-88854-10-8
Edition: **2019**
Published by: **Discovery Publishing House Pvt. Ltd., New Delhi (India)**

3 Analysis of Agricultural Soil Quality with Special Reference to Heavy Metals

[1]Dr. Pawan Kumar 'Bharti'

ABSTRACT

The rapid growth of industrialization and urbanization has created negative impacts on the environment especially in the last three decades. The industrial wastes containing organic pollutants and heavy metals in their effluents have been polluted surface and ground water. In India, the industrial effluents have contributed a major source of pollution. Textile effluent when discharged into the pond and through pond they percolated to the ground water. Thus, contaminated ground water has deteriorated immensely the drinking utilities, post agriculture irrigation and impacts on soil systems and crop productivity. The aim of this study was to emphasized on the transfer of heavy metals and extent of heavy metal contamination of soil due to irrigation with contaminated ground water affected by textile industrial effluents, on agricultural land. Metal transfer factors from effluent to ground water, from ground water to irrigated agricultural soil and from soil to vegetation are described in a simplified method in water, soil and plants.

Key words: Heavy metals, industry, agriculture soil, transfer factor.

Introduction

Textile effluents have consisted high concentrations of heavy metals, organic and inorganic pollutants and toxic colours, which may alter the surface water quality of the region. Toxic pollutants may percolate down via soil profile and reach in ground water, which ultimately cause the health hazards among human being and livestock after consumption as daily drinking requirements. The waste water without any treatment may cause adverse effect on the health of human, domestic animals, wildlife and environment (Sharma *et al.*, 1999). Thus, contaminated ground water has deteriorated immensely the drinking utilities, post agriculture irrigation and impacts on soil systems and crop productivity. It is essential to know the status and functions of heavy metals discarding from textile industries in to surface, ground water, soil and crop plant vegetation for health safety of regional people, which may help in recent research in the field of soil and water pollution by industries and for advance alarming against pollution to public, NGOs and GOs. The present paper deals with the distribution and transfer of heavy metals between water and soil. Regarding human consumption and irrigation practices ground water may cause the human and livestock health hazards and reduce soil fertility and agricultural plant productivity.

Dye houses waste water of generally discharged openly into Binjhole pond water, thus polluted the surface water quality of the region (Malik *et al.*, 2006). After delaying for a long period of time the heavy metal contents may leach down in to ground water regime through soil profile very slowly. Because the ground water movement is very slow (CPCB, 2003), so metal contents remain in ground water for a long period even in toxic form. Thus metals reach in local ground water and deteriorated the ground water quality of neighborhood area. Metals reach in agricultural soil through repeated irrigation by contaminated ground water. Some concentrations of metals again percolate in to ground water and some of them delay in soil water. Soil particles bound a huge amount of heavy metals due to adsorptive nature, which remain in capillary water and easily available for plants. Plants absorb the sufficient amount of water for their different requirements. Metals present in this available water arrive in plant tissues with water and accumulate in various parts of plant bodies (Malik *et al.*, 2004). These metal contents may affect the plants activities and generate some physiological changes in plants sometimes (Garg and Kaushik, 2006). In other cases, accumulated amount of heavy metals may reach in livestock and human beings after continuous uptake of these crop parts.

Soil of agricultural fields requires sufficient irrigation for high production in agricultural fields. Irrigation water with poor quality can result in the alteration of physico-chemical characteristics of irrigated agricultural soil. Several minerals such as chloride, sulphate, bicarbonate, sodium, calcium and magnesium in irrigation water may change the soil quality with its continuous application on soil. These minerals contained in the irrigation water can build up the soil's trophic level and ultimately influence the agriculture productivity (Malik and Bharti, 2007; Bharti, 2007).

Historical Resume

Several researchers from India and abroad have been discussed various aspects of heavy metals pollution of water and soil in term of characteristics of water bodies, affected agricultural soils and bottom sediments from time to time. This review includes some of important contribution made in the field of industrial pollution, with references to heavy metals parameters of ground water, surface water, characterization of textile industrial effluents, contaminated agricultural irrigated soil and bottom sediment soils by different authors of country and abroad. Aggarwal and Mehrotra (1952) surveyed the soil and soil water affected by effluent in some selected regions of Uttar Pradesh. Richards

(1954) evaluated the quality of saline and alkali soils and gave a technique for the improvement of these sick soil systems in the agricultural sector for good performance of agriculture productivity. Kanwar (1961) assessed the quality of irrigation water as an index of suitability for irrigation purposes.

Darra *et al.*, (1964) evaluated the water quality of irrigation water used in Rajasthan. Saksena *et al.*, (1966) evaluated the quality of ground waters for irrigation in Ahor developmental block, Jalore. Bhakuni and Bopardikar (1967) stated the method of recovery Zinc from the spinning bath waste of Viscos reyon factory by using ion exchange method and found it significant useful in metal removal process. Williums (1972) described the characteristics and various properties of Metals. Katz (1975) highlighted the effect of heavy metals on some environmental components and biotic organisms of aquatic environment in New York. Dowedy and Larson (1975) reported the availability of some metals in various vegetable crops in a polluted region in the vicinity of an industrial area. Dulka and Risby (1976) stated ultra trace metals in some environmental and biological systems in the vicinity of textile industrial sector. Shivakumar *et al.*, (1977) made a geo-graphical approach for toxic trace element pollution in ground water around Patancheru and Bollaram Industrial area, A.P., India. Martin and Cougherty (1982) stated the basic monitoring techniques for detection of heavy metals pollution through the biological agents. Ireland (1983) described the heavy metals uptake and their distribution in tissues of organisms. Numberg (1984) studied on the volumetric approach in trace metal chemistry of natural waters and atmospheric precipitation. Nriagu and Pacyna (1988) carried out a study on the quantitative assessment of worldwide contamination of air, water and soil with trace metals.

Mishra *et al.*, (1990) reported the occurrence of heavy metals in crop plants of Sanagar more than the permissible limits presence of which may cause the adverse effect on the plant/human health and may cause high mortality of fish population in affected aquatic environment. Singh *et al.*, (1994) highlighted the degradation of water and soil quality of Parwanoo area with respect to heavy metals. Sharma and Patel (1996) determined copper in water of Raipur with the help of spectrophotometer. Prasad and Chandra (1997) studied well water quality status of Hyderabad and Khurshid and Shabeer (1997) observed water quality degradation due to heavy metal pollution. Mohan *et al.*, (1998) observed heavy metals (Fe, Pb, Ca & Zn) in the ground water of Naini industrial area; Dist. Allahabad, U.P. Kashem and Singh (1999) had also found the decreasing concentration of Cu, Mn, Pb and Zn with increasing distance from disposal point. Stetzenbach *et al.*, (1999) evaluated the heavy metals in ground water and used multivariate statistical analysis. Tyagi and Budhi (2000) postulated the degradation of ground water quality due to heavy metals in industrial area of India.

Kumar *et al.,* (2001) studied on the impact of textile industry on ground water quality of Sanagar, Jaipur and found the high amount of chemicals (e.g. sulphuric acid and acetic acid) and dyes (e.g. chrome and metal dyes) suspended solids and toxic metals in the waste which may enter in the groundwater and deteriorate its quality. Siddiqui and Pathania (2002) made some studies on heavy metals in surface and ground water of Jalandhar and Ludhiana districts of Punjab state. Shrivastava *et al.,* (2003) collected soil samples from surface of the soil from different agriculture fields in the Khandesh region and Tapi River sediment samples were also collected from five different stations which were 7-8 km away from each other and detected the concentrations of heavy metals have been determined by ICP-AES. Khan *et al.,* (2003) harvested some *Solanum melongena* plant in a laboratory experiment using five different levels of textile waste water and observed the contamination of heavy metals as 1.417 mg/g of Zn, 1.003 mg/g of Cu, 0.378 mg/g of Ni, 0.378 mg/g of Cd, 0.773 mg/g of Cr, 1.139 mg/g of Pb and 0.427 mg/g of Co in the soil of pots treated with highest ratio of distilled water and waste water. Yadav and Sumanlata (2003) indicated the heavy metal pollution in ground water in Bahadurgarh block of districts Jhajjar, Haryana. Malik *et al.,* (2004) evaluated the accumulation of heavy metals in crop plants through irrigation of contaminated ground water in Panipat region and emphasized on bioremediation processes for combat ground water pollution. Chao *et al.,* (2005) reported the heavy metal contaminated site in Taiwan and described the status and distribution of heavy metals in environment. It is necessary to reduce the levels of toxic metals from industrial effluents before discharging into surface waters. The general methods of treating wastewater-containing metals are coagulation, ion exchange, reverse osmosis and adsorption. Adsorption is a highly effective physico-chemical treatment for removing heavy metals for effluents.

Due to high cost of activated carbon, efforts are being directed towards finding low cost adsorbents. Recently much interest has been shown for removal of heavy metals using a large number of low cost materials. Coal fly ash, the solid waste of power plants is one of the cheapest and non-conventional adsorbents (De, 2005).

Zheng *et al.,* (2006) assessed the heavy metals pollution of agricultural soil in Guanzhong district of China. Lokeshwari and Chandrappa (2006) evaluated the impact of heavy metals contamination of a Lake on soil and cultivated vegetation near Bangalore and found the presence of some heavy metals in rice and vegetables, beyond the limit of Indian Standards and calculated metal transfer factors from soil to vegetation are found significant for Zn, Cu, Pb and Cd. Hedge *et al.,* (2006) revealed the provenance of heavy minerals with special reference to ilmenite of the Honnevar beach in central west coast of India and observed some trace heavy elements like Co, Cr, V and Ni in the sandy soil of the beach. Singh (2006) indicated the contamination of ground water of Ganges-

Brahmaputra river basin in north east India and found the ground water unfit for direct human consumption and noticed the rice and vegetable fields irrigated by ground water received a large amount of arsenic through shallow tube wells in the affected areas of north 24 *Parganas* and Murshidabad, West Bangal. Malik *et al.,* (2007) assessed the migration of heavy metals in the ground water regime of Panipat industrial area on the behalf of different spatial variations the heavy metals were found in maximum quantities at point source of pollution.

Malik and Bharti (2007) studied on soil quality of irrigated agricultural fields in a textile industrial area of Panipat city. Va´zquez, *et al.,* (2007) monitored the heavy metal pollution in San Antonio Bay, Rẏ´o Negro, Argentina. Obiri (2007) determined the heavy metals in water from boreholes in Dumasi in the Wassa West District of Western Region of Republic of Ghana. Huang *et al.,* (2007) indicated the speciation and mobility of heavy metals in mud in coastal reclamation areas in Shenzhen in China. Walker *et al.,* (2007) identified the influence of heavy metals and mineral nutrient supply on *Bituminaria bituminosa.* Golia *et al.,* (2007) measured the accumulation of metals on tobacco leaves (primings) grown in an agricultural area in relation to soil.

Mico *et al.,* (2007) described the comparison of two digestion methods for the analysis of heavy metals by flame atomic absorption spectroscopy. Padmavathiamma and Li (2007) explained the phytoremediation technology through the hyper-accumulation metals in plants and different aspects of phytoremediation technology and the biological mechanisms underlying phyto-remediation.

Study Area

Dye houses are situated on Jatal road in industrial area, these are quite famous for handloom business in Panipat city. Textile dying industries in Panipat region consume large quantities of water and discharge it into a common effluent drain, which ends up in to a large pond situated near Binjhole village. Since last five or six years, it was noticed that ground water quality is degrading day by day of the regions and local people think that the dye waste water is the major source of heavy metal pollution in area. But these heavy metals are travelling from wastewater to ground water and ground water to soil system and from soil system to agricultural crop tissues. In this paper, the route of heavy metals in soil and water is highlighted with proper illustrations and flow diagrams.

Methodology

Metals that are naturally introduced into the water body come primarily from such sources as rock weathering, soil erosion, or the dissolution of water-soluble salts. Naturally occurring metals move through aquatic environments independently of human activities, usually without any detrimental effects. Humans consume metallic elements through both water and food. Some metals such as sodium, potassium, magnesium, calcium, and iron are found in living tissue and are essential to human life-biological anomalies arise when they are depleted or removed. Probably less well known is that currently no less than six other heavy metals including molybdenum, manganese, cobalt, copper and zinc, have been linked to human growth, development, achievement and reproduction (Vahrenkamp, 1979; Friberg *et al.*, 1979). Even these metals, however, can become toxic or aesthetically undesirable when their concentrations are too great. Several heavy metals, like cadmium, lead, and mercury, are highly toxic at relatively low concentrations, can accumulate in body tissues over long periods of time and are nonessential for human health.

The toxic heavy metals entering the ecosystem may lead to geo-accumulation, bioaccumulation and biomagnifications. Heavy metals like Fe, Cu, Zn, Ni and other trace elements are important for proper functioning of biological systems and their deficiency or excess could lead to a number of disorders. Food chain contamination by heavy metals has become a burning issue in recent years because of their potential accumulation in biosystems through contaminated water, soil and air. Therefore, a better understanding of heavy metal sources, their accumulation in the soil and the effect of their presence in water and soil on plant systems seem to be particularly important issues of present-day research on risk assessments (Lokeshwari and Chandrappa, 2006). Path of heavy metals in various trophic levels may be different due to the nature of heavy metals and quality of host abiotic components. Transfer rate may be evaluated by the calculation of concentrations of heavy metals between two different trophic levels. Transfer factor between plants and soil may be calculated for each metal according to the following formula:

$$TF = Ps\ (\mu g\ g{-}1\ dry\ wt)/St(\mu g\ g{-}1\ dry\ wt),$$

Where, *Ps* is the plant metal content originating from the soil and *St* is the total metal content in the soil (Lokeshwari and Chandrappa, 2006). Thus transfer factor (coefficient) may evaluate also between every two trophic levels of ecosystem.

Analysis of Metals

Collected, preserved, diluted water samples were prepared for the evaluation of metal concentrations with the help of AAS 4129. In the case of soil samples, a suspension (1:5) should be prepared in the distilled water; rest processes are like surface water and ground water samples. Metals enter in the surface, ground water and soil/sediments through the disposing of toxic textile effluents of dye houses. For every metal a standard was required and concentration may be detected by AAS. Diluted and completely digested samples were required for metal detection by AAS 4129. Metal elements were determined with the help of Atomic absorption spectrophotometer (Model AAS 4129). Alan Walsh first developed the technique of atomic absorption spectrophotometry in 1955, and since then it has emerged as a powerful tool in quantitative analysis of more than 70 metals. The major advantages of the method are that it is free from any kind of interferences and very small concentrations are possible to be measured (De, 2002). The AAS is based on the principle that atoms of elements, which normally remain in ground state under flame condition, absorb energy when subjected to radiation of specific wavelength. The absorption of radiation is proportional to the concentration of atoms of the element. The absorption of radiation by the atoms is independent of the wavelength of absorption and temperature of the atoms. These to feature provide AAS a distinct advantage over flame spectroscopy.

Copper (Cu)

Copper in the natural waters also results in higher concentration due to pollution. It is used with sulphate as a pesticides and also separately as an algicide. Although, it passes as such through the body but there is evidence of accumulation of trace quantities in liver. The limits of it in the standards are not due to its toxic effects but are due to its taste producing capacity.

Preparation of 1000 Cu (μg/ml) standard: Dissolve 1 gm of Cu in 50 ml of 6N of HNO_3 and dilute to 1 L to give 1000 μg/ml Cu.

Cadmium (Cd)

Cadmium is fairy dense silver white malleable and most toxic metal, which melts at 320.9°C. Cadmium is used for dye and paint pigment production, batteries, ceramic industries, wooden industries and plastic production. The Cd found in a sample of Ca is likely in a inorganic form and may be relatively less toxic to plants and animals, while same amount of Cd when present in zinc or phosphates may be highly toxic to plants and animals, especially when there is calcium deficiency in soil or livestock rations.

Preparation of 1000 Cd (μg/ml) standard: Dissolve 1 gm of Cd Metal in 20 ml of 5N HCl containing 0.5 ml of concentrated HNO_3 and dilute to 1 L to give 1000 μg/ml Cd.

Iron (Fe)

Iron is one of the most abundant elements of the rocks and soil, ranking fourth by weight. All kinds of waters including ground water have appreciable quantities of iron. Iron has more solubility at acidic pH, therefore large quantities of iron are leached out from the soils by acidic waters. In the alkaline medium iron remain comparatively low in soluble phase.

Preparation of 1000 Fe (μg/ml) standard, dissolve 1.000 g of iron wire in 50 ml of (1+1) HNO_3 and dilute to 1 liter with de-ionized water to give 1000 μg/ml Fe.

Manganese (Mn)

Although not a toxic metal, Mn imparts objectionable and tenacious stains to laundry plumbing fixtures and clothing. It occurs in domestic waste water, industrial effluents, acid mine drainage and receiving strums and therby enters water bodies. Mn is relatively non-toxic to animals, but toxic to plants at higher levels.

Preparation of 1000 Mn (μg/ml) standard: Dissolve 1 gm of Mn in 50 ml of 6N of HNO_3 and dilute to 1 L to give 1000 μg/ml Mn.

Nickel (Ni)

At high concentrations, nickel has toxic properties. Aquatic organisms have varying sensitivities to nickel salts depending on the water's pH, hardness, alkalinity and type of nickel compound under consideration. Nickel as a metal is a carcinogen.

Preparation of 1000 Ni (μg/ml) standard: Dissolve 1 gm of Ni metal in 50 ml of 6N of HNO_3 and dilute to 1 L to give 1000 μg/ml Ni.

Lead (Pb)

It is a dense soft metal and is quite resistant to corrosion. It has melting point of 327°C. Major source of lead is PbS (Galena). Lead is used for pipes, solders, electrodes, batteries, newsprint, and pigments in paints. Lead is also used in insecticides, beverages, ointments and synthetic dyes. The chemical form of lead determines its solubility in water and biological fluids, the extent of its fixation on soil and type of chemical reactions occurring in atmospheric, aquatic as well as soil environment.

Preparation of 1000 Pb (μg/ml) standard: Dissolve 1 gm of Pb metal in 20 ml of 6N of HNO_3 and dilute to 1 L to give 1000 μg/ml Pb.

Zinc (Zn)

Zinc is present in high concentrations in the wastes from pharmaceuticals, paint, galvanizing, cosmetics, dyes and pigments, etc., and their discharge increases its concentration in appreciable amounts in the waters. Zinc is very essential micronutrient in human beings and only at very high concentration it may cause some toxic effects. Zinc salts produce an undesirable taste to the water and causes water to appear milky and on boiling, a greasy surface scum may also form in the water (Mani *et. al.*, 2005).

Preparation of 1000 Zn (μg/ml) standard: Dissolve 1 gm of Zn metal in 40 ml of 5N HCl and dilute to 1 L to give 1000 μg/ml Zn.

Standards and Calibration

Possible metals and metals oxides are to be preferred in the preparation of standards. This enables the analyst to dissolve them that samples and standards will contain identical elements and hence minimizes any chemical or physical interference effects.

Only concentrated standards (above 1000 µg/ml) should be held in storage. Working standards should be diluted from standards stock solutions only when needed. At low concentrations (less than 10 µg/ml) solutions have been found to deteriorate quite quickly because of the absorption on the walls of the container. Similar standard addition solutions can be prepared containing all of the required elements. This will avoid multiple splitting of the sample for individual elements and reduce the amount of time spent in preparing standards. Before weighting, standards materials should be treated to ensure that they are in a standard state.

Metals: Wash with acetone and ether to remove any oil layers. Remove any oxide coating by abrasion with emery cloth or by acid pickling and drying.

Oxides: Dry at 110 °C for two hours. If necessary, heat to evaluated temperatures to remove bound water.

Compounds: Equilibration at constant water content, or drying at 110 °C for two hours to remove any water.

Standards of known concentrations were prepared and evaluated the concentration of metal in water/ soil digested sample. Every metal has some specific properties and atomic weight, so for every metal different condition of standard and calibration was applied for every metal (ECIL methods manual, 2004).

Observations

Experimental Site

Heavy metals in agriculture soil

Cadmium (ppm): The cadmium concentration in agricultural soil was recorded maximum 3.4 ± 0.7 in summer 2006 and minimum 0.70 ± 0.60 in monsoon 2005 ranged between 0.1 to 4.0 ppm. The highest value of cadmium in agricultural soil was found 4.0 ppm during June 2006 and lowest 0.1 ppm in August 2005.

Copper (ppm): The concentration of copper in agricultural soil was recorded maximum 36.3 ± 7.4 in summer 2005 and minimum 13.4 ± 6.0 in winter 2005-06 ranged between 5.0 to 42.5 ppm. The highest value of copper in agricultural soil was found 42.5 ppm during June 2006 and lowest 5.0 ppm in December 2005.

Iron (ppm): The concentration of iron in agricultural soil was recorded maximum 82.8 ± 18.1 in summer 2006 and minimum 26.8 ± 10.8 in monsoon 2005 ranged between 14.40 to 100.5 ppm. The highest value of iron in agricultural soil was found 100.5 ppm during May 2006 and lowest 14.40 ppm in October 2005.

Manganese (ppm): The concentration of manganese in agricultural soil was recorded maximum 13.6 ± 1.4 in summer 2005 and minimum 5.8 ± 1.7 in winter

2006-07 ranged between 2.0 to 15.0 ppm. The highest value of manganese in agricultural soil was found 15.0 ppm during June 2005 and lowest 2.0 ppm in December 2005.

Nickel (ppm): The concentration of nickel in agricultural soil was recorded maximum 10.5 ± 0.8 in summer 2005 and minimum 5.3 ± 1.1 in winter 2006-07 ranged between 3.8 to 12.1 ppm. The highest value of nickel in agricultural soil was found 12.1 ppm during May 2006 and lowest 3.8 ppm in December 2006.

Lead (ppm): The concentration of lead in agricultural soil was recorded maximum 62.4 ± 10.9 in summer 2005 and minimum 25.1 ± 6.7 in winter 2006-07 ranged between 16.0 to 73.5 ppm. The highest value of lead in agricultural soil was found 73.5 ppm during June 2006 and lowest 16.0 ppm in November 2005.

Zinc (ppm): The concentration of zinc in agricultural soil was recorded maximum 19.4 ± 4.7 in monsoon 2006 and minimum 7.7 ± 2.8 in winter 2005-06 ranged between 4.3 to 23.5 ppm. The highest value of zinc in agricultural soil was found 23.5 ppm during July 2006 and lowest 4.3 ppm in January 2006.

Control Site

Heavy metals

Cadmium (ppm): The cadmium concentration in soil on control site was recorded maximum 2.23 ± 0.31 in summer 2005 and minimum 0.225 ± 0.21 in winter 2006-07 ranged between 0.00 to 2.80 ppm. The highest value of cadmium in agricultural soil was found 2.80 ppm during June 2006 and lowest 0.00 ppm in September 2006.

Copper (ppm): The concentration of copper in soil on control site was recorded maximum 27.4 ± 5.7 in summer 2005 and minimum 10.0 ± 4.1 in winter 2005-06 ranged between 3.5 to 32.0 ppm. The highest value of copper in agricultural soil was found 32.0 ppm during May 2005 and lowest 3.5 ppm in December 2006.

Iron (ppm): The concentration of iron in soil on control site was recorded maximum 68.6 ± 17.5 in summer 2005 and minimum 18.4 ± 9.0 in winter 2006-07 ranged between 6.90 to 84.50 ppm. The highest value of iron in agricultural soil was found 84.50 ppm during April 2005 and lowest 6.90 ppm in October 2005.

Manganese (ppm): The concentration of manganese in soil on control site was recorded maximum 11.5 ± 1.1 in summer 2005 and minimum 4.8 ± 1.5 in winter 2006-07 ranged between 3.2 to 12.5 ppm. The highest value of manganese in agricultural soil was found 12.5 ppm during June 2005 and lowest 3.2 ppm in December 2006.

Nickel (ppm): The concentration of nickel in soil on control site was recorded maximum 8.43 ± 1.2 in summer 2005 and minimum 2.6 ± 1.87 in winter 2006-07 ranged between 0.00 to 9.20 ppm. The highest value of nickel in agricultural soil was found 9.20 ppm during June 2006 and lowest 0.00 ppm in November 2006.

Lead (ppm): The concentration of lead in soil on control site was recorded maximum 42.3 ± 3.1 in summer 2005 and minimum 18.25 ± 5.9 in winter 2006-07 ranged between 11.3 to 46.8 ppm. The highest value of lead in agricultural soil was found 46.8 ppm during June 2006 and lowest 11.3 ppm in November 2005.

Zinc (ppm): The concentration of zinc in soil on control site was recorded maximum 16.5 ± 3.3 in monsoon 2006 and minimum 7.3 ± 0.8 in summer 2007 ranged between 5.1 to 19.1 ppm. The highest value of zinc in agricultural soil was found 19.1 ppm during July 2006 and lowest 5.1 ppm in January 2006.

Correlation Coefficient

Correlation was found maximum 0.8421 and 0.7499 for cadmium with water holding capacity and sodium respectively. Correlation for copper was found maximum 0.9134 and 0.9454 with temperature and Electric conductivity respectively. Correlation for iron was found maximum 0.8736 and 0.8436 with water holding capacity and sodium respectively. Correlation for manganese was found maximum 0.8162 and 0.9076 with temperature and Electric conductivity respectively. Correlation for nickel was found maximum 0.7798 and 0.8286 with water holding capacity and Electric conductivity respectively. Correlation for lead was found maximum 0.8483 and 0.8596 with water holding capacity and Electric conductivity respectively. Correlation for zinc was found maximum 0.8513 and 0.7586 with temperature and Electric conductivity respectively.

For cadmium correlation was found maximum 0.8706 and 0.7532 with water holding capacity and Electric conductivity respectively. Correlation for copper was found maximum 0.9142 and 0.8290 with temperature and chloride respectively. Correlation for iron was found maximum 0.8397 and 0.8795 with water holding capacity and sodium respectively. Correlation for manganese was found maximum 0.8814 and 0.7925 with temperature and chloride respectively. Correlation for nickel was found maximum 0.7267 and 0.6699 with temperature and water holding capacity respectively. Correlation for lead was found maximum 0.8608 and 0.8055 with water holding capacity and Electric conductivity respectively. Correlation for zinc was found maximum 0.8704 and 0.7613 with temperature and chloride respectively. For cadmium correlation was found maximum 0.7611 and 0.6466 with cadmium and lead respectively. Correlation for copper was found maximum 0.9733 and 0.9121 with iron and nickel respectively. Correlation for iron was found maximum 0.8074 and 0.8628 with manganese and lead respectively. Correlation for manganese was found maximum 0.9279 and 0.9548 with nickel and zinc respectively. Correlation for nickel was found maximum 0.9458 and 0.9475 with manganese and nickel respectively. Correlation for lead was found maximum 0.9482 and 0.9664 with copper and manganese respectively. Correlation for zinc was found maximum 0.8065 and 0.5301 with iron and nickel respectively. For cadmium correlation was found maximum 0.7650 and 0.7646 with copper and manganese respectively. Correlation for copper was found maximum 0.2703 and 0.2542 with cadmium and iron respectively. Correlation for iron was found maximum 0.2989 with cadmium. Correlation for manganese was found maximum 0.7224 and 0.5619 with cadmium and iron respectively. Correlation for nickel was found maximum 0.8617 and 0.8799 with cadmium and iron respectively. Correlation for lead was found maximum 0.8432 and 0.7390 with copper and manganese respectively. Correlation for zinc was found maximum 0.7216 and 0.8553 with manganese and lead respectively.

Metals Accumulation Factor

Metal accumulation factor for cadmium was found maximum 8.56 in winter 2006-07 and minimum 0.91 in monsoon 2005. For copper metal accumulation factor was found maximum 3.15 in summer 2005 and minimum 1.31 in monsoon 2005. Metal accumulation factor for iron was maximum 1.49 in winter 2006-07 and minimum 1.12 in summer 2005. For manganese metal accumulation factor was maximum 1.31 in summer 2007 and minimum 1.11 in monsoon 2005. Metal accumulation factor for nickel was found maximum 2.05 in winter 2006-07 and minimum 1.17 in monsoon 2005. For lead metal accumulation factor was found maximum 1.48 in summer 2005 and minimum 1.28 in monsoon 2005. Metal accumulation factor for zinc was maximum 1.20 in monsoon 2005 and minimum 1.02 in winter 2006-07.

Discussion

Waste waters from textile industries have the high amount of the heavy metals entering them most hazardous for soil plant and other organisms including human beings (Sial *et al.,* 2006). Many effects of Cd action results from interactions of various micro and macro elements as it antagonizes to Cu, Zn and Fe and also interferes with Ca absorption. Cadmium found in a sample of Ca is likely in an inorganic form and may be relatively less toxic to flora and fauna, while same amount of Cd when present in zinc or phosphates may be highly toxic to plants and animals, especially in calcium deficiency in soil. The use of contaminated water into irrigation may be increase the cadmium status in agricultural soil (Mani *et al.,* 2005). An increasing number of ground water wells were found to be contaminated by chemical waste from point sources and also widespread known point source pollution from fertilizers was threatening the water resources in extensive areas (Lagas *et al.,* 1989 and Meier and Mull, 1989).

Cadmium concentrations in textile industrial effluent (0.005-0.052 ppm), pond water (0.001-0.012 ppm) and agricultural soil (0.7-3.4 ppm) turn down in rainy season due to the dilution factor, while in the ground water system its impact seems after monsoon and cadmium concentration reduces. Cadmium slightly fluctuated and remains mostly constant in pond sediment (4.0-5.7 ppm) and drain sediment (4.2-5.8 ppm). Transfer factor for cadmium (0.12-1.5) from textile industrial effluent to ground water was recorded high in winter months (after monsoon). In geo-accumulation index cadmium (3.77-3.81) laid in between 3 to 4 mean strongly polluted by cadmium. Metal accumulation factor for ground water (57.1-250.0) was found mostly very high or infinite for cadmium, because in most samples of control sites cadmium was absent.

Transfer factor of cadmium from ground water to agricultural soil on control site was found infinite, because cadmium was almost absent in ground water and agricultural soil at control site. So, any correlation between ground water and agricultural soil was not noticed. Cadmium transfer is due to some other non-point sources of cadmium pollution. Figure-5.4.6 showing the transfer factor of cadmium from ground water to agricultural soil clearly indicated the transfer level of metal. During the last decade, the industrial use of Cd has increased and can create both acute and chronic cases of clinically identifiable toxicity in humans. In human, absorption of dietary Cd is limited up to 15 % and that of inhaled Cd is high 40 % and not absorbed from skin (Mani *et al.*, 2005). When the animal kept on contaminated feed along with the industrial polluted environment for long time, they suffer from its toxicity symptoms which may be sub clinical or clinical. The retention time of Cd is quite high, half life being 40 years. Cadmium is produced as inevitable by-product of zinc (or occasionally lead) refining (lenntech.com). Cd was found slightly high in ground water for drinking purposes, because it should not be more than 0.003 mg/l for health views, while it should be less than 1 µg/l generally in drinking water (WHO, 2006). Helena (1999), Umar and Ahmad (2000), Kumar *et al.*,(2001) and Yadav *et al.*,(2002) observed the high Cd concentrations in industrial area like the present study of ground water, while Krebs *et al.*, (1999), Singh *et al.*,(1994) and Fakayode and Oniyawa (2002) in soil and Bordas and Bourg (1998), Vazquez *et al.*, (2007) and Korfali and Davies (2004) in sediment.

During the last decade, the industrial use of Cd has increased and can create both acute and chronic cases of clinically identifiable toxicity in humans. In human, absorption of dietary Cd is limited up to 15 % and that of inhaled Cd is high 40 % and not absorbed from skin (Mani *et al.*, 2005). When the animal kept on contaminated feed along with the industrial polluted environment for long time, they suffer from its toxicity symptoms which may be sub clinical or clinical. The retention time of Cd is quite high, half life being 40 years. Cadmium is produced as inevitable by-product of zinc (or occasionally lead) refining (lenntech.com). Cd was found slightly high in ground water for drinking purposes, because it should not be more than 0.003 mg/l for health views, while it should be less than 1 µg/l generally in drinking water (WHO, 2006). Helena (1999), Umar and Ahmad (2000), Kumar *et al.*,(2001) and Yadav *et al.*,(2002) observed the high Cd concentrations in industrial area like the present study of ground water, while Krebs *et al.*, (1999), Singh *et al.*,(1994) and Fakayode and

Oniyawa (2002) in soil and Bordas and Bourg (1998), Vazquez *et al.,* (2007) and Korfali and Davies (2004) in sediment.

Concentrations of copper in textile industrial effluent are due to the residues of some dyes especially used for blue or green colours. Copper concentrations in textile industrial effluent (0.16-0.44 ppm) were found parallel or sometimes higher than iron. Most of the part of copper content reach in pond water (0.25-0.43 ppm) and rest settle down on drain sediment (45.8-54.8 ppm). Copper in pond sediment (38.6-52.4 ppm) also settled down after some time. Transfer factor of copper from pond water to ground water (0.97-1.17) and ground water to agricultural soil (0.45-0.82) was found higher than other microelement except cadmium. In geo-accumulation index copper was not recorded in polluted condition. Metal accumulation factor for copper was recorded high in winter season (3.28) for ground water; while in agricultural soil high metal accumulation factor was found in summer months (1.20).

Copper is sometimes found in insufficient quantity in soil (Miller and Turk, 2002) but it may be added in to soil system by some anthropogenic activities. Copper may accumulate in living organisms and their various body parts (Kudesia, 1992). High amount if heavy metals like cu and Zn may harm to living organism of existing ecosystem (Aslam *et al.,* 2004).

However, Cu concentration was not detected high in ground water samples as described by WHO (2006) in drinking water i.e. 2.0 mg/l. The Cu concentrations level in study area have compared with those observed by Yusus and Sonibare (2004), Aslam *et al.,* (2004), Helena (1999), Umar and Ahmad (2000), Kumar *et al.,*(2001) and Yadav *et al.,*(2002) in ground water; Krebs *et al.,* (1999), Singh *et al.,*(1994) and Fakayode and Oniyawa (2002) in soil and Bordas and Bourg (1998), Nasr *et al.,*(2006), Vazquez *et al.,* (2007) and Korfali and Davies (2004) in sediments. Ather and Vohra (1985) reported that heavy metal enters in water system by various ways in natural resources like erosion, weathering, volcanic activities and anthropogenic activities that include direct emissions of heavy metal by different industries.

Iron is one of the most abundant elements of the rocks and soil, ranking fourth by weight. All kinds of waters including ground water have appreciable quantities of iron. Iron has more solubility at acidic pH, therefore large quantities of iron are leached out from the soils by acidic waters. In the alkaline medium iron remain comparatively low in soluble phase. Excess calcium can reduced the activity of iron in soil and soil aeration may influence the availability of iron to plants (Miller and Turk, 2002).

In ground waters most of the iron remains in ferrous state due to general lack of oxygen. In alkaline conditions in ground waters, the iron is mostly ferrous bicarbonate, which is a colourless substance. When the ground water with higher concentrations of iron is tapped, it quickly oxidizes to ferric state in the form of insoluble ferric hydroxide, a brown substance. If appreciable quantities of ferrous bicarbonates are present in ground water, and they come in contact with oxygen at surface, the hydroxides are formed, CO_2 is released and hence it increases the pH, facilitating the oxidation processes (Minhas and Gupta, 1992). Generally, movement of iron compounds take place downward through the soil profile and reach in to ground water table (Miller and Turk, 2002). However, iron was not found in high concentration in textile industrial effluents (0.24-0.54 ppm), but the high concentrations of iron were observed in effluent drain sediment (5656.0-8467.7 ppm) due to the continuous settlement and abundantly natural occurrence in earth crust materials. Iron in shallow ground water samples (1.5-3.8 ppm) was found higher to textile effluents, while iron in deep ground water (0.48-1.05 ppm) and control ground water (0.363-0.868 mg/l) was not detected in high concentrations. Iron was present in high quantity in pond sediment (3803.5-6013.4 ppm) and effluent drain sediment (5656.0-8467.7 ppm). Iron concentration in agricultural soil was analyzed comparatively higher than other metals.

Iron's transfer factors were found very high from textile industrial effluent to ground water (5.93-9.64), from textile industrial effluent to pond water up to 25.00, while iron was transferred from pond water to ground water with highest 0.40 coefficient. However, transfer factor of iron was noticed low in comparison to other metals from shallow ground water to agricultural soil. Metal enrichment factor in all seasons and in all sediment samples was calculated 1000.0 due to the comparative parameter for other metals for determination metals enrichment factor. In geo-accumulation index for drain sediment and pond sediment iron was not indexed at very high rank, it was found very low because the natural occurrence of iron in earth crust shale was very high, so iron was not a pollution causing agent in industrial area during the present study. Metal accumulation factor of iron was found from 2-4 for ground water in Panipat region. Iron was detected in ground water with 2-4 times high quantities in comparison to control site's ground water. Iron in textile industrial effluent and pond water was found very high, while in ground water samples it was also found very high for drinking purposes (WHO, 2006) Helena (1999), Yusus and Sonibare (2004), Umar and Ahmad (2000), Kumar *et al.*,(2001) and Yadav *et al.*,(2002) observed the similar trends of iron concentrations in ground water and Singh *et al.*,(1994) in agricultural soil of industrial area.

Manganese was found as a second abundant element in the effluent drain and pond sediment after iron. However, manganese was comparatively low in textile industrial effluent (0.11-0.31 ppm) and very low in ground water samples (0.28-0.55 ppm). In ground water samples manganese remains below 1.0 during the study even in shallow aquifer. In agricultural soil, manganese was comparatively low in concentrations (5.8-13.6 ppm) regarding other metals. Manganese was third most enriched element in ground water samples. Mn was found slightly high at experimental sites in the case of soil samples. Manganese has positive relationship with all the physico-chemical parameters of ground water as correlated with temperature (0.6892), total solids (0.8508) electric conductivity (0.8544), total alkalinity (0.7074) except dissolved oxygen.

Transfer factor of Mn from textile industrial effluent to pond water was noticed from 1to 4 almost in all seasons, while below 1 in winter season. Transfer factor was calculated near 1 in all seasons from pond water to ground water. Transfer factor from ground water to agricultural soil was noticed very low at experimental sites as well as at control site. Enrichment factor of Mn was found around 100-200, highest after Fe in drain sediment, while enrichment factor was noticed higher in pond sediment. The value of Mn in geo-accumulation index was noticed always below 1 with negative rank even highest value in drain sediment as well as pond sediment due to the high natural shale value of Mn in earth crust. Metal accumulation factor of Mn in ground water was high and ranged between 2 to 4, while in soil environment it was found below 2 always. Mn was found slightly high in ground water for drinking purposes, because it should not be more than 0.5 mg/l for health views in drinking water (WHO, 2006).

Mathess (1974) reported that fresh ground water constitutes 0.00-0.007 ppm cadmium, WHO (1984) recommended Cd concentration should not exceed maximum of 0.01 ppm in raw drinking water supply, 0.5 ppm in irrigation water. USEPA (1990) recommended maximum permissible Cd concentration as 0.04 and 0.02 ppm to protect aquatic life including fish. Hart (1982) reported a concentration range of Pb 0.0003-0.03 ppm in natural fresh water, while Frostner and Wittman (1979) the likely level as 0.002 ppm. Siddiqui and Pathania (2002) reported that the high value of Pb, Cr and other trace metals in ground water in Jalandhar and Ludiana industrial area.

Manganese, Iron and potassium may deficient in alkaline soil (Miller and Turk, 2002), while manganese and iron is soluble in acidic soil (Brady, 1995). Manganese usually is present in sufficient quantity in most soils and need not be added for plant growth (Miller and Turk, 2002). Yusus and Sonibare (2004), Umar and Ahmad (2000), Kumar *et al.,*(2001) and Yadav *et al.,*(2002) gave a report of Mn status in ground water, Fakayode and Oniyawa (2002) in soil system and Nasr *et al.,*(2006) in sediments of aquatic system affected by industrial pollution.

Nickel is one of the second trace elements of the present study after cadmium. As it is very toxic to plants and animals in low concentrations and has a tendency to accumulate in body parts. However Ni was presented in very minor concentrations in textile industrial effluent (0.007-0.067 ppm), and pond water (0.047-0.13 ppm), it was found comparatively high due to the regular input. Ni concentrations in pond were noticed higher during the summer season due to the loss of water by vaporization from pond system. About similar conditions were observed in ground water samples. In deep ground water, Ni was almost absent like cadmium. In agricultural soil all metals were found higher than ground water so, nickel was also found high (5.3-10.5 ppm). Ni was found very high like other metals due to the settling of metals on bottom beds in pond sediment (49.0-63.7 ppm) and drain sediment (58.0-75.0 ppm). Nickel has no positive correlations with any physico-chemical parameter of soil and water except total alkalinity, Calcium, electric conductivity and water holding capacity. Highest transfer factor of Ni from textile industrial effluent to pond water and ground water (14.14) was found in monsoon seasons. However, transfer factor from pond water to ground water (0.83-1.29) was not found effective comparative to transfer factor of other metals from ground water to agricultural soil at control site. Like cadmium, Ni was sometimes found infinitive in winter seasons.

Enrichment factor of Ni (7.35-11.7) was not effective in comparison to iron in drain sediment, but in pond sediment (8.38-14.85) it was slightly high due to the high retention time of wastewater in pond. The observations of present study reveals that Ni never reflected the pollution load in drain or pond sediment through the geo-accumulation index because it was found always below than 1. Metal accumulation factor in agricultural soil was recorded around 1-2, while in ground water it was found slightly high or sometimes infinitive. Ni was found high in ground water for drinking purposes, because it should not be more than 0.07 mg/l for health views, while it should be less than 0.02 mg/l generally in drinking water (WHO, 2006). Nickel may accumulate in aquatic life but its presence is not magnified along food chains (lenntech.com). So, there is not so big fear of nickel toxicity to higher animals including human beings, but agricultural plant health will be affected in contaminated agricultural soil. This trend of Ni concentrations in present study have been supported on the basis of recommendation of Kumar *et al.,* (2001) and Yadav *et al.,*(2002) in ground water, Kasem and Singh (1999), Singh *et al.,*(1994) and Fakayode and Oniyawa (2002) in soil and Nasr *et al.,* (2006) in sediment. Jayabaskeran and Sree Ramulu (1996) observed a great heavy metal movement in sewage irrigating light textured soil than in heavy textured soil. It may be pointed out that the builds up of heavy metal like Cr, Pb, Ni warrant toward continuous monitoring and suitable measures are needed before these become toxic.

Lead was found highest in textile industrial effluent, but it accumulated in drain sediment in comparatively less quantity. Lead mostly remained in effluent (0.25-0.50 ppm) and fluctuated in pond (0.5-1.8 ppm). Rest quantity of lead settled down on bed sediment of drain and pond, so, the lead concentration was found low in pond sediment (44.0-69.0 ppm) and high in drain sediment (47.2-70.0 ppm). Lead was the second most abundant metal species after iron. Lead was found in high concentrations in shallow ground water (0.85-1.84 ppm) in comparison to deep ground water (0.28-0.41 ppm). Pb was also second most enriched element after iron in agricultural soil (25.1-62.4 ppm) due to the high distribution of these metals in earth crust. Lead is deposited mostly in bones and some soft tissues. High concentrations of lead may create toxicity in human (Kudesia, 1992).

Pb was found slightly high in ground water (0.85-1.84 ppm) for drinking purposes and also in pond water (0.50-1.8 ppm), because it should not be more than 0.01 mg/l for health views, while it should be less than 0.1 mg/l generally in drinking water (WHO, 2006). Helena (1999), Umar and Ahmad (2000), Kumar *et al.*,(2001) and Yadav *et al.*,(2002) were observed the same trend of occurrence of Pb concentrations in ground water, Fakayode and Oniyawa (2002), Krebs *et al.*, (1999) and Singh *et al.*,(1994) in soil environment and Bordas and Bourg (1998), Nasr *et al.*,(2006) and Vazquez *et al.*, (2007) in sediment.

However, zinc was not found so high in textile industrial effluent (0.11-0.34 ppm) in comparison to lead, but it was found in very high concentrations in drain sediment (143.5-260.0 ppm). Similarly, it was found in less quantity in pond water (0.11-0.2 ppm) and accumulated in very high quantity in bed sediment (116.2-240.0 ppm) of pond. Zinc concentration was fluctuated in pond sediment (116.2-240.0 ppm) season to season, while in drain sediment (143.5-260.0 ppm) the fluctuation of zinc concentrations was not observed in high concentration. Zinc concentration (0.13-0.22 ppm) was found at fifth position in ground water samples among the all seven metals, while zinc concentration was found at fourth position in agricultural soil (7.7-19.4 ppm) among all metals studied. However, the concentrations of zinc in agricultural soil was found manifold than ground water, pond water and textile industrial effluent due to the natural occurrence of zinc in soil profile. During the study, in all experimental soils zinc concentration was found slightly higher than those at control soil (7.3-16.5 ppm). Positive correlations were found between zinc and temperature (0.8704), electric conductivity (0.2569), Cl (0.7613), pH (0.4955) in agricultural soil. Positive relationship was noticed between heavy metals of ground water with Zn. Transfer factor of zinc from textile industrial effluent to pond water was not found more than 1. However, transfer factor of Zn was found more than 1 from pond water to ground water during almost all seasons.

Transfer factor of Zn from ground water to agricultural soil was found slightly higher than 1 at experimental sites, while it was also found higher even more than 2 at control site. Enrichment factor of zinc in drain sediment was ranked at third position, while it was noticed slightly high in pond sediment due to the long retention time. In geo-accumulation index, the value of zinc was found more than 1.0 in all seasons, and ranked below 1 in geo-accumulation index in drain sediment.

Metal accumulation factor of Zn was calculated between 2 to 3 in ground water samples, while metal accumulation factor was found near 1 in the case of agricultural soil and always remain below 2. Zn was found low in ground water and in pond water for drinking purposes, because it should not be more than 3.0 mg/l for health views, while it should be less than 5.0 mg/l generally in drinking water (WHO, 2006).

Zinc is sometimes found in insufficient quantity in soil (Miller and Turk, 2002). Zinc salts are relatively non-toxic, but high concentrations may cause health problems like vomiting, renal damage, etc. (Kudesia, 1992). High amount of Zn may harm to living organism of that ecosystem (Aslam *et al.*, 2004). Helena (1999), Umar and Ahmad (2000), Kumar *et al.*, (2001), Yadav *et al.*,(2002), Yusus and Sonibare (2004) and Aslam *et al.*, (2004) reported the same fluctuations of Zn concentrations in ground water, Singh *et al.*,(1994), Krebs *et al.*, (1999) and Fakayode and Oniyawa (2002) in soil and Bordas and Bourg (1998), Nasr *et al.*,(2006), Vazquez *et al.*, (2007) and Korfali and Davies (2004) in sediment.

Heavy metals added to the soil in the field strongly absorbed by first component of upper part of undisturbed soil horizons. Subsequent redistribution to lower soil layers probably takes a very long time due to slow adsorption and heavy metals in upper layer tend to increase with time (Alumaa *et al.*, 2001). The trace heavy metal ions activities, depends on the solubility in the soil and often a much better indicator of heavy metal in soil solution reflected the soil metal fraction, that is most directly available for plants uptake, absorption by soil biota or leaching to ground water (McBride *etal.*, 1997; Cances *et al.*, 2003 and Lofts *et al.*, 2004).

Minor or secondary elements such as magnesium, manganese, calcium, zinc, copper, boron, iron, and perhaps others are essential but except in certain specific cases either they are injurious to crop and soil in large quantity. If any element is lacking in soil or it is present in improper proportions normal plant growth will not occur (Miller and Turk, 2002). It is urgently required that industries should continuously monitor textile effluent and take necessary actions to properly treat waste water prior their disposal to water bodies and save already depleting natural water resources (Aslam *et al.*, 2004).

Transfer of Heavy Metals

In the recent years there has been a growing concern with environmental protection. This can be achieved either by decreasing the afflux of pollutants to the environment or by their removal from contaminated media. The former is a feasible choice only for pollutants of anthropogenic origin, whereas, the latter is unavoidable for those of natural origin (Gomez-Serrano *et al.*, 1998). The presence of heavy metals in the aquatic environment has been of great concern to scientists and engineers because of their increased discharge, toxic nature, and other adverse effects on receiving waters (Singh, 2006).

In heavy metals analysis, the total concentrations of the metals are often determined (Okonwo *et al.*, 1999, 2001; Castro Dentros *et al.*, 2003). However, total concentration of trace metals provides no information concerning the fate of the metal in the terms of its interaction with sediments, its mobility, bioavailability, or resultant toxicity (Christie, 1995). It is now widely accepted that measuring total metal concentrations cannot fully assess the role of aquatic sediments as a sink or as a source of pollutants. In addition, determination of total elements does not given an accurate estimate of the likely environmental impact. Instead, it is desirable to have information on the potential availability of metals (whether toxic or essential) to biota under various environmental conditions. Since the mobility of heavy metals, as well as their bioavailability and related eco-toxicity to plants, critically depends upon chemical forms in which, a metal is present in the sediment, considerable interest exists in trace element speciation (Davidson *et al.*, 1994).

Heavy metals are introduced into aquatic system from various anthropogenic sources. Heavy metals constitute a special group of contaminants of aquatic systems and deserve special attention. Since metals are not removed by natural degradation processes, they may become enriched in sediments over time. Metal contamination of sediments is an issue of growing concerns worldwide (NRC, 1989). Both natural processes and anthropogenic activities are responsible for introducing metals in to the aquatic system (Nriagu, 1989). Many contaminants discharged into surface waters rapidly become associated with the particulate matter and incorporated in sediments. Metals in aquatic systems become part of the water-sediment system and their distribution is controlled by a dynamic set of physical-chemical interactions and equilibrium, largely governed by pH and type of legends and chelating agents, oxidation state of the mineral components and the redox conditions of the system. Metal contaminated sediments may release heavy metals back to the overlying water column and, thus, pose risk to aquatic life and ecosystems. Due to their particle reactivity, heavy metals tend to accumulate in sediment as a result may persist in the environment long after their primary sources have been removed (Forstner and Wittman, 1981).

Heavy metals travel from one level to another in the ecological system due to the accumulation in abiotic and biotic components. In the study area, basically anthropogenic source of heavy metals are the dye houses in textile industrial area. Heavy metals reach in effluent drain and also its bottom sediment and further into pond and bed sediment of pond near village Binjhole adjoining to textile industrial area of Panipat. Heavy metals percolate slowly from the bed sediment of Binjhole pond towards the ground water table and there may be a threat to deep aquifers also by leaching process of metals. As the ground water was mostly used in irrigation and drinking purposes in most rural parts of Haryana, which have affected the agricultural soil health after irrigation by contaminated ground water and ultimately influence on the agricultural productivity, vegetation health and grain quality also. The use of ground water for drinking purposes of human and cattle in contaminated conditions, a threat of various health hazards and diseases have occurred to public at present. Some of the diseases caused by toxic heavy metals have been lethal to living organisms.

Accumulation of Heavy Metals

Due to the industrialization, a huge quantity of waste materials discarded outside from the industries, in which various toxic substances including heavy metals are present. These large quantities of discarded heavy metals have been created havoc in the environmental ecosystem and affected all biotic components of the surrounding water and agricultural system. The accumulating processes of run-off derived metals from the point and non-point pollution sources and their significant accumulation in the sediment of drain and pond with furthermore retention in agricultural soil has been observed by many investigators (Harper *et al.*, 1984; Nightangle, 1987 and Yusuf *et al.*, 1986). The extent of contamination due to heavy metal deposition in different industrial sites in relation to quite vulnerable metal toxicity among soil biota and plants have been investigated by Moon *et al.*, (1991) and recorded Cd, Cu, Pb, Zn level in the industrial drain and top soil of agricultural fields.

Heavy metals have a tendency to accumulate and store in a component or trophic levels. The storage of heavy metals has created harmful effects for biotic components. The heavy metals accumulated in sediment and percolated down in to ground water known as bio-accumulation of metal. From ground water, heavy metals may turn into two ways; one is though irrigation and second is through drinking by human beings. The accumulation of heavy metals through the food chain is called the bio-magnifications. The concentrations of metal increased at every next trophic level, whereas metals can cause various harmful effects on irrigated agricultural soil, human beings and livestock by alteration in some biochemical reaction in body cells (De, 2002).

In the present study, heavy metals in pond water were observed slightly lower than textile industrial effluents, whereas the heavy metal concentrations in effluent drain were higher than pond sediment. Shallow ground water of about 40 ft depth was highly polluted in comparison to increasing depth of water table. Although the effect of spatial variation was also found in the study, when the heavy metals concentrations in ground water and soils at control site were presented comparatively in less or very less quantities. Some metals like cadmium and nickel were not detected in ground water at control site. After all, if the conditions will be same in textile industrial area then definitely there is a fear to contamination of ground water into horizontal direction also and this will affect the ground water of surroundings and deep aquifers with the time.

Table 3.1: Seasonal Variation of Heavy Metals in Agricultural Irrigated Soil

Heavy metals	Unit	Summer 2005		Monsoon 2005		Winter 2005-06		Summer 2006		Monsoon 2006		Winter 2006-07		Summer 2007	
		Mean	SD	Mean	SD	Mean	SD	Mean	SD	Mean	SD	Mean	SD	Mean	SD
Cad-mium (Cd)	ppm	3.333	0.611	0.667	0.551	1.780	0.444	3.350	0.686	1.200	1.153	1.925	0.350	2.650	0.212
Copper (Cu)	ppm	36.300	7.422	30.200	5.345	13.400	5.968	34.875	9.309	32.333	5.498	14.350	4.916	20.850	3.748
Iron (Fe)	ppm	76.667	16.805	26.767	10.772	28.800	13.221	82.825	18.097	30.400	12.375	27.450	10.051	62.100	13.859
Manga-nese (Mn)	ppm	13.567	1.401	10.233	2.380	5.900	2.799	13.075	1.910	11.033	1.960	5.775	1.676	10.450	1.768
Nickel (Ni)	ppm	10.467	0.757	7.633	1.137	5.780	1.244	10.525	1.812	8.067	1.504	5.325	1.056	9.050	1.061
Lead (Pb)	ppm	62.400	10.922	39.333	11.675	25.340	9.226	61.300	11.385	44.933	15.791	25.100	6.733	46.150	4.738
Zinc (Zn)	ppm	13.167	3.911	18.533	5.150	7.680	2.805	13.025	3.471	19.400	4.747	9.150	3.101	8.000	1.697

Table 3.2: Seasonal Variation of Heavy Metals in Soil at Control Site

Heavy metals	Unit	Summer 2005		Monsoon 2005		Winter 2005-06		Summer 2006		Monsoon 2006		Winter 2006-07		Summer 2007	
		Mean	SD	Mean	SD	Mean	SD	Mean	SD	Mean	SD	Mean	SD	Mean	SD
Cadmium (Cd)	ppm	2.233	0.306	0.733	0.473	0.460	0.351	2.000	0.770	1.233	0.451	0.225	0.206	1.400	0.141
Copper (Cu)	ppm	11.533	15.396	23.000	4.036	9.980	4.141	20.525	13.495	22.733	4.966	10.250	5.637	15.800	4.667
Iron (Fe)	ppm	68.633	17.539	19.000	11.207	20.940	12.563	66.450	15.315	21.133	11.208	18.400	9.038	48.250	9.263
Manganese (Mn)	ppm	11.500	1.114	9.200	1.833	4.962	2.028	10.775	1.791	9.533	2.159	4.800	1.490	7.950	1.202
Nickel (Ni)	ppm	8.433	1.172	6.533	1.026	3.380	1.846	8.050	1.313	6.767	1.026	2.600	1.867	6.300	0.283
Lead (Pb)	ppm	42.267	3.121	30.633	8.999	19.000	7.316	41.925	3.677	31.400	7.602	18.275	5.934	34.600	4.101
Zinc (Zn)	ppm	12.100	1.500	15.400	3.830	7.460	2.475	11.700	2.655	16.467	3.275	8.950	2.885	7.250	0.778

Table 2.3: Mean Values (±SD) of Heavy Metals in Soil at Control and Experiment Sites

Heavy metals	Unit	2005-06				2006-07			
		Control Site	SD	Experi-mental sites	SD	Control Site	SD	Experi-mental sites	SD
Cadmium (Cd)	ppm	1.033	0.819	1.950	1.098	1.183	0.893	2.292	1.099
Copper (Cu)	ppm	14.317	9.218	24.100	11.451	17.050	9.744	26.075	11.391
Iron (Fe)	ppm	35.267	25.354	43.150	25.433	36.975	24.866	49.417	29.212
Manganese (Mn)	ppm	7.984	3.215	9.283	3.850	8.158	3.086	9.908	3.601
Nickel (Ni)	ppm	5.675	2.527	7.608	2.161	5.767	2.731	8.133	2.611
Lead (Pb)	ppm	29.317	11.729	39.967	17.818	30.508	11.188	43.750	18.264
Zinc (Zn)	ppm	10.667	4.148	11.867	5.640	11.525	4.195	12.833	5.460

Table 2.4: Correlation Between Heavy Metals and Physico-chemical Parameters of Agricultural Soil

Parameters	Tempera-ture	WHC	Bulk density	Soil moisture	pH	EC	Cl	Na	K
Cadmium (Cd)	0.2211	0.8421	-0.5639	-0.8066	-0.2848	0.3965	0.3654	0.7499	0.6852
Copper (Cu)	0.9134	0.5300	-0.0815	0.0914	0.3754	0.9454	0.8479	0.0853	-0.1689
Iron (Fe)	0.3455	0.8736	-0.6445	-0.6449	-0.4051	0.4198	0.3249	0.8436	0.7116
Manganese (Mn)	0.8162	0.6657	-0.2403	-0.0712	0.2034	0.9076	0.7254	0.3169	0.0611
Nickel (Ni)	0.7218	0.7798	-0.3816	-0.2585	0.0187	0.8286	0.6603	0.4813	0.2623
Lead (Pb)	0.7091	0.8483	-0.4542	-0.2607	0.0462	0.8596	0.6972	0.4876	0.2369
Zinc (Zn)	0.8513	0.0750	0.3246	0.5031	0.6535	0.7586	0.7744	-0.4581	-0.6269

Table 2.5: Correlation between Heavy Metals of Agricultural Soil

	Cadmium (Cd)	Copper (Cu)	Iron (Fe)	Manganese (Mn)	Nickel (Ni)	Lead (Pb)	Zinc (Zn)
Cadmium (Cd)	1						
Copper (Cu)	0.3719	1					
Iron (Fe)	0.7981	0.5348	1				
Manganese (Mn)	0.4834	0.9502	0.6730	1			
Nickel (Ni)	0.6368	0.8904	0.8093	0.9581	1		
Lead (Pb)	0.6911	0.8811	0.7809	0.9274	0.9566	1	
Zinc (Zn)	-0.1615	0.7484	-0.0190	0.5876	0.4374	0.466065186	1

Table 2.6: Metal Accumulation Factor for the Agricultural Soil of Panipat Region

	Summer 2005	Monsoon 2005	Winter 2005-06	Summer 2006	Monsoon 2006	Winter 2006-07	Summer 2007
Cadmium (Cd)	1.49	0.91	3.87	1.68	0.97	8.56	1.89
Copper (Cu)	3.15	1.31	1.34	1.70	1.42	1.40	1.32

Iron (Fe)	1.12	1.41	1.38	1.25	1.44	1.49	1.29
Manganese (Mn)	1.18	1.11	1.19	1.21	1.16	1.20	1.31
Nickel (Ni)	1.24	1.17	1.71	1.31	1.19	2.05	1.44
Lead (Pb)	1.48	1.28	1.33	1.46	1.43	1.37	1.33
Zinc (Zn)	1.09	1.20	1.03	1.11	1.18	1.02	1.10

Conclusion

The study indicates that there was heavy metals pollution in pond water and sediment, which affected the ground water of the industrial area of Panipat region. Beside this, the bottom sediment of common effluent drain stored the heavy metals in high quantities, which have no secure or pre-managed future. Thus, textile industrial effluents discharging from dye houses contaminated the surface water, drain sediment, pond sediment and ground water also. Furthermore, the impact of heavy metals reflected negative impacts on agricultural soil after irrigation by contaminated ground water. Heavy metals remained in upper part of soil horizons mostly but moved in to lower soil layers probably after a long time due to slow adsorption (Alumaa *et al.*, 2001). Heavy metals strongly absorbed by first component to which they make contact and plants uptake them. So there is a fear to accumulate the heavy metals in different body parts of vegetation. High quantity of heavy metals accumulated in organisms may be harmful for health of organisms and create various diseases, which may magnify through food web of the water and agricultural ecosystems.

Heavy metals from textile industries affected the shallow ground water quality in shallow badly, while deep ground water affected slightly. Vertically, heavy metals contamination decreased with the increasing depth of water table. In the case of horizontal distribution, the heavy metal concentrations decrease with increasing distance from pollution source. In the circle of 1 Km from pollution source almost heavy metals level was found higher than the outer wide circle in the industrial area. Heavy metals contamination was found to be low in soil at control site and also in outer circle of textile industrial area. However, the area of around 1 Km from textile industrial area was found highly affected by heavy metals in Panipat region. Textile industrial effluent or contaminated ground water has been altered the physico-chemical parameters of agricultural soil. It was indicated that the comparison of agricultural soil to control soil that some characteristics were influenced by contaminated irrigated ground water. Heavy metals in agricultural soil were found slightly higher than control soil. Due to the regular discharging of metals residues in the textile industrial area, threat have been appear on plant vegetation, livestock and human beings also of the region. So, some appropriate measures for the amendment and control of textile pollution should be adopted by industrialists, municipality, government,

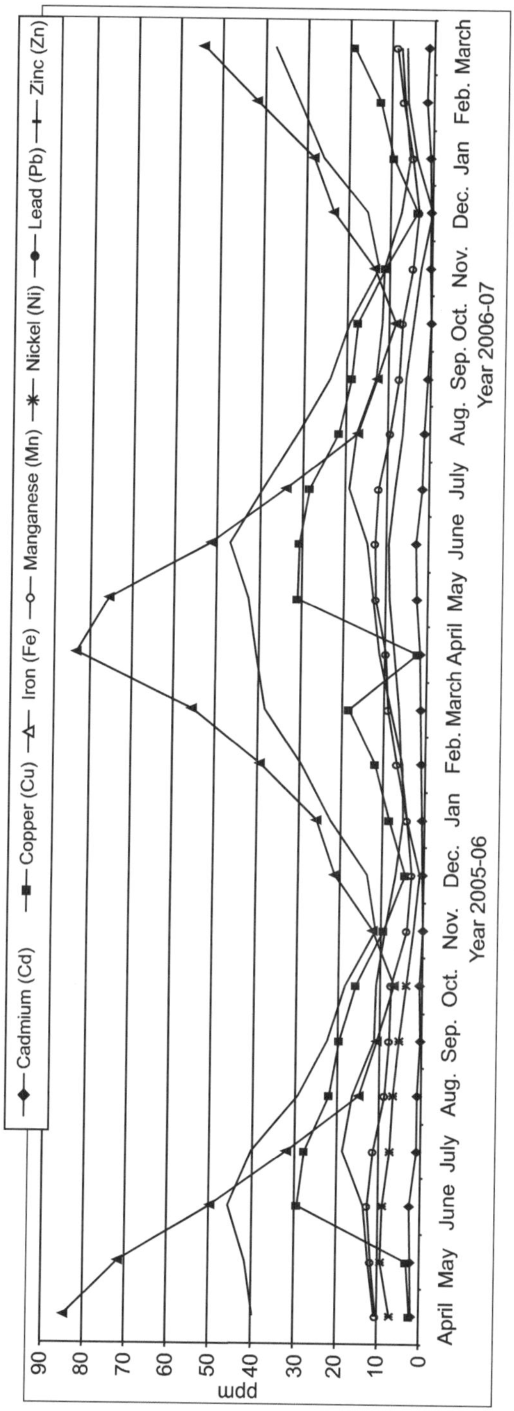

Fig. 3.1: Heavy metals fluctuation in agricultural soil

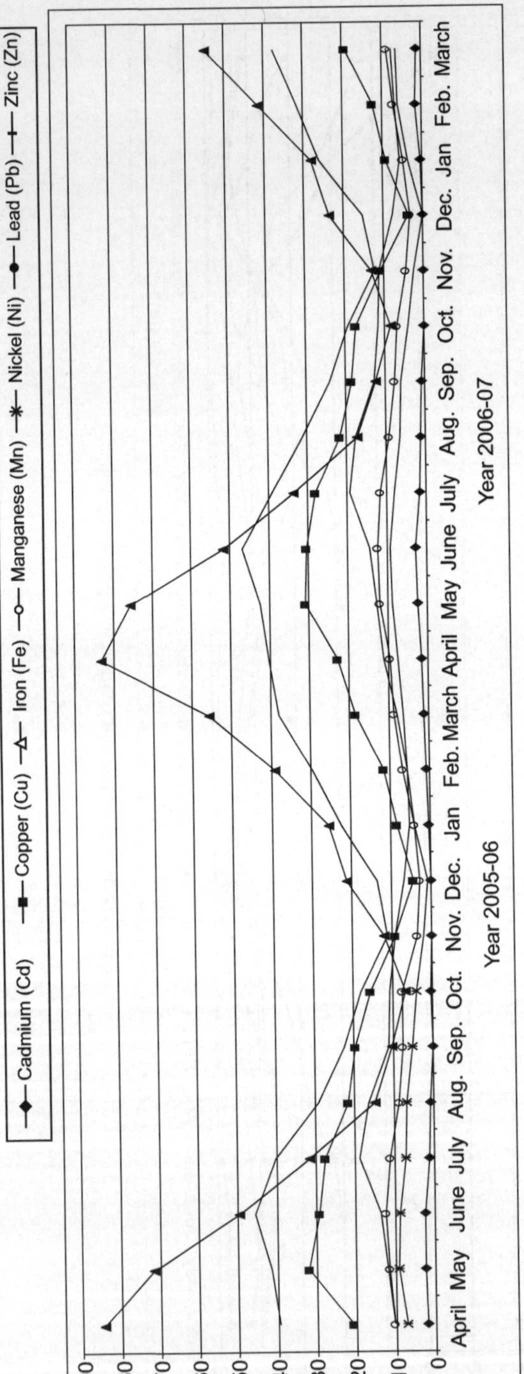

Fig. 3.2: Heavy metals fluctuation in soil at control site

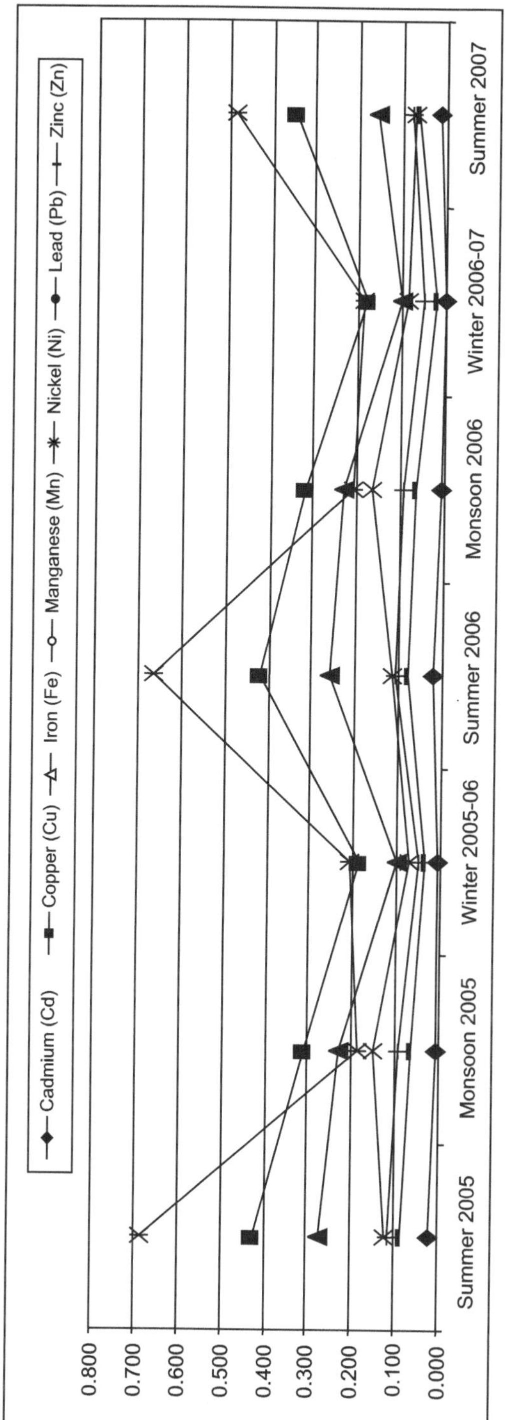

Fig. 3.3: Seasonal fluctuation of heavy metals in soil at control site

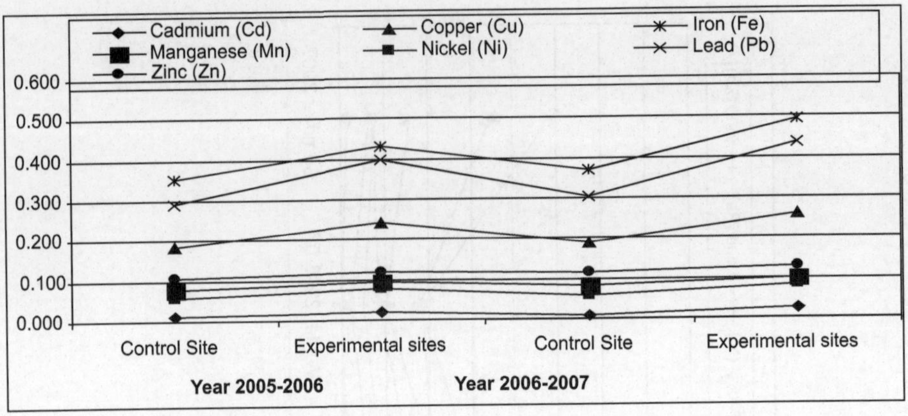

Fig. 3.4: Mean values of heavy metals in soil at control and experimental sites

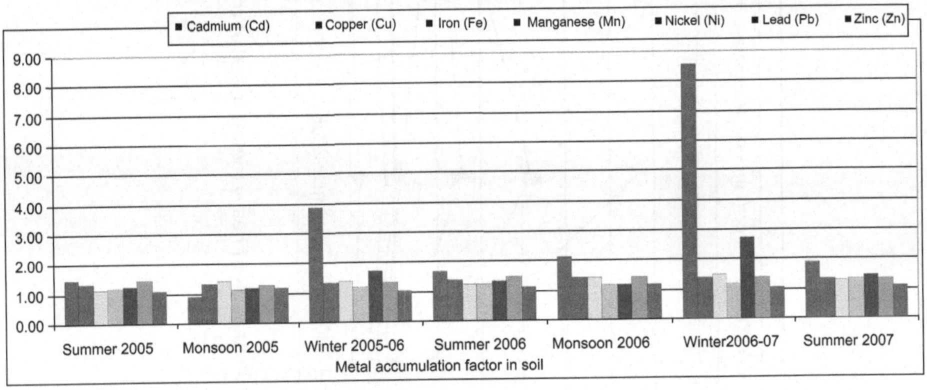

Fig. 3.5: Accumulation factor for various metals in agricultural soil of Panipat region

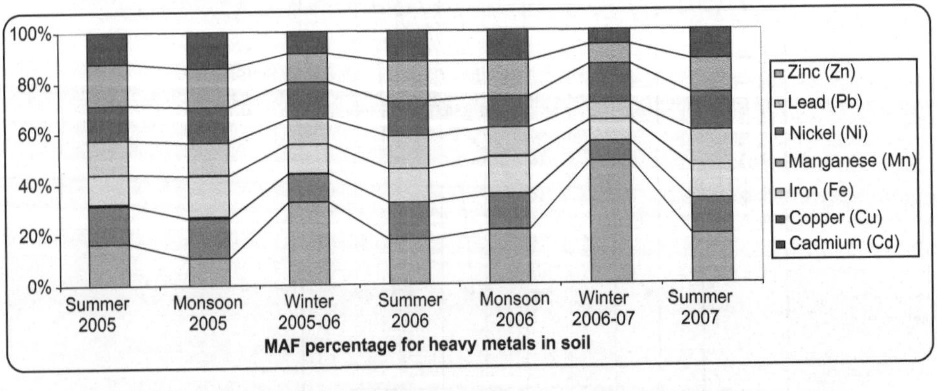

Fig. 3.6: Percentage MAF for various metals in agricultural soil of Panipat region

NGOs and local people also at various levels for the protection of environmental components.

An effluent treatment plant of appropriate capacity must be installed in the industrial area for the primary and biological treatment of for composite effluent from textile industries. Unlike most organic pollutants, heavy metals are generally refectory and cannot be degraded or readily detoxified biologically. Hence the safe and effective disposal of wastewater containing heavy metals is always a challenge to industrialists and environmentalists, since cost-effective treatment alternative are not available (Manahan, 1984). However, some researchers like Singh (2006) developed a low cost adsorbent of heavy metals from some cheap byproducts.

Restoration of affected agricultural soil is still an environmental aspect for Haryana state. Almost agricultural soils were noticed alkaline already, however, the soil in the industrial area of selected location was not so alkali, but its pH was more than 7. All the above observation and data indicated that the qualities of effluents sometimes do not meet the CPCB, BIS, MINAS and WHO specified norms. The effluents may also cause various health problems among the human being through contaminated ground water supply by municipal tube wells water scheme. In order to achieve the standards it is suggested to install the effluent treatment plants for the treatment of composite effluents of the textile industries.

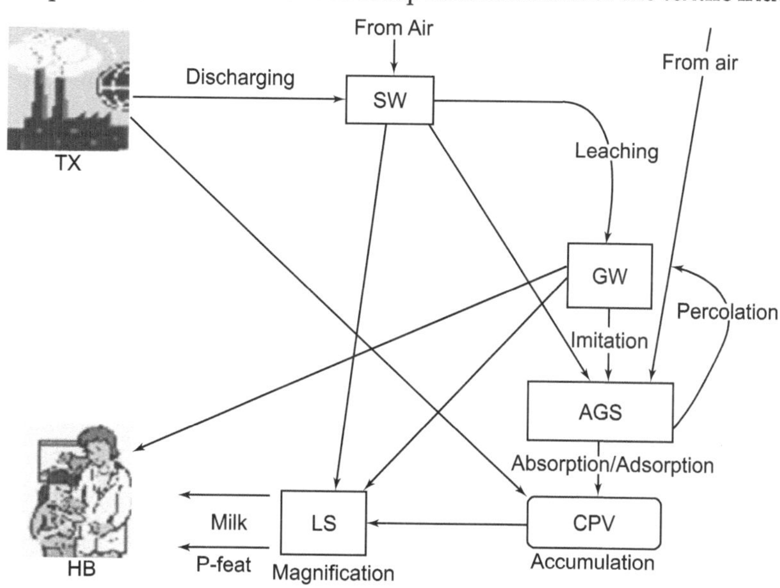

Fig. 3.7: Basic mechanism of heavy metal transfer between water and soil

On the basis of all above given facts, formula and functions related to water, soil, plants and heavy metals, it is concluded that heavy metals travel among all the abiotic environmental components and ultimately reach in livestock and human beings. Available figure may also express the movement of heavy metals from textile industrial waste to surface water, from surface water to ground water, from ground water to agricultural soil, then in crop plants and at last to livestock and human beings. In nature, every element has a natural cycle in the environment but these heavy metals have not any appropriate recycle way in industrial environment, which may be hazardous to all living and non-living components of ecosystem.

REFERENCES

Aboulhassan, M.A.; Souabi, S.; Yaacoubi, A. and Baudu, M. (2005): Treatment of Textile Wastewater using a Natural Flocculants, *Environmental Technology*. 26: 705-711.

Abson, J.N.; Furness, C.D. and Howe, C. (1967): Development of the Simicar Resipirometer and its Application to Waste Treatment, *Waste Poll. Control*, 66: 607.

Aggarwal, R.R. and Mehrotra, R.R. (1952): Soil Survey and Soil Water in Uttar Pradesh, *Suptd. Printing and Stationery*, Aallahabad, pp: 361-372.

Ajmal, M. and Khan, A.U. (1985): Effects of a Textile Factory Effluent on Soil and Crop Plants, *J. Env. Poll.*, 37(2): 131-137.

Al-Degs, Y.; Khraisheh, M.A.M.; Allen, S.J. and Ahmed, M.N. (2000): Effect of Carbon Surface Chemistry on the Removal of Reactive Dyes from Textile Effluent, *Water Research*, 34(3): 927-935.

Alumaa, P.; Steinnes, E.; Kirso, U. and Petersell, V. (2001): Heavy Metal Sorption by Different Estonian Soil Types at Low Equilibrium Solution Concentrations, *Proc. Estonian Acad. Sci. Chem.*, 50(2): 104–115.

Ameta Suresh C., Punjabi Pinki Bala, Kothari Shilpa, Sancheti Anjali (2003): Effect of Untreated and Photocatalytically Treated Dyeing Industry Effluent on Growth and Biochemical Parameters of *Allium Cepa* (Onion), *Poll. Res.*, 22(3): 389-392

Annadurai, G.; Juang, R.S. and Lee, D.J. (2002): Use of Cellulose Based Wastes for Adsorption of Dyes from Aqueous Solutions, *J. Haz. Mat.*, B92: 263-274.

APHA (2005): Standard Methods for the Examination of Water and Waste Water, *American Public Health Association*, 21st Edition, 1015, Fifteenth Street, NW, pp: 1170.

Aslam, M.M.; Baig, M.A.; Hassan, I.; Qazi, I.A.; Malik, M. and Saeed, H. (2004): Textile Wastewater Characterization and Reduction of Its COD and BOD by Oxidation, *Electron. J. Environ. Agri. Food Chem.*, 3(6): 804-811.

Ather, M. and Vohra, S.B. (1985): Heavy Metals and Environment, *New Age International Publisher Limited, Wiley Eastern Limited, New Delhi*, pp: 635.

Aurangabadkar, K.; Swaminathan, K.; Sandhya, S; Uma, T.S.; Jothikumar, N. and Paramasivam, R. (2001): Ground Water Quality Around a Municipality Solid Waste Dumping Site at Chennai, *IJEP*, 21(4): 323-327.

Bachmat, Y. (1994): Ground Water as Part of the Water System. In: Ground Water Contamination and Control, ed. V. Zoller. Marcel Dekker, Inc, New York, pp: 1-560.

Bae, W.; S.H. Lee; and G.B. Ko (2004): Evaluation of Predominant Reaction Mechanisms for the Fenton Process in Textile Dyeing Waste. *Water Sc. and Tech.* 49 (4): 91-96.

Baruah N.K.; Kotoki, P.; Bhattacharya, K.G. and Borah, G.C. (1996): Metal Speciation in Jhanjhi River Sediments. *Sci. Total Environ.*, 193: 1-12.

Basu, A.K.; Rao, C.G.S.; Dhaneshwar, G; Mukharjee, M.K.A.; Kutty, D. Ray and Trivedi, R.C. (1973): Study on Hooghly Estuaries Pollution in the Vicinity of Tissue Mill, *Proc. Symp. on Environ. Poll.*, pp: 24-26.

Beven, K. (2000): On the Future of Distributed Modeling in Hydrology, *Hydrological Processes*, 14: 3183-3184.

Bhakuni, T.S. and Bopardikar, M.V. (1967): Method of Recovery Zinc from Spinning Bath Waste of Viscos Reyon Factory by Ion Exchange Process, *Env. Health*, 9(4): 327-338.

Bhargava, G.P.; Singhla, S.K. and Abrol, I.P. (1972): Characteristics of Some Typical Saline Sodic Soils Occurring in Karnal District Haryana State, Report No. 2, Division of Soils and Agronomy; *CSSRI, Karnal*, pp 35.

Bharti, P.K. (2007): Effect of Textile Industrial Effluents on Groundwater and Soil Quality of Panipat (Hariyana), *Thesis Submitted to Gurukula Kangri University, Haridwar*, pp: 192.

Bhat, R. and Kulkarni, R. (2005): COD Reduction of Dye Industry Effluent, *J. Ind. Poll. Control*, 21 (1): 147-150.

Bordas, S, and Bourg, C.M. (1998): A Critical Evaluation of Sample Pretreatment of Contaminated Sediments to be Investigated for the Potential Mobility of their Heavy Metal Load, *Water, Air and Soil Pollution*, 103: 137-149.

Bousselmi, L.; Gelsson S.V. and H. Schroeder (2004): Textile Wastewater Treatment and Reuse by Solar Catalysis: Results from a Pilot Plant in Tunisia, *Water Sc. & Tech.*, 49(4): 331-337.

Brady, N.C. (1995): The Nature and Properties of Soils, Prentice Hall of India Pvt. Ltd., New Delhi, pp: 621.

Cances, B.; Ponthieu, M.; Castrec-Rouelle, M.; Aubry, E. and Benedatty, M.F. (2003): Metal Ion Speciation in a Soil and its Solution: Experimental Data and Modal Results, *Geoderma*, 113: 341-355.

Canter, L.W. (1987): Ground Water Quality Protection, *Lewis Publications*. Inc., Chelsea, Ml, pp: 1-650.

Castro Dentros, T.S. Dentos Neto, A.A. Moura, M.C., P.A. Barros Neto, E$.I., Forte K.R., Leite, R.H.L. (2003): Heavy Metals Extraction by Micromulsion, *Wat. Res.*, 37: 2709-2717.

Chao, Keh-Ping; Tsai, Ching-Tsan; Wang, John H.C.; Lin, Shaw-Tao and Chiang, Chow-Feng (2005) Health Risk Assessment of a Heavy Metal Contaminated Site in Taiwan. *Jr. Practice Periodical of Hazardous, Toxic, and Radioactive Waste Management*, pp: 167-171.

Christie, S.L. (1995): Speciation, In: Fitfield, F.W., Haines. P.J. (Eds). *Environmental Analytical Chemistry*, Chapman and Hall, UK, pp: 245-273.

Chung, K.T. (1983): The Significance of Azo-reduction in the Mutagenesis and Carcinogenesis of Azo Dyes, *Mutation Research*, 114: 269-279.

Considine, D.M. (1974): Chemical and Process Technology Encyclopedia, *McGraw Hill Book Co.*, New York, pp: 655.

CPCB (2003): Ground Water, *Central Pollution Control Board, Parivesh Bhawan*, Delhi, pp: 56.

CPCB (2003): Parivesh: Ground Water, *Central Pollution Control Board*, Delhi-32, July, pp: 40.

Darra, B.L.; Mehta, K.M. and Pareek, B.L. (1964): Quality of Irrigation Water in Rajasthan, *J. Indian Soc, Soil Sc.*, 12: 121-130.

Dash, S.K. and Sahoo, H.K. (1998): Quality Assessment of Groundwater in a Part of Sundargarh District, *Indian J. Environmental Protection*, 19(4): 273-278.

Davidson, C.M., Thomas R.P., McVey, S.E., Perala, R., Littlejohn, D. and Ure, A.M. (1994): Evaluation of a Sequential Extraction Procedure for the Speciation of Heavy Metals in Sediments. *Anal.Chim. Acta.*, 291: 277-286.

Dayama, O.P. (1987): Influence of Dyeing and Textile Water Pollution on Nodulation and Germination of Gram, *J. Acta. Ecol.*, 9(1-2): 34-37.

De, A.K. (2002): Environmental Chemistry, New Age International (P) Limited Publishers, pp. 392.

De, A.K. (2005): Adsorption of Cadmium and Zinc on Coal Fly Ash, *J. Ind. Poll. Control*, 21 (1): 27-30.

Desh, D. (1981): Activated Sludge Treatment of Liquid Waste- A Review, *J. IAWPC Tech.*, Vol-VII, pp: 69-72.

Dhar, N.R.; Khoda, A.K.M.B.; Khan, A.H.; Bala, P. and Karim, M.F. (2005) A Study of Effect of Acid Activated Saw Dust on the Removal of Different Dissolved Tannery Dyes (Acid Dye) From Aqueous Solutions. *Journal of Environ. Sci. & Engg.* 47 (2): 103-108.

Doneen, L.D. (1954): Stalinization of Soils of Salts in Irrigation Waters, *Trans. Geophys. Union*, 35: 943-952.

Dowedy, R.H. and Larson, W.E. (1975): The Availability of Sludge Borne Metals in Various Vegetable crops, *J. Env. Qual.*, 4: 278-282.

Dulka, J.J. and Risby, T.H. (1976): Ultra Trace Metals in Some Environmental and Biological Systems, *Analytical Chemistry*, 48(8): 640-653.

Dutta, P.S. (1999): Ground Water Situation in Delhi- Red alert, Nuclear Research Laboratory, *IARI, New Delhi*, pp: 39.

Dutta, P.S. (2005): Ground Water Ethics for its Sustainability, *Current Science*, 89 (5): 812-817.

Dwivedi, A.K.; Shashi and Singh, J. (2005): Water Pollution and Ground Water Recharging, *Current Science*, 91 (4): 407-408.

Eaton, F.M. (1950): Significance of Carbonates in Irrigation Waters, *Soil Sc.*, 39: 123-133.

ECIL Methods Manual (2004) Methods Manual, Atomic Absorption Spectrophotometer, AAS 4129, *Electronic Corporation of India Limited*, Hyderabad-500062, pp: 85.

Eckenfelder, W.W. and Bornad, J.L. (1971): Treatment Cost Relationship for Industrial Waste, *Chemical Engg. Progress*, 67(9): 76.

Fakayode, S.O. and Onianwa, P.C. (2002): Heavy Metal Contamination of Soil, and Bioaccumulation in Guinea Grass (*Panicum Maximum*) Around Ikeja Industrial Estate, Lagos, Nigeria, *Environmental Geology*, 43: 145-150.

Fetter, C.W. (1994): Applied Hydrology, 3rd Edition, Macmillan, New York.

Florence, T.M. (1982): The Speciation of Trace Elements in Waters, *Talanta*, 29: 345-369.

Forstner, U. (1985): Chemical forms and Reactivities of Metals in Sediments in Chemical Methods for Assessing Bioavailable Metals in Sludge and Soils, In: Leschber, R., Davies, R.D. and Hermite, L.P. (Eds), *Elsevier, London*, pp: 1-30.

Forstner, U. and Wittman, G.T.W. (1981): Metal Pollution in the Aquatic Environment, Second ed. *Springer, Berlin*, pp: 486.

Forstner, U.; Ahlf, W.; Calmano, W.; Kersten, M. and Schoer, J. (1990): Assessment of Metal Mobility in Sludge and Soild Wastes, In: Metal Speciation in The Environment (Eds.- Broeckaert, J.A.C; Gucer, S. and Adams, F.) Springer, Berlin, pp: 1-41.

Fransson, Åsa (2007): A Case Study to Verify Methods for Estimating Transmissivity Distributions along Boreholes, *Hydrogeology Journal*, 15: 307–313,

Fraser, B.G. and Williams, D.D. (1998): Seasonal Boundary Dynamics of a Ground Water/ Surface-Water Ecotone, *Ecology*, 79(6): 2019-2031.

Frostner, U., and Wittman, G.T.W. (1979) Metal Pollution in the Aquatic Environment, *Berlin Germany, Springer- Verlag.*, pp: 545.

Gardner, W.R. (1957): Some Steady State Solutions of the Unsaturated Moisture Flow Equation with Application to Evaporation from a Water Table, *Soil Sci.*, 85: 228-232.

Garg, V. K; Sharma, I.S. and Bishnoi, M.S. (1998): Fluoride in Under Ground Water of Uklana Town, District Hisar, Haryana, *Poll. Res.* 17(2): 149-152.

Garg, V.K. and Kaushik, P. (2006): Influence of Short-term Irrigation of Textile Mill Wastewater on the Growth of Chickpea Cultivars, *Chemistry and Ecology*, 22(3): 193-200.

Garg, V.K.; Chaudhary, A.; Deepshikha and Dahiya, S. (1998): An Appraisal of Ground Water Quality in Some Villages of District Jind, *Indian J. Environmental Protection*, 19(4): 267-272.

Gharaibeh, M.A.; Eltaif, N.I. and Bayan Al-Abdullah (2007): Impact of Field Application of Treated Wastewater on Hydraulic Properties of Vertisols, *Water Air Soil Pollut*, DOI-10.1007/s11270-007-9423-z.

Golia, E.E.; Dimirkou, A. and Mitsios, I.K. (2007): Accumulation of Metals on Tobacco Leaves (Primings) Grown in an Agricultural Area in Relation to Soil, *Bul.l Environ. Contam. Toxicol.*, DOI 10.1007/s00128-007-9111-0.

Goltenboth, F. (1994): Impact of Textile Factory in Salatiga on Ledok River System, Central Java, *J. Environ. Toxicol.*, South East Asia, pp: 301-317.

Gomez-Serrano, Garcia-Macias, A., Espinosa-Mansilla, A. and Valenzuela-Calahorro (1998): Adsorption of Mercury, Cadmium and Lead from Aq9uoes Solution on Heat Treated and Sulphurized Activated Carbon. *Wat. Res.*, 32:1-4.

GoogleEarth (2006): Software for Satellite Imagery, Available at http://www.google.com.

Gopal, B. (1994): Conservation of Inland Water in India: An Overview. Verh. Internet. Verein. *Hydrobiologia*, 384: 267.

Govindan, V.S. and Sundarlingam, V.S. (1979) Studies on Treatment of textile Mill Waste Water by Stabilization Pond Method. *J. Pollution Control*, 5 (2):137-145.

Gray, C. W. and Mclaren, R. G. (2006): Soil Factors Affecting Heavy Metal Solubility in Some New Zealand Soils, *Water, Air and Soil Pollution*, 175: 3-14.

Groff, K.A. (1993): Textile Waste, *Environmental Research*. 65: 421.

Gupta, R.K., Singh, R.R. and Abrol, I.P. (1989): Influence of Simultaneous Changes in Sodicity and PH on Hydraulic Conditions of an Alkali Soil, *Soil Science*, 147: 28-33.

Harper, H.H.; Yusuf, Y.A. and Wanielista, M.P. (1984): Fate of Heavy Metals in Stromwater Management System, In: *Lake and Reservoir Management, USEPA, Washington*, pp: 329-334.

Hart, B.T. (1982): Trace Metals in Natural Waters, *Speciation Chem. Australian*, 49: 260-265.

Hedge, V.S.; Shalini, G. and Kanchanagouri, D.G. (2006): Provenance of Heavy Minerals with Special Reference to Ilmenite of the Honnevar Beach, Central West Coast of India, *Current Science*, 91 (5): 644-648.

Helena, B.A.; Vega, M.; Barrado, E.; Parado, R. and Fernandez, L. (1999): A Case of Hydro-Chemical Characterization of an Alluvial Aquifer Influenced by Human Activities, *Water, Air and Soil Pollution*, 112: 365-387.

Hesse, P.R. (1994): A Textbook of Soil Chemical Analysis, *CBS Publishers and Distributors*, 485, Bholanathnagar, Shahdhra, Delhi-110032, pp: 520.

Hitz, H.R.; Huber, W and Rud, R.H. (1978): The Absorption of Dyes on Activated Sludge, *Journal of Society of Dyers and Colorists*, February: 71-76.

Horing, R.H. (1976): Characterization and Treatment of Textile Dyeing Wastewaters, In: Proceedings of National Technical Conference, *American Association of Textile Chemists and Colorist*, pp: 100-104.

Hoston, A.K. (1965): An Index Number system for Rating Water Quality, *J. Wat. Poll. Cont. Fed.*, 37(3): 300-306.

http//:www.engg.ksu.edu as access on 16 november, 2006

Huang, J.; Huang, R.; Jiao, J.J. and Chen, K. (2007): Speciation and Mobility of Heavy Metals in Mud in Coastal Reclamation Areas in Shenzhen, China, *Environ. Geol.*, DOI 10.1007/s00254-007-0636-7.

Hynes, H.B.N. (1970): The Ecology of Running Waters, *Liverpool University Press, Liverpool, 4th Impression*: 1-555.

Ireland, M.P. (1983): Heavy Metals Uptake and Tissue Distribution, In: Earthworm Ecology-from Darwin to Vermiculture (Ed.- Satchell, J.E., *Chapman and Hall*), pp: 135-147.

IUPAC (1994): Atomic Weights of the Elements, 1993, International Union of Pure and Applied Chemistry, *Pure Appl. Chem.*, 66: 2423.

Jain, C.K. (2004): Metal Fractionation Study on Bed Sediments of River Yamuna, India, *Wat. Res.* 38: 569-578.

Jayabaskeran, K. J. Sree Ramulu U. S. (1996): Distribution of Heavy Metals in Soil of Various Sewage Farms in Tamil Nadu, *J. Indian Soc. Soil. Sci.*, 44: 401-404.

Jha, M.N. and Pandey, P. (1984): Impact of Growing Eucalyptus and Soil Monocultures on Soil in Natural Sal Area of Doon Valley, *Ind. For.*, 110: 16-18.

Judlins, J.F. and Hornsby, J.S. (1978): Color Removal from Textile Dye Waste using Magnesium Carbonate, *Journal of Water Pollution Control Federation*, 50: 2446-2456.

Kalra, Y.P. and Maynarol, D.G. (1991): Methods Manual for Forest Soil and Plant Analysis. *For. Can., Northwest Reg. North. For. Cent. Edmonton, Alberta. Inf. Rep. Nor. X-319*, pp: 1-65.

Kanwar, J.S. (1961): Quality of Irrigation Water as an Index of Suitability for Irrigation Purposes, *Potash Review*, 13: 1-13.

Karle, K.K.; Bhusal, S.S.; Gunjal, P.S. and Kuchekar, S.R. (1992): Studied on Ground Water Quality in Pravaranagar Area of Ahmednagar District, *Poll. Res.* 11(2): 65-68.

Kashem, M.A. and Singh, B.R. (1999): Heavy Metal Contamination of Soil and Vegetation in the Vicinity of Industries in Bangladesh, *Water, Air and Soil Pollution*, 115: 347-361.

Kataria, H.C. (1996): BOD and COD Contents in Bore Well Water of Bhopal (M.P.), *Natcon*, 8(1): 69-72.

Kataria, H.C.; Gupta, S.S. and Jain, O.P. (1995): Water Quality of Bore Wells in B.H.E.L. area of Bhopal, *Poll. Res.* 14 (4): 455-462.

Katz, M. (1975): The Effect of Heavy Metals on Fish and Aquatic Environment. (Ed.- Krenkel, P.A.), *Pregamon Press, New York*, pp: 637-645.

Kaushik, M.P. (2006): Vanaspati Vigyan, Prakash Prakashan, Muzaffarnagar, 834.

Khan T.I., Marwari Richa, Singh N. (2003): Impact of Textile Wastewater on *Solanum Melongena* Var-FI- Hybrid Kanhaiya in pot Experiment with Special Emphasis on Analysis of Heavy Metals. *Dimensions Polln*, 2: 108-116.

Khurshid, Zaheeruddin and Mohd. Usman Shabeer (1997): Degradation of Water Quality Due to Heavy Metals Pollution in Faridabad District, Haryana, India, *Poll. Res.* 16(1): 41-43.

Korfali, S.I. and Davies, B.D.E. (2004): The Relationship of Metals in River Sediments (Nahr-Ibrahim, Lebanon) and Adjacent Floodplain Soil, *the CIGR J. of Scientific Research and Development*, Manuscript LW 04 010, 6: 1-22.

Krebs, R.; Gupta, S.K.; Furrer, G. and Schulin, R. (1999): Gravel Sludge as an Immobilizing Agent in Soils Contaminated by Heavy metals: A Field Study, *Water, Air and Soil Pollution*, 115: 465-479.

Krishna, A. K. and Govil, P. K. (2004) Heavy Metal Contamination of Soil Around Pali Industrial area, Rajasthan, India, *Environmental Geology*, 47: 38-44.

Krull, R. and E. Dopkens (2004): Recycling of Dye House Effluents by Biological and Chemical Treatment, *Water Sc. And Tech.* 49(4): 311-317.

Kudesia, V.P. (1992): Water Pollution, *Pragati Prakashan, Meerut*, pp: 407.

Lofts, S.; Spurgeon, D.J.; Svendsen, C. and Tipping, E. (2004): Deriving Soil Critical Limits for Cu, Zn, Cd, and pH: A Method Based on Free Ion Concentration, *Environ. Sci. Tech.*, 38: 3623-3631.

Lokeshwari, H. and Chandrappa, G.T. (2006): Impact of Heavy Metal Contamination of Bellandur Lake on Soil and Cultivated Vegetation, *Current Science*, 91(9): 622-627.
Lokeshwari, H. and Chandrappa, G.T. (2006): Impact of Heavy Metal Contamination of Bellandur Lake on Soil and Cultivated Vegetation, *Current Science*, 91(9): 622-627.
Loska, K. and Wiechula, D. (2002): Speciation of Cadmium in the Bottom Sediment of Rybnik Reservoir, *Water, Air Soil Pollut.*, 141: 73-89.

Lung, W. (1990): Speciation Analysis – Why and How? *Fresenius J. Anal. Chem.* 337: 557-564.

Malik, D.S. and Bharti, P. K. (2007): Soil Quality of Irrigated Agricultural Fields in Textile Industrial Area of Panipat City, *Asian Journal of Experimental Sciences,* 21 (2): 445-451.

Malik, D.S.; Bharti, P.K. and Grover, S. (2006): Alteration in Surface Water Quality near Textile Industries at Panipat (Haryana), *Environment Conservation J.*, 7(2): 65-68.

Malik, D.S.; Bharti, P.K; Kamboj, N. and Yadav, R. (2007): Quantification of Heavy Metals Migration in Ground Water Regime Due to Discharge of Textile Industrial Effluents in Panipat area, Haryana, *Pollution Research,* 26 (4): 123-125.

Malik, D.S.; Yadav, R. and Bharti, P.K. (2004) Accumulation of Heavy Metals in Crop Plants through Irrigation of Contaminated Ground water in Panipat Region, *Environmental Conservation Journal* 5 (3): 101-104.

Manahan, S. (1984): Environmental Chemistry, Brooks/Colei, CA, USA, pp: 638.

Manchanda, H.R. (1990): Significance of the Type of Salinity for Growing Pulses Under Saline Conditions, *Indo-Pak Workshop on Soil Salinity and Water Management,* Feb, 10-14, pp: 2-3.

Mani, V.; Kaur, H. and Mohini, M. (2005): Toxic Metals and Environmental Pollution, *J. Ind. Poll. Cont.*, 21(1): 101-107.

Martin, J.M. and Whitfield, M. (1983): The Significance of the River Input of Chemical Elements to the Ocean, In: Wong, C.S.; Boyle, E.; Bruland, K.W.; Burton, J.D. and Goldburg, E.D. (Eds.), Trace Metals in sea Water, *Plenum Press, New York,* pp: 324-331.

Martin, M.H. and Cougherty, P.J. (1982): Biological Monitoring of Heavy Metals Pollution, *Applied Science Publishers,* pp: 463.

Masters, G.M. (1998): Introduction to Environmental Engineering and Science, *Prentice-Hall India,* pp: 460.

Mathess, G. (1974): Heavy Metals as Trace Constituents in Natural and Polluted Ground Water, *Goel mijnbouw, New Jersy, USA,* 53: 149-155.

McBride, M., Sauve, S. and Hendershot, W. (1997): Solubility Control of Cu, Zn, Cd, and Pb, in Contaminated Soils, *Euro. J. Soil Science,* 48: 337-346.

Mico, C; Recatal, L.; Peris, M. And Sanchez, J. (2007): A Comparison of two Digestion Methods for the Analysis of Heavy Metals by Flame Atomic Absorption Spectroscopy, *Spectroscopy Europe,* 19 (1): 23-26

Mido, Y. and Satake, M, (1995): Chemicals in the Environment, *Discovery Publishing House, New Delhi,* pp: 491.

Millar, C.E. and Turk, L.M. (2002): Fundamentals of Soil Science, Biotech Books, Delhi-35, pp: 462.

Minhas, P.S. and Khosla, B.K. (1986): Solute Displacement in a Silt Loam Soil as Affected by the Method of Water Application under Different Evaporation Rates, *Agric. Wat. Mgmt,* 12: 63-75.

Mohan, R.; Chopra, N. and Chowdhary, G.C. (1998): Heavy Metals (Fe, Pb, Cd, Zn) in the Ground Water of Naini Industrial Area, Dist. Allahabad, U.P., *Poll. Res.* 17(2): 167-168.

MPCA (2001): Effects of Land Use on Ground Water Quality, St. Cloud Area, Minnesota – Short Report, *Minnesota Pollution Control Agency,* Ground Water Monitoring and Assessment Program, pp: 1-29.

Muller, G. (1979): Schwermetalle in den Sedimenten Des Rheinsveranderungen Seit, *Umschau*, 79: 778-783.

Nasr, S.M.; Okbah, M.A. and Kasem, S.M. (2006): Environmental Assessment of Heavy Metal Pollution in Bottom Sediments of Aden Port, Yemen, *International Journal of Oceans and Oceanography*, 1(1): 99-109

National Research Council (NRC) (1989): Contaminated Marine Systems- Assessment and Remediation, *National Academy Press, Washington*, D.C. pp: 185.

Navarro, A. and Font, X. (1993): Discriminating different Sources of Ground Water Contamination Caused by Industrial Waste in the Besos River Basin, Barcelona, Spain, *J. Applied Biochemistry*, APPGEY, 8: 277.

Nedunuri, K.V.; Govindaraju, R.S.; Erickson, L.E. and Schwab, A.P. (1995): Modeling of Heavy Metal Movement in Vegetated, Unsaturated Soils with Emphasis on Geochemistry, In: Proceedings of the 10th Annual Conference on Hazardous Waste Research, pp: 57-66.

Nongkynrih, P.; Dkhar, P.S. and Khathing, D.T. (1996): Micronutrients Elements in Acid Alfisols of Meghalaya Under Rice Cultivation, *J. Soil Si.*, 44(3): 455-457.

Nriagu, J.O. and Pacyna, J.M. (1988): Quantitative Assessment of Worldwide Contamination of Air, Water and Soil with Trace Metals, *Nature*, 333: 134-139.

Numberg, H.W. (1984): The Volumetric Approach in Trace Metal Chemistry of Natural Waters and Atmospheric Precipitation, *Analyst. Chim. Acta*, 164: 1-21.

Obiri, Samuel (2007): Determination of Heavy Metals in Water from Boreholes in Dumasi in the Wassa West District of Western Region of Republic of Ghana, *Environ Monit Assess*, 130: 455–463

Padmavathiamma, P.K. and Li, L.Y. (2007): Phytoremediation Technology: Hyper-Accumulation Metals in Plants, *Water Air Soil Pollut.*, DOI- 10.1007/s11270-007-9401-5.

Palanivelu, K.; Priya, M.N.; Selvan, A.M. and Natesan,U. (2006): Water Quality Assessment in the Tsunami Affected Coastal Areas of Chennai, *Current Science*, 91 (5): 583-584.

Prasad, S. (2003): Fundamentals of Biostatistics (Biometry), *Emkey Publication, Delhi-51*, pp: 168.

Pujari, G.K. and Sinha, B.K. (1999): Studies on the Water and Soil Quality of Some Villages of Attabira area Irrigated by Bargarg Main Canal Originated from Hirakund Reservoir of Orissa, *J. of Env. and Poll.*, 6(1): 71-76.

Rao, K.V.G.K.; Gupta R.K. and Kamra, S.K. (1987): Reclamation of Waterlogged High SAR Saline Soil, CSSRI, Karnal, A Feasibility Report for *CIRB, Hissar, CSSRI, Karnal*, pp: 21.

Rhoades, J.D. (1987): Use of Saline Water for Irrigation, *Wat. Qual. Bull.*, 12: 14-20.

Richards, L.A. (1954): Diagnosis and Improvement of Saline and Alkali Soils, US Deptt. Agri., Edited Handbook, No. 60: 160.

Saxena, M.M. (1994): In: Environmental Analysis Water, Soil and Air, *Agro Botanical Publishers*. pp: 1-180.

Schroeder, W.H. (1989): Development in the Speciation of Mercury in Natural Waters, *Trends Anal. Chem.* 8: 339-342.

Sharma, D.R. (1978): Testing of a Model for Prediction Sodium Hazards of Irrigation Waters, *J. Indian Soc. Soil Sci.*, 27: 204-208.

Sharma, D.R. and Parihar, S.S. (1973): Effect of Depth and Salinity of Ground Water on Evaporation and Soil Salinization, *Indian J. Agric. Sci.*, 43: 582-586.

Shrivastava V.S. and Patil B.H. (2003): Metallic and Some Physico-chemical Studies of Soil and Aquatic Sediments, *Eco Env Conserv*, 9(1): 75-77

Singh, B. and Bhumbla, D.R. (1968): Effect of Quality of Irrigation Water on Soil Properties, *J. Res.* (Punjab Agri. Univ.), 5: 166-171.

Singh, B. Rana, D.S. and Bajwa, M.S. (1977): Salinity and Sodium Hazards of Underground Irrigation Waters of Bhatinda District (Punjab), *Indian J. Ecol.*, 4: 32-41.

Singh, K.N.; Bains, S.S. and Dayanand (1969): Salinity Problem in High Water Table Areas- An Appraisal, *Indian J, Agron.*, 14: 31-34.

Singh, K.S. and Sharma, R.P. (1971): Studies on the Effects of Saline Irrigation Waters on Physico-chemical Properties of Some Soils of Rajasthan, *J. Indian Soc. Soil Sci.*, 18: 345-356.

Singh, T.B.; Jadon, S.P.S. and Mishra, G.J. (1994): Degradation of Water and Soil Quality of Parwanoo Area with Respect to Heavy Metals, *IJEP*, 14 (4): 282-287.

Srinivasan, M. and Murali, M. (1996): Some Studies on Effect Pollutants on Properties of Soils, *IJEP*, 16(7): 522-523.

Tan, K.H. and Nopamornbodi, O. (1981): Electron Microbeam Analysis and Scanning Electron Microscopy of Soil-root Interfaces, *Soil Sci.*, 131: 100-106.

Taylor, S.R. (1964): Abundance of Chemical Elements in the Continental Crust – A new Table, *Geochim. Cosmochim. Acta.* 28: 1273-1275.

Trevors, J.T. and Saier Jr., M.H. (2007): Regulation of Pollution, *Water Air Soil Pollut*, DOI 10.1007/s11270-007-9344-x.

Trivedi, R.K. and Goel, P.K. (1984): Chemical and Biological Methods for Water Pollution Studies Karad, *Environmental publication*, pp: 1-251.

USEPA (1990): Operation and Quality Control Manual, Environmental Protection Agency (EPA), Athens, GA 30613.

Va´zquez, N.N.; Gil, M.A.; Esteves, J. L. and Narvarte, M. A. (2007): Monitoring Heavy Metal Pollution in San Antonio Bay, Rý´o Negro, Argentina, *Bull. Environ. Contam. Toxicol.*, DOI 10.1007/s00128-007-9084-z.

Walker, D.J.; Bernal, M.P. and Correal, E. (2007): The Influence of Heavy Metals and Mineral Nutrient Supply on *Bituminuria bituminosa, Water Air Soil Pollut*, DOI 10.1007/s11270-007-9422-0.

Walker, R. (1970): The Metabolism of Azo Compounds: A Review of the Literature, *Food Cosmetics Toxicology*, 8: 659-661.

WHO (2006) Standards for Drinking Water, Available at http//:www.lenntech.com

Williums, D.R. (1972): Metals, Ligands and Cancer, *Chemical Review*, 72 (3): 203-213.

Wint, A. (1981): The Disposal of Toxic Wastes, In: Industrial Effluent Treatment Vol-I (Eds.- Watler, J.K. and Wint, M.), pp: 1-19.

Yadav, R.K.; Goyal, B.; Sharma, R.K.; Dubey, S.K. and Minhas, P.S. (2002): Post-irrigation Impact of Domestic Sewage Effluent on Composition of Soils, Crops and Ground Water- A Case Study, *Environment International*, 28: 481-486.

Yuandong, Z.; Shirong, L. and Jiangming, M. (2006): Water-holding Capacity of Ground Covers and Soil in Alpine and Sub-Alpine Shrubs in Western Sichuan, China, *ACTA Ecologica Sinica*, 26(9): 2775-2782.

Zheng, G.; Yue, L.; Li, Z and Chen, C. (2006): Assessment on Heavy Metals Pollution of Agricultural Soil in Guanzhong District, *J Geographical Sciences*, 16, (1): 105-113.

Soil Environment and Conservation **Pages 72-92**
Edited by: **Dr. Ashok K. Rathoure; Dr. Pawan Kumar 'Bharti' and Dr. Alka Chauhan**
ISBN: 978-93-88854-10-8
Edition: **2019**
Published by: **Discovery Publishing House Pvt. Ltd., New Delhi (India)**

4

Advances and Application of Soil Fertility for Sustainable Crop Production

Dr. Prasann Kumar[1], Shweta Pathak[2], Mohit Naik[1], Sunil Kumar[1]

ABSTRACT

Soil is popularly called as soul of infinite life. Characteristics differ from the layers above and beneath. Each soil type usually has three or four horizons. Horizons are defined in most cases by obvious physical features, chiefly colour and texture. These may be described both in absolute terms (particle size distribution for texture, for instance) and in terms relative to the surrounding material (i.e., "coarser" or "sandier" than the horizons above and below). The differentiation of the soil into distinct horizons is largely the result of influences, such as air, water, solar radiation and plant material, originating at the soil-atmosphere interface. Since the weathering of the soil occurs first at the surface and works its way down, the uppermost layers have been changed the most, while the deepest layers are most similar to the original parent material.

Keywords: Agriculture, Biotic, Crop, Density, Energy, Forage, Gap.

Introduction

Sustainable agriculture integrates three main goals—

- Environmental health.
- Economic profitability.
- Social and economic equity.
- Agriculture continues to be mainstay of India's economy.
- Future increase in agricultural production has to come by way of increasing productivity of land already under cultivation.
- Vital role of fertilizers for increasing agricultural productivity is universally recognized.
- Share of fertilizers for increasing foodgrain production is 41%.

Essential Elements

CHO: Carbon is supplied in the gaseous form from the atmosphere, hydrogen and oxygen are supplied 90-95% by water.

1 Department of Agronomy, School of Agriculture Lovely Professional University, Jalandhar, Punjab, 144411, India
2 Department of Plant Physiology, I.Ag. Sci., BHU., Varanasi, 221005, U.P., India

N P K Ca Mg S: Macro element phosphorus, potassium, calcium and magnesium, sulphur, are supplied by the breakdown of organic matter, through soil and fertilizers. Nitrogen is also supplied by the breakdown of organic matter and by fixation (synthesis from the atmosphere).

Micro-elements: zinc, iron, manganese, copper, molybdenum, boron, cobalt, chlorine, sodium, through soil and fertilizers (Figure 4.1).

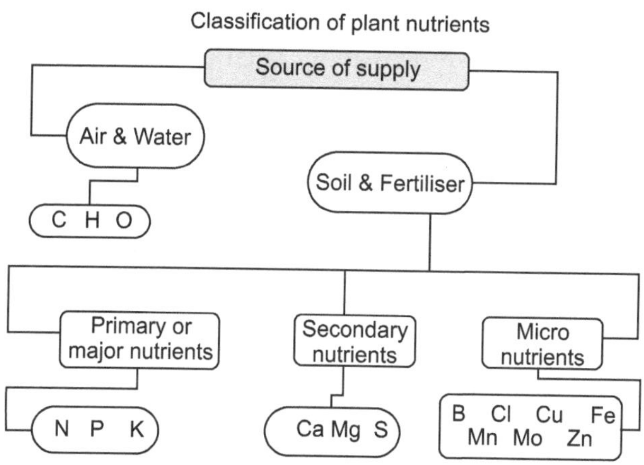

Fig. 4.1: Classification of plant nutrients
(Source: Based on Review of Literature, 2018)

Criterion of Essentiality (D I Arnon)

- In the absence of essential nutrient, plant will not be able to complete its life cycle.
- Deficiency for that element will not be corrected by any other element.
- The element should be directly involved in plant's Metabolic Processes.

Additional Mineral Elements: Following elements are beneficial to plants but not necessarily essential:

1.	Sodium	Na	
2.	Cobalt		Co
3.	Vanadium	Vn	
4.	Nickel		Ni
5.	Selenium	Sl	
6.	Aluminum	Al	
7.	Silicon		Si

Mobility of Nutrients in Plant.

- Very mobile: N & K.
- Moderately mobile: S & Mg.

- Relatively immobile: Ca, B, & Fe.
- Immobile: P

Reasons for Declining Crop Response

- Inadequate and imbalanced fertilizer use.
- Negative nutrient balance between crop removal and fertilizer addition.
- Increasing multi-nutrient deficiency.
- Lack of farmers' awareness about balanced plant nutrition.
- Lack of varietal breakthrough.
- Poor crop management (Excess fertilizer is not the substitute of poor management, Table 4.1).

Table 4.1: All India Demand Forecast of Fertilizer Products ('000 tons) 2015-16 to 2019-20

Year	Urea	DAP	NP/NPKs	SSP	MOP*
2015-16	32858	12212	11142	5513	4643
2016-17	33677	12413	11420	5948	4793
2017-18	33754	12764	11841	6476	4934
2018-19	34536	12950	12318	6626	5048
2019-20	35307	13014	12799	7096	5086

(Source: Based on Review of literature, 2018)

1. *For direct consumption.
2. Source: Working Group Report on Fertilizer Industry for Twelfth Five-Year Plan

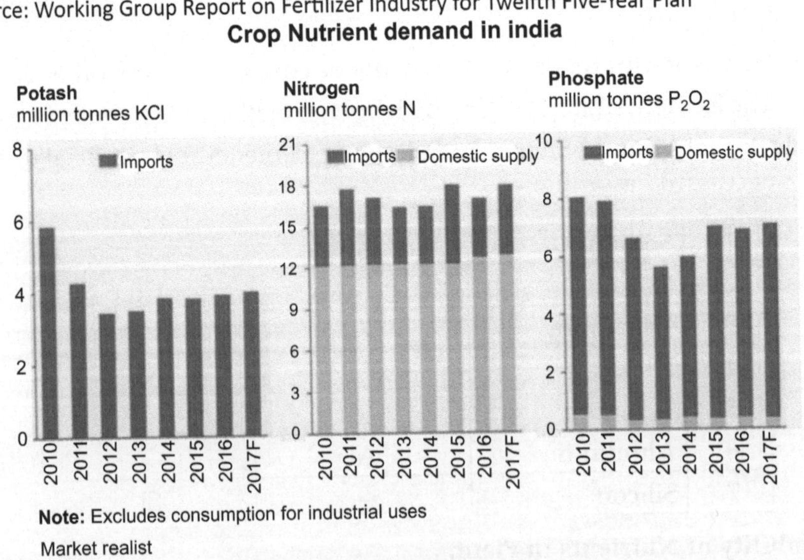

Fig. 4.2: Crop Nutrient Demand in India

(Source: Based on Review of literature, 2018)

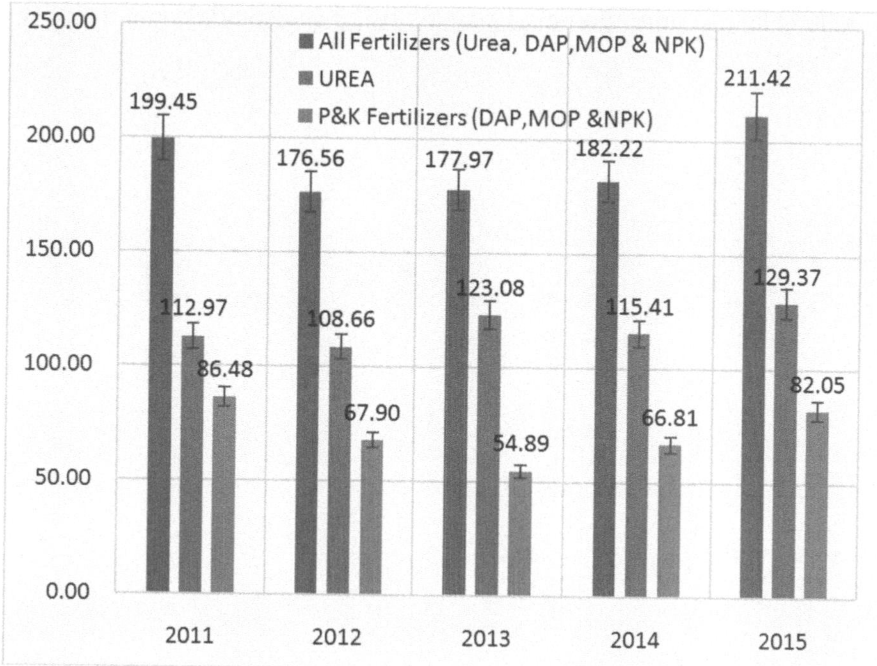

Fig. 4.3: Fertilizer Sales trend in last 5 years during 2010-11 to 2015-16 (April to August) (Source: Based on Review of literature, 2018)

where, Figures in Lakh Metric Tonnes, National Conference on Agriculture for Rabi 2015-16.

Department of fertilizer, GOI

Total fertilizer nutrient consumption increased by 5.6% during 2015-16 over the previous year. Supply from indigenous production increased significantly, urea in particular. Production of urea recorded all time high level of 24.5 million tonnes, nearly 2 million tonnes higher over the previous year's level.Imports of major fertilizerscontinued to remain high in 2015-16 with the exception of lower import of MOP (Figure 4.2, 4.3, 4.4 and 4.5).

Balance Fertilization

The Nutrient need of the crop plant and its chemical behavior in soil decides:

How much to apply?

Recommended dose based on soil test.

When to apply?

- N application is matched to grand growth stage of the crop. It is more prone to loss, hence recommended for application in split doses.
- P_2O_5 is less mobile so its basal application is suggested.

- K_2O being cation do not get easily lost, it is also advisable to apply as basal.

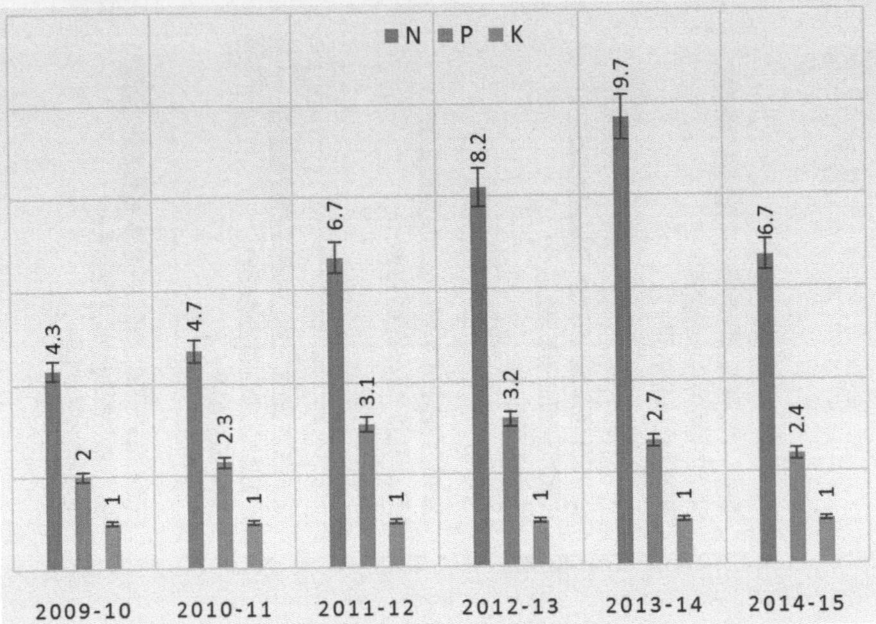

Fig. 4.4: Total fertilizers consumption
(Source: Based on review of literature, 2018)

- How to apply?
- Placement
- Broadcasting
- Foliar Application
- Fertigation

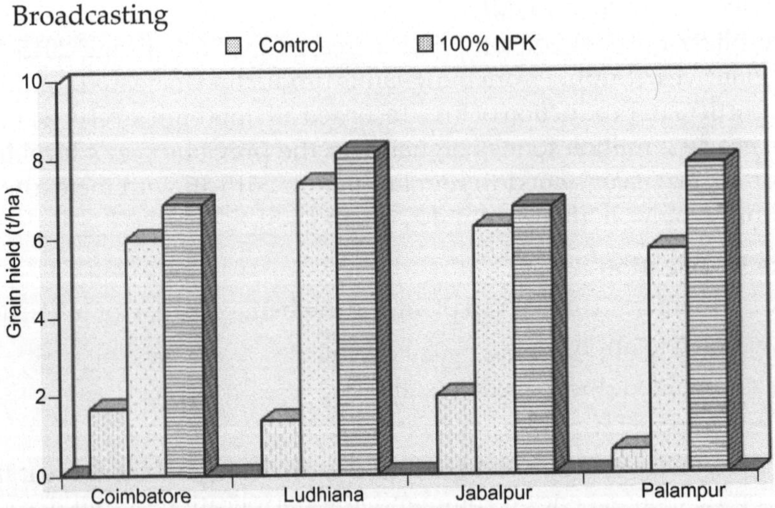

Fig. 4.5: Total mean grain yield of rice-wheat cropping under long-term fertilization and manuring
(Source: Based on review of literature, 2018)

- Soil and Water Testing
- Soil testing laboratories
- State Department of Agriculture
- District and sub-division levels and Agricultural Universities
- IFFCO, KRIBHCO, and other fertilizer agencies
- Soil testing –tool to assess the status of soil to supply plant nutrients
- Quantity and methods of fertilizer application
- Reclamation of kallar (Saline, sodic) soil
- Suitability of soil for particular crop
- Suitability of soil for use of particular quality of irrigation water

Methods of Taking Soil samples

- Scrap away surface litter, if any
- Take a uniform core of soil from surface to plough depth (15cm) by auger.
- Kassi or Kurpa- dig a V shape hole.
- Take soil from 8-10 spots at random in a zig-zag pattern
- In standing crop, the samples should be taken between the rows of plants.
- Mix well the soil collected from different spot and take a composite sample about 1/2kg to give representative sample
- Each sample should be labeled and should have address and field number

Environmental Concern Through

Leaching of Applied Urea in Soil

Leaching..................... as NO_3

Up to 80 cm depth with total of 15 cm irrigation in sandy soil

Nitrification

Refer to biochemical conversion of NH_4 to $NO_{3\text{ in}}$ soil

NH_4 ----------------------! NO_2 ----------------! NO3

Nitrosomonas Nitrobacter

Factors affecting Nitrification

Soil pH, soil moisture temperature, aeration and crop residues

N Leaching Varies with Soil Type

To avoid leaching losses, applied N must be either utilized by crop or retained in soil.

There should be regulated nitrification.

Volatilizations

Volatilizations.................. as NH_3

Loss up to 30% of applied N Broadcast: 30-40%, Drilled: 5%

Denitrification

Refers to biochemical conversion of NO_3 into gaseous forms of N. it occurs under anaerobic conditions (as in paddy fields).

$$NO_3 \xrightarrow[\text{Bacteria}]{\text{Lack of Oxygen}} NO, N_2O, N_2$$

To Reduce Denitrification Losses

Avoid use of $NO_{3\ sources}$, use nitrification inhibitors, In rice - apply N in soil in reduced zone before puddling and use slow release N sources or coated materials.

Factors Affecting Volatilizations

Type of N fertilizer, method of application, soil pH, soil moisture content, soil temperature, $CaCO_3$ content in soil and organic matter status

Factors Affecting Denitrification

Soil pH, soil moisture content, oxygen level in soil and organic matter status.

N Stabilizer

It block the conversion of:

$$NH_4 \text{------------x----------}\rightarrow NO_3$$

Thus keeps the more stable NH_4 form in the soil

Phosphorus

P is immobile in soil and therefore its movement occurs primarily through erosion and run-off.

P pollution is associated through its effect or eutrophication.

Increases in residues reduces soil P losses

Follow practice which increase residues in soil and reduce erosion and run-off.

When erosion is stopped, P run-off loss and thereby environment pollution from P is minimized.

Follow conservation plan with

- Cover crops
- Conservation tillage

- Terracing
- Contour strip cropping
- Grass waterways
- Water basins & diversions.

Table 4.2: Low Nutrient Use Efficiency & Associated Causes

Nutrient	Efficiency (%)	Cause of low efficiency
Nitrogen	30-50	Immobilization, volatilization, denitrification, Leaching
Phosphorus	15-20	Fixation in soils Al – P, Fe – P, Ca – P
Potassium	70-80	Fixation in clay - lattices
Sulphur	8-10	Immobilization, Leaching with water
Micro nutrients (Zn, Fe, Cu, Mn, B)	1-2	Fixation in soils

(Source: Based on Review of Literature, 2018)

Factors influencing FUE

- Soil management.
- Liming of acid soils.
- Saline and Sodic soil amelioration.
- Agronomic management:
- Proper Crop Management Practices.

Fertilizer management:

- Suitable combination of Organic and inorganic sources.
- Suitable time, quantity and method

Neem Coated Urea

Government of India made it mandatory for all indigenous producers of urea to produce 100% of their total production of subsidised urea as *neem* coated urea as notified on 25th May, 2015. Imported urea is also required to be *neem coated* before despatch from the ports.

Band Placement

Placing fertilizers below the seeds without touching the seeds stimulates early growth of seedlings. For application of phosphate fertilizers as phosphates are less mobile. Broadcast application will result in unavailability to roots. More availability of phosphates to crops grown in acidic soils where fixation of phosphates is a problem. Early root development will be rapid and extensive and plant growth will be stimulated. Under rainfed conditions, due to extensive and deeper root development, plants will be able to draw moisture from lower depths of soil and better withstand drought.

Broadcasting

- On all crops with a dense stand and not sown in rows.
- In the case of plants whose roots spread widely in the soil.
- On very fertile soils
- When high rate of fertilizers are used
- When readily soluble nitrogenous fertilizers are applied
- When potassic fertilizers are applied in light soils.

Drawbacks with Broadcast Application?

May stimulate weed growth with the result that the crop does not derive full benefit of fertilizers. Fertilizers may come in contact with a large volume of soil and are likely to be fixed and unavailable for that crop. This is particular in the case of super phosphate application

Foliar Application of Fertilizers

- Only those fertilizers that do not scorch (burn) leaves are sprayed.
- Usually micronutrients, which are required in low rates, are foliar sprayed.
- Urea sprays are used for supplying nitrogen.
- Ammonium phosphate fertilizer is also used to spray to improve seed setting in multicut fodder legumes like Berseem.
- For the reason that low concentration of fertilizers needs to be sprayed most of the fertilizers are not used for foliar application.

Fertilizers

- Nitrogen
- Urea (46% N), Ammonium Sulphate (21%), Calcium ammoniumnitrate (26% N), Ammonium chloride (25% N)
- Phosphorus
- DAP (46% P_2O_5, 18% N), SSP (16% P_2O_5) and TSP (46% P_2O_5)
- Potassium,
- Muriate of Potash (60% K_2O)
- Sulphate of Potash (48% K_2O)

Items Under Essential Commodity Act

Cattle fodder, including oil cakes and other concentrates. Coal, including coke and other derivatives. Components parts and accessories of automobiles. Cotton and woollen textiles. Foodstuffs, including edible oilseeds and oils. Iron and Steel, including manufactured products of Iron & Steel. Paper, including newsprint, paperboard and strawboard. Petroleum and Petroleum products. Raw Cotton, either ginned or unginned and cotton seed. Raw Jute. The following commodities are also declared as essential through notifications: Jute textiles. Fertilizer, whether inorganic, organic or mixed. Yarn made wholly from cotton. Seeds of food crops and seeds of fruits and vegetables, seeds of cattle fodder and Jute seeds.

Nitrogen

- Necessary for formation of amino acids, the building blocks of protein
- Essential for plant cell division, vital for plant growth
- Directly involved in photosynthesis
- Necessary component of vitamins, carbohydrates

Deficiency Symptoms

Older leaves are affected, Leaf blades uniformly

- Light green to yellow.
- Tip and margin of older leave become necrotic.
- Vegetative growth slowed down stalks become short and slender.
- 3% Urea solution sprayed 2-3 times at 8 to 10 days interval

Sulphur

- S is essential for synthesis of amino acids, protein and
- Vitamins
- Deficiency Symptoms
- Young leaves affected
- Apical merisetms remains alive, immature leaves
- having varying degree are chlorosis but do not wilt
- Young leaves uniformly chlorotic and develop faint
- Purplish tinge. Leaves are shorter than normal.

Phosphorus

- Cell division–stalks and root elongation.
- P deficiency the poorly developed root system-poor.
- Plant growth and finally low sugar yield.
- Complementary element to N.
- Deficiency Symptoms.
- Older leaves are affected.
- Leaf blades dark to blue green, red or purple colour at the tip and margin exposed to sunlight.
- Leaves narrower and shorter than normal poor to no tillering.

- Older leaves yellow and eventually die-back from tip along the margin.
- Root system poorly developed.

Potassium

Potassium plays important role for Respiration, Chlorophyll development, Maintenance of water content in the leaves, Translocation of sugar and starch

Deficiency Symptoms

Deficiency symptoms usually appears first on older leaves while younger leaves usually remains green.Symptom begins as a pale yellow chlorosis on the tips of older leaves and cover marginal tissue (inverted V). K fertilizers (MOP) should be applied along the plant rows fallowed by irrigation and hoeing at vattar.

Zinc

Zn is essential for biosynthesis of plant growth regulator. Activity of various enzymes also depended upon the presence of zinc.

Deficiency Symptoms

Young leaves affected. Apical meristems remains alive, immature leaves having varying degree are chlorosis but do not wilt. Broad band of yellowing in the leaf blade. The mid rib and leaf remain green except when deficiency is severe. Red lesions are often noticed. The lesions may be associated with a fungus which prefers to grow in Zn deficent tissue.

Iron

Iron is essential for the synthesis of chlorophyll. Serve as an electron carrier in nitrogen fixation.

Deficiency Symptoms

Iron deficiency in sugarcane is manifested as iron chlorosis, Young leaves are affected first. Apical meristems remains alive, immature leaves having varying degree are chlorosis but do not wilt Interveinal chlorosis from tip to base of leaves and appearance of alternate stripes. Entire leaves may become Chlorotic and turn papery. In severe deficiency leaf tip dies, whole plant become chlorotic and plant growth is checked.

Manganese

Mn is activator of many enzymes involve in protein synthesis.

Deficiency Symptoms

Young leaves affected, Interveinal chlorosis from tip toward middle of leaves, Entire plant may become chlorotic.

Soil Health

Soil health is an appropriate balance of the physical, chemical and biological aspects of soil. A healthy soil would ensure proper retention and release of water and nutrients, promote and sustain root growth, maintain soil biotic habitat, respond to management and resist degradation

Table 3: Integrated Nutrient Supply System

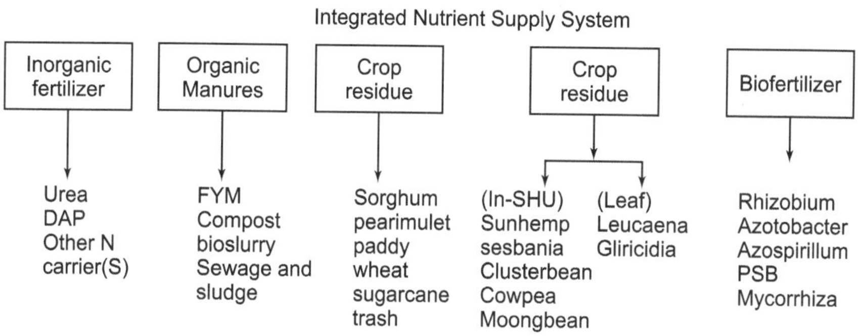

(**Source:** Based on a review of literature, 2018)

Table 4.4: Components of IPNS

Components	Desirable effect	Other effect
Fertilizers	Concentrated sources	Causes nutritional imbalances
Organic manures	Low nutrients but improves soil physical properties	Immediate crop need cannot be met.
Green manure	Source of N from atmosphere	Loose one crop
Crop residues	Source of K, mulching & improves soil physical properties	Immobilization of nutrients, more fertilizer N
Crop rotation	N fixed by legumes	Small amount of N
Biofertiliser – N	Symbiotic and a symbiotic N fixation	Small amount of N
Biofertiliser – P_2O_5	VAM, PSB	Small amount of P_2O_5

(**Source:** Based on a review of literature, 2018)

Table 4.5: Nutrients Contents of Commonly Used Organic Manures

Manures	N(%)	P_2O_5(%)	K_2O(%)
FYM	1.0	0.5	1.0
Poultry	1.8	1.2	1.3
Daincha	3.5	0.6	1.2
Press Mud	2.9	0.8	0.4
Cane trash	0.5	0.4	0.3
Municipal	0.4	0.6	0.4

(**Source:** Based on a review of literature, 2018)

PROMOTION OF CITY COMPOST

Department of Fertilizers notified the policy on promotion of city compost in February, 2016. Market Development Assistance of ₹ 1500/MT of city compost was provided for encouraging production and consumption of city compost. Initially, the marketing and promotion of city compost would be done through the existing fertiliser companies. In due course, compost manufacturers and other marketing entities recognized by the concerned State Government would be included.

Biofertilizer for Nitrogen Fixation

Symbiotic
Leguminous plant + Rhizobium
Blue-green algae and water fern (Azolla) in rice fields
Non-Symbiotic
Blue-green algae: Nostoc, Anabaena, etc.
Bacteria: Aerobic – Azotobacter, Azospirillum, Bacillus, Polymyxa, etc.
Anaerobic – Clostridium, Rhodosprillum, Clorobium, etc.

Table 4.6: Crop Residues Burnt in Haryana 2008-09 (Mt/yr)

Crop residues burnt in Haryana 2008-09 (Mt/yr)		
Residue burned		**Residue burned**
(based IPCC defautl coefficients)		**(based on jain et all 2014**
coefficients)	6.85	9.18
Total Residues generated Mt/yr		
Cereal crop	24.73	
Fiber crop	7.58	
Oil Seed	2.15	
Sugarcane	1.93	

IPCC (Intergovernmental Panel on Climate Change) (2000). Good Practice Guidance and Uncertainty Management in National Greenhouse Gas Inventories (Cambridge University Press, New York).
Niveta Jain*, Arti Bhatia, Himanshu Pathak 2014 Aerosol and Air Quality Research, 14: 422-430
(**Source:** Based on a review of Literature, 2018)

Table 4.7: Crop Wise Residue Generated in Haryana

	Production (000 tons)*	Ratio**	Total Residues (000 tons)
Rice	4145	1.5	6218
Wheat	16075	1.7	27328
Sugarcane	9120	0.4	3648
Coton	2676	2.15	5753
Oil Seed	1141	3	3423

(**Source:** Based on a review of Literature, 2018)
Source: * Department of Agriculture Haryana
**Niveta Jain*, Arti Bhatia, Himanshu Pathak 2014
Aerosol and Air Quality Research, 14: 422–430

Agricultural crop residue burning contribute towards the emission of greenhouse gases (CO_2, N_2O, CH_4, air pollutants (CO, NH_3, NOx, SO_2, NMHC, volatile organic compounds), particulates matter and smoke thereby posing threat to human health (Jain *et al.*, 2014). Burning of Rice residues causes 70%CO_2, 7%CO, 0.66% CH_4 and 2.09% N_2O (Gupta *et al.*, 2004). Balanced and integrated nutrient management involving all the essential nutrients, organic manures, biofertilizers and amendments. Soil & water testing for the status of the nutrients in the soil, fertilizer recommendation and soil and water management. Knowledge of multi-nutrient deficiency and their management in different crops. Creating awareness amongst farmers on benefits of balanced fertilization. Availability of the fertilizer to meet out the nutrient requirements of the crop. Proper soil management and agro agronomic practices for enhancing the fertilizer use efficiency.

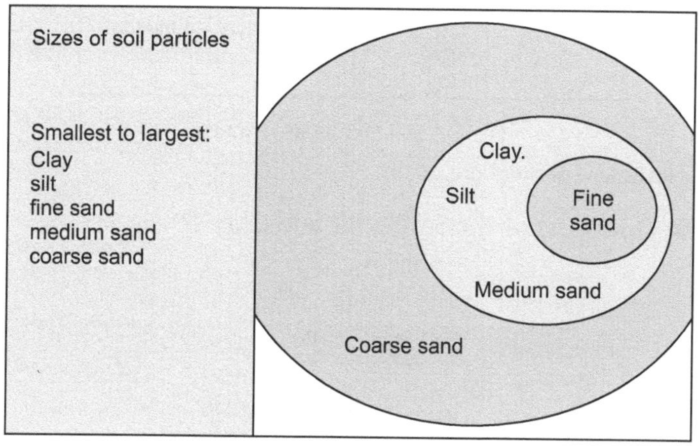

Fig. 3.6: Sizes of the soil particles

(**Source:** Based on Review of Literature, 2018)

Identification of Soil Texture

1. Spread soil on newspaper. Remove all rocks, trash, roots, etc. Crush all lumps.
2. Fill a tall, slender jar ¼ full of soil.
3. Add water until the jar is ¾ full.
4. Add a teaspoon of non-foaming dishwasher detergent.
5. Put on a tight fitting lid and shake hard for 10-15 minutes. This shaking breaks apart the soil aggregates and separates the soil into individual mineral particles.
6. Set the jar where it will not be disturbed for 2-3 days.
7. Soil particles will settle out according to size.
8. After **1 minute**, mark on the jar the depth of the sand.

9. After **2 hours**, mark the depth of silt.
10. When the water clears (**1-3 days or more**), mark the clay levels.
11. Measure the thickness of sand, silt, and clay layers and calculate the percentages of each.
12. Refer to the soil texture triangle and identify your soil.

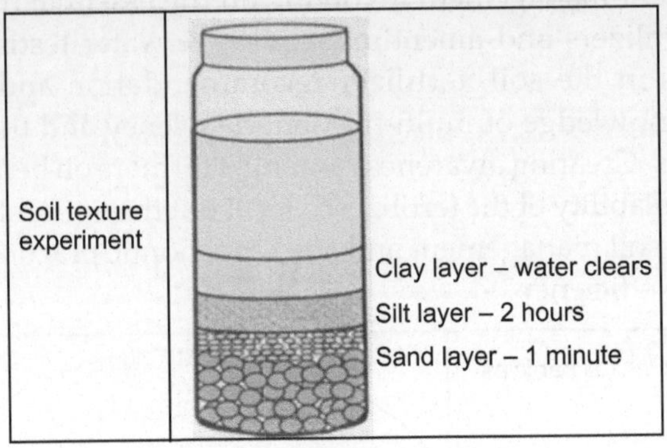

Fig. 4.7: Soil texture experiment

(**Source:** Based on Review of Literature, 2018)

Measure the Thickness of the Sand, Silt and Clay

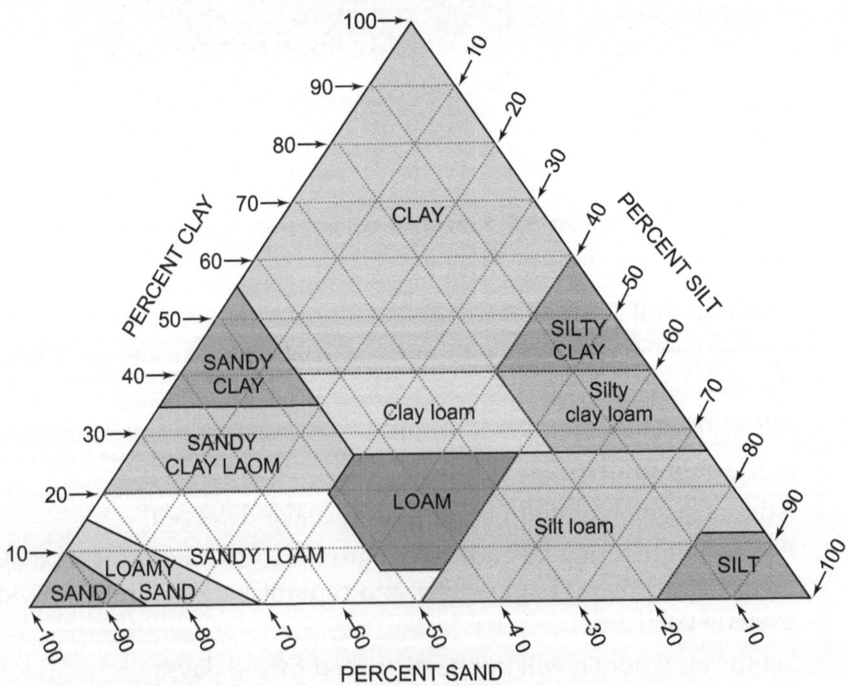

Fig. 4.8: Soil Texture Triangle

(**Source:** Based on Review of Literature, 2018)

A natural resource made up of minerals and small rocks, gases, water, and organic matter = soil

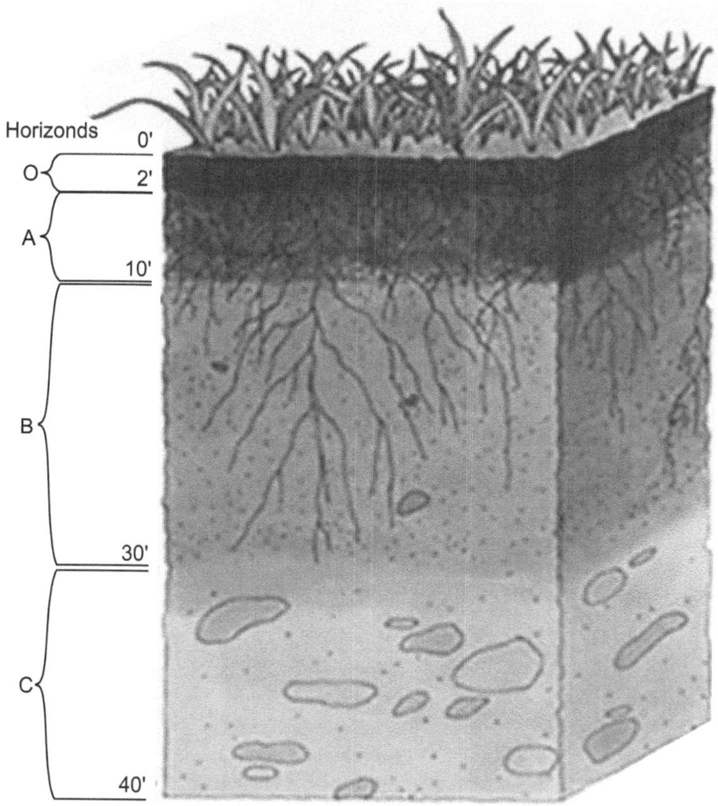

Fig. 4.9: Different horizon of soil

(**Source:** Based on a review of literature, 2018)

Flashback to the 1930'S

Drought caused big problems for farmers. Without rain, land was extra dry. Because farmers planted their crops in long, straight lines, the wind blew through their fields more strongly and blew their topsoil away. Crops could not grow!

Protecting Topsoil

Contour plowing: soil is plowed in curved rows that follow the shape of the land. This decreases wind and water damage to the land. Farmers keep soil in place by planting cover crops. This is what happens: Soil sticks to plant roots. Stems & leaves protect the soil from wind. Farmers protect soil that is lost from moving down hills by using terrace farming. Crops are planted on level sections.

Fig. 4.10: Aragonite-rich soil

(**Source:** Based on a review of literature, 2018)

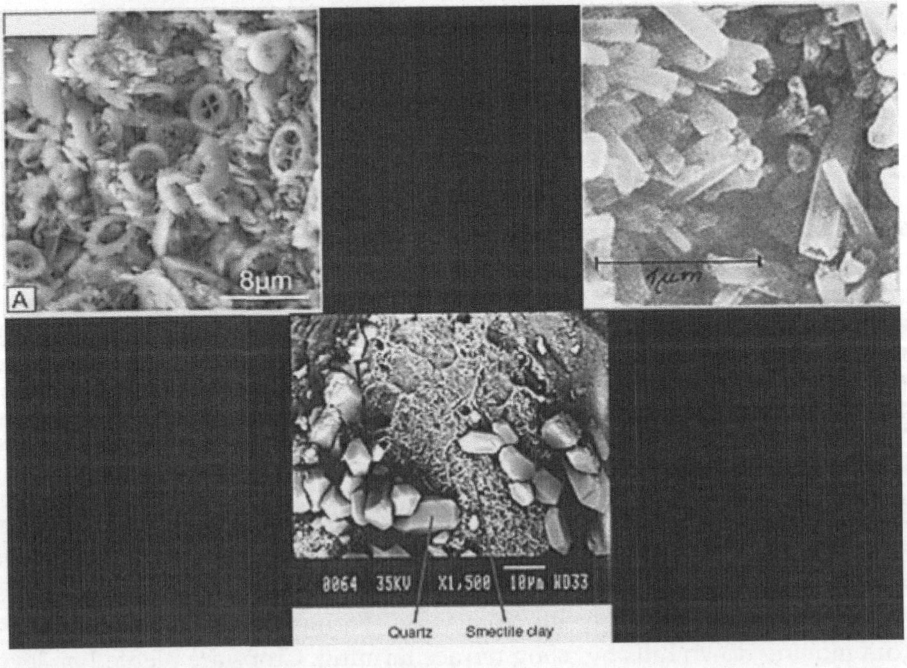

Fig. 4.11: Quartz and smectite clay

(**Source:** Based on a review of Literature, 2018)

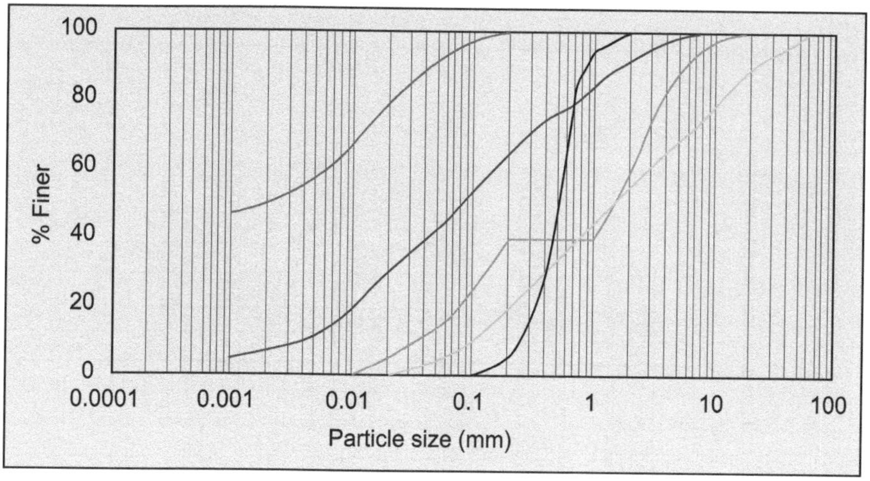

Fig. 4.12: Grading curve

(**Source:** Based on a review of Literature, 2018)

Atterberg's Limits

Particle size is not useful for fine grained soils.

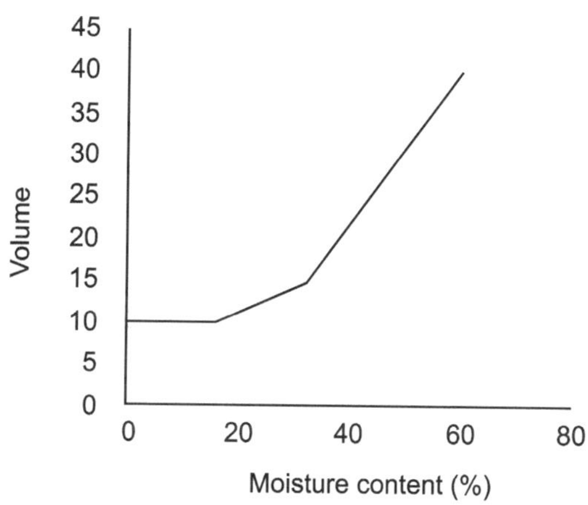

Fig. 4.13: Graph of Atterberg's Limit

(**Source:** Based on Review of Literature, 2018)

Assessment of Carbon Sequestration Potential of Soil

Main objective: Identify which Crop has the Highest Soil C Sequestration Potential

- Root biomass production and distribution along the soil profile
- Assessment of SOC stock variation and its degree of stabilization

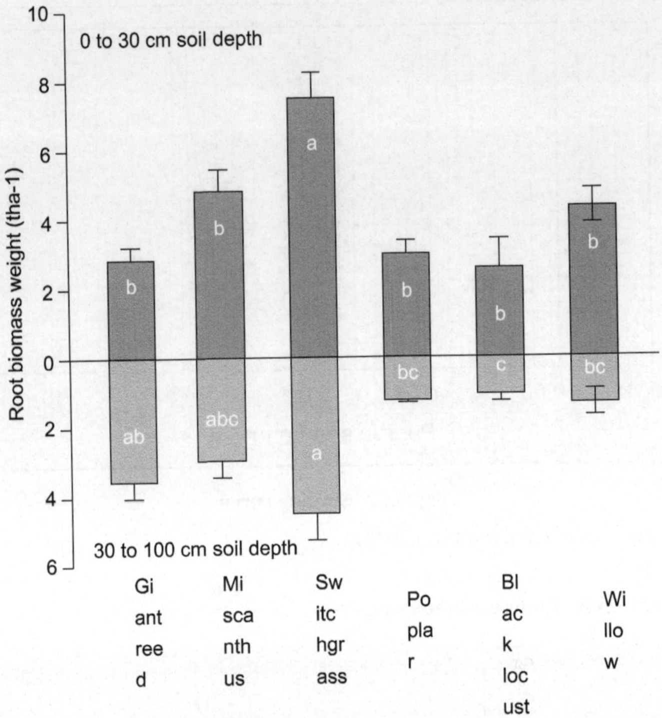

Fig. 4.14: Root Biomass Weight (t ha^{-1})

(**Source:** Based on Review of Literature, 2018)

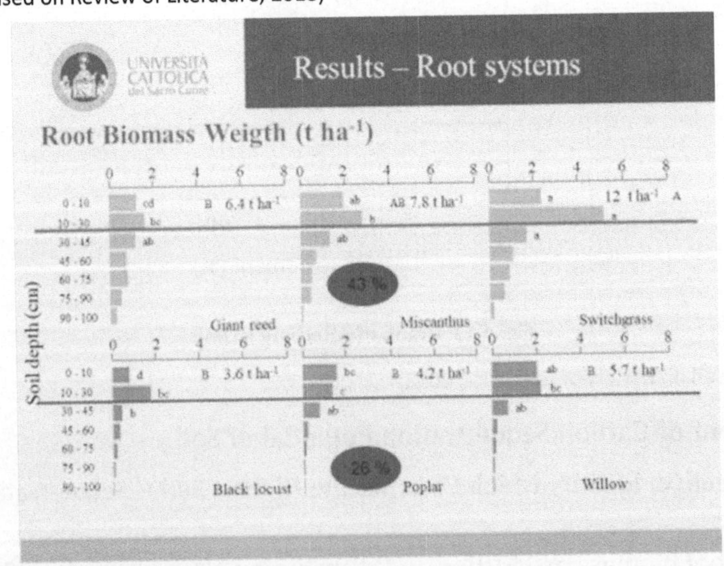

Fig. 4.15: Results of Root Biomass of different plants grown for the purpose of carbon sequestration

(**Source:** Based on Review of Literature, 2018)

UNIVERSITÀ CATTOLICA del Sacro Cuore

SOC fractions and stabilization mechanisms

Wet sieving, density and ....

- **cPOM** (2000 – 250 μm) and fPOM (250 – 53), unprotected SOC fractions
- **iPOM** (250 – 53 μm), physically protected SOC fractions

.... chemical fractionation

- **HC ds + c** chemically protected SOC fraction
- **HC μs + c** chemically protected SOC fraction
- **NHC ds + c** biochemically protected SOC fraction
- **NHC μs + c** biochemically protected SOC fraction

Fig. 4.16: SIC fractions and Stabilization mechanisms

UNIVERSITÀ CATTOLICA del Sacro Cuore

Results – SOC

Total Soil Organic Carbon Content

Depth (cm)	Pr (>F)
0 – 10	< 0.001
10 – 30	0.53
30 – 60	0.41
60 – 100	0.84

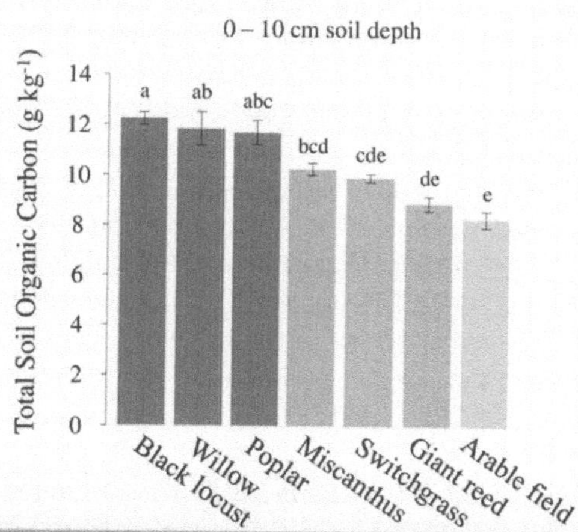

Fig. 4.17: Total soil organic carbon content

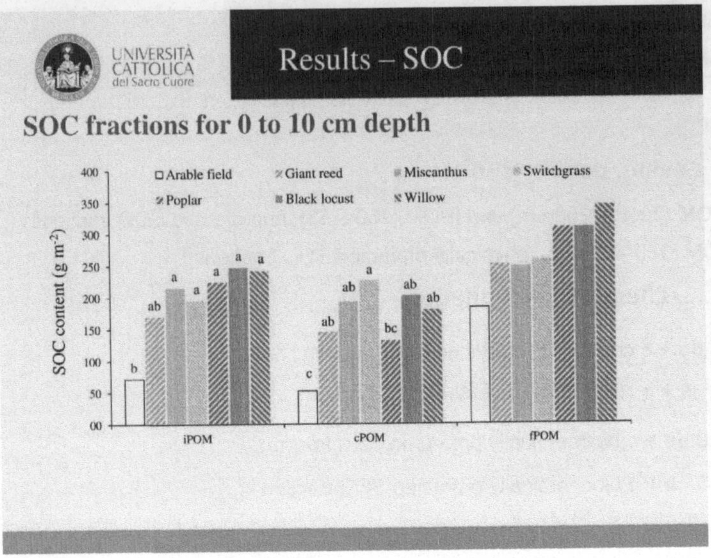

Fig. 4.18: SOC fraction for 0 to 10 cm depth

(**Source:** Based on Review of Literature, 2018)

Conclusion

Woody species showed the greatest SOC sequestration potential in the first soil layer, but their ability to allocate root biomass in the deeper soil layers was limited. Herbaceous species allocated a high amount of root biomass in the deeper soil layers, but only switch grass and miscan thus sequester C in the first soil layer.

REFERENCES

FAO (2014). *"World Reference Base For Soil Resources 2014*. World Soil Resources Reports 106. Rome: Food and Agriculture Organisation of the United Nations. ISBN 978-92-5-108369-7. ISSN 0532-0488 (https://www.worldcat.org/issn/0532-0488).

Nikiforoff, C. C. (1931). "History of A, B, C". *Bulletin of the American Soil Survey Association*. 12: 67–70.

Soil Survey Staff (1999). *Soil Taxonomy: A Basic System of Soil Classification for Making and Interpreting Soil Surveys*. Agriculture Handbook Number 436 (second ed.). Washington, DC: United States Department of Agriculture Natural Resources Conservation Service.

Johnson, D.L., J.E.J. Domier, and D.N. Johnson. 2005. Reflections on the Nature of Soil and Its Biomantle. Annals, Association of American Geographers, v. 95 (1), pp. 11–31.

Wilkinson, M.T. and G.S. Humphreys. 2005. Exploring Pedogenesis via Nuclide-based Soil Production Rates and OSL-based Bioturbation Rates. Australian Journal of Soil Research, v. 43, pp. 767–79.

Soil Survey Staff. 1992. *Keys to Soil Taxonomy*. United States Department of Agriculture, Soil Conservation Service, Soil Management Support Services Technical Monograph No. 19. Fifth edition. Pocahontas Press, Blacksburg, VA.

Soil Environment and Conservation **Pages 93-101**
Edited by: Dr. Ashok K. Rathoure; Dr. Pawan Kumar 'Bharti' and Dr. Alka Chauhan
ISBN: 978-93-88854-10-8
Edition: 2019
Published by: Discovery Publishing House Pvt. Ltd., New Delhi (India)

5 Impacts of Phosphate Amendments at a Contaminated Site

[1]Dr. Ashok K. Rathoure

Introduction

Rock phosphate is an important mineral resource with numerous uses and applications in agriculture and the environment. It is used in the manufacture of detergents, animal feed, and phosphate (PO_4^{3-}) fertilizers. Leaching or runoff losses from rock phosphate products like PO_4^{3-} fertilizers, animal feeds, and detergents could cause eutrophication of surface waters enriched in PO_4^{3-} by these losses. Although direct application of rock phosphate reduces pollution by acting as a slow-release fertilizer, its effectiveness is limited by several factors. The major limitation of rock phosphate in direct application is its low solubility, which reduces its availability for soil reactions or plant uptake. Strategies used to increase the effectiveness of directly applied rock phosphate are based on increasing acidity, as this increases rock phosphate solubility. The application of rock phosphate in agriculture may have adverse effects because it contains hazardous elements that could be transferred to the soil through the application of fertilizers, especially after long term use. Chemical analysis of Rock phosphate obtained from top rock phosphate-producing countries, however, shows that hazardous elements contained therein are below tolerable limits for PO_4^{3-} fertilizers. Studies have also reported that the radionuclides in rock phosphate do not pose any radiological risk. The presence of these elements in rock phosphate can be put to positive use if they are extracted before they are applied to farmlands. This makes rock phosphate a source of rare earth metals and radionuclides that could be used in technological development and as a future energy source. The affinity of rock phosphate for metals makes it a useful adsorbent for the removal of metals from aqueous solutions and an excellent material for metal immobilization in contaminated soils. Rock phosphate is a very important finite resource but its applications have adverse environmental implications.

[1] Eco Chem Sales & Services, New Civil Road, Surat (GJ), India

Soil Amendments

Soil amendments can be used to cost-effectively reduce the bioavailability and mobility of toxic metals in contaminated soils. One study was conducted at a Pb-contaminated site to evaluate the effectiveness of P-induced Pb immobilization by Cao *et al.*, 2002. Phosphate was applied at a 4.0 molar ratio of P to Pb with three treatments: T1, 100% of P from H_3PO_4; T2, 50% P from H_3PO_4 + 50% P from $Ca(H_2PO_4)_2$; and T3, 50% P from H_3PO_4 + 5% phosphate rock. Phosphate amendments effectively transformed soil Pb from the nonresidual (sum of exchangeable, carbonate, Fe/Mn, and organic) to the residual fraction, with residual Pb increase by 19"48% for T1, 22"50% for T2, and 11-55% for T3, respectively. Lead immobilization was attributed to the P-induced formation of chloropyromorphite $[Pb_{10}(PO_4)_6C_{12}]$, which was identified in the surface soil, subsurface soil, and plant rhizosphere soil. Occurrence of chloropyromorphite was evident 220 days after P addition for T1 and T2 treatments and 330 days for T3. Visual MINTEQ model and activity-ratio diagram indicated that lead phosphate minerals controlled Pb2+activities in the P-treated soils. Phosphate treatments significantly reduced Pb translocation from the roots to the shoots in the St. Augustine grass (*Stenotaphrumsecundatum*), possibly via the formation of chloropyromorphite on the cell walls of roots. In this field observation, the researcher suggested that P amendments are efficient in reducing Pb mobility via in situ formation of insoluble chloropyromorphite minerals at a field setting. Lead immobilization shows a long-term stability. A mixture of H_3PO_4 and phosphate rock yields the best overall results for in situ Pb immobilization, with less soil pH change and less P leaching. Application of combined H_3PO_4 with phosphate rock may provide an effective alternative to the current phosphate remediation technologies for contaminated soils.

Metal Immobilization

The contact of soluble metal species with microbial cells results in *in-situ* transformations of the targeted species. As a consequence, the metals are immobilized by the microbial biomass. Soluble metal and metalloid species may be sequestered from water streams via their interaction with microbial cells by active (i.e. metabolic/energy dependent) and passive (i.e. non metabolic/ energy independent) processes.Metabolically mediated immobilisation of metal species by active microbial cells includes different mechanisms such as bioprecipitation and biological reduction/oxidation. Passive metal uptake by microbial cells is described by the general term biosorption and includes different mechanisms of physico-chemical interaction between the microbial cell biopolymers and the metal species such as complexation, chelation, ion exchange and precipitation.

Both living/metabolizing and non-metabolizing microbial cells may be used in technology development for:

1. The removal of metals from aqueous industrial effluents
2. Metal recovery from industrial process streams
3. Bioremediation of contaminated surface waters and groundwater

Among the existing microorganisms in nature, bacteria, fungi, yeasts and algae are used in most cases for metal and metalloid sequestering from water streams. Microorganisms influence the chemical state - speciation and hence the mobility of the metals by numerous and complex mechanisms ranging from direct processes like metal transformation and intracellular uptake, to more indirect processes via production of substances that render the metals more or less mobile.

Microbially-mediated metal transformations

- May involve phase changes of metals;
- Are responsible for metal cycling in ecosystems.
- Are of use in biohydrometallurgy and bioremediation
- Are much more often caused by prokaryotes than by eukaryotes

A great number of microbially-mediated metal transformations exist. The mechanism and influence on metal mobility is not clear in all cases. Many terms that are used for classification are overlapping and there is some confusion in terminology (Johnson, 2006).

- Assimilation/adsorption and mineralization
- Dissolution and precipitation
- Oxidation and reduction
- Methylation and dealkylation

Other commonly used terms describing microbially-mediated metal transformations are not always consistent with the previous classification. These terms seem often to be used to describe biotechnologies like applied microbially-mediated metal transformations within biohydrometallurgy:

- Bioleaching
- Biotransformation
- Microbiological separation processes like
- Biosorption
- Bioprecipitation
- Bioaccumulation

Bioremediation

Bioremediation is one of the most promising technological approaches to the problem of hazardous waste. It is a technology for removing pollution from environment, restoring contaminated site and preventing future pollution.

Bioremediation can be performed in situ or ex situ. Microorganisms directly degrade contaminants rather than merely transferring them from one medium to another, employ metabolic degradation pathways and can be used in situ to minimize disturbance of the clean-up site. Hence, microorganisms can be effective, economical and non-disruptive tools for eliminating hazardous chemicals. Its advantage generally outweigh the disadvantage, therefore may be used as management tool. The microorganisms can improve phytoextraction by increasing plant biomass or by enhancing the availability of heavy metals to the plant. However, use of microorganisms to improve plant biomass via improved N or P nutrition can have a significant positive impact on phytoextraction. Those soils, which are contaminated and possess the higher amount of toxic metal than plant tolerance, then at such sites phytoremediation through rhizobacteria is preferred and carried out. This method not only increases the plant tolerance towards metals but also stabilizes the growth of plants involving the remediation of metal polluted soil. The soil fertility which is being lost due to heavy metal accumulation has been restored through this method. As the role of plant growth-promoting rhizobacteria is known however a lot remains there to understand regarding the mechanism of phytoremediation. While on the other hand, bioremediation through rhizobacteria is an economic and ecological friendly process. In order to survive in heavy metal polluted environments, many microorganisms have developed resistance to toxic metal ions. These mechanisms include: metal exclusion by permeability barriers, active transport of the metal away from the cell organism, intracellular sequestration of the metal by protein binding, extracellular sequestration, enzymatic detoxification of the metal to a less toxic form and reduction in metal sensitivity of cellular targets. The detoxification mechanisms may be directed against one metal or a group of chemically related metals. Furthermore, the detoxification mechanisms may vary depending on the type of microorganism. Most microorganisms are known to have specific genes for resistance to toxic ions of heavy metals. Mostly, the resistance genes are found on plasmids or on chromosomes. Plasmid encoded metal resistance determinants have been reported to be inducible.

Biosorption

Among the recent studies biosorption by filamentous fungi is the most frequently used technology to treat waste water contaminated with mercury. The technology has been used to meet regulatory cleanup levels, is commercially available to treat waste water, and generates a residual that typically does not require further treatment before disposal. There is always a scope of improvement and addition of new technologies or process improvement, the intent of this chapter is to call for action with the development of sound efficient and economical methods to reduce the contamination of mercury.

Chloropyromorphite Formation with Metal

Conversion of soil Pb to pyromorphite [Pb5(PO4)3Cl] was evaluated by Ryan *et al.*, 2001 by reacting a Pb contaminated soil collected adjacent to a historical smelter with hydroxyapatite [Ca5(PO4)3OH]. In a dialysis experiment where the soil and hydroxyapatite solids were placed by researchers in separate dialysis bags suspended in 0.01 M $NaNO_3$ solution a crystalline precipitate, identified as chloropyromorphite, formed on the dialysis membrane containing the soil. The aqueous composition of the solution indicated that dissolution of solid-phase soil Pb was the rate-limiting step for pyromorphite formation. Addition of hydroxyapatite to the soil caused a decrease in each of the first four fractions of sequential extractable Pb and a 35% increase in the recalcitrant extraction residue. After 240-day incubation at field-moisture content there was a further increase in the recalcitrant extraction residue fraction of the hydroxyapatite-amended soil to 45% of the total soil Pb. The increase in the extraction residue fraction in the hydroxyapatite amended 0-d incubated soil as compared to the control soil illustrates that the chemical extraction procedure itself caused changes in extractability. Therefore, the chemical extraction procedure cannot easily be utilized to confirm changes occurring in amended soils. The further increase after the 240-d incubation implies that the reaction also occurs in the soil during incubation. Extended X-ray absorption fine structure (EXAFS) spectroscopy indicated that after the 240-d incubation the hydroxyapatite treatment caused a change in the average, local molecular bonding environment of soil Pb. Low-temperature EXAFS spectra (chi data and radial structure functions " RSFs) showed a high degree of similarity between the chemical extraction residue and synthetic pyromorphite, providing additional evidence that the change of soil Pb to pyromorphite is possible by simple amendments of hydroxyapatite to soil.

Impact of Metal on Soil

Heavy metal pollution is a serious global environmental problem as it adversely affects plant growth and genetic variation. It also alters the composition and activity of soil microbial communities. The objectives of this study were to determine the soil microbial diversity, bermudagrass genetic variation in Cd contaminated or uncontaminated soils from Hunan province of China, and to evaluate Cd-tolerance of bermudagrass at different soils. The Biolog method, hydroponic experiments and simple sequence repeat markers were used to assess the functional diversity of microorganisms, Cd-tolerance and the genetic diversity of bermudagrass, respectively. Four of the sampling sites were heavily contaminated with heavy metals. The total bioactivity, richness, and microbial diversity decreased with increasing concentration of heavy metal. The hydroponic experiment revealed that bermudagrass populations collected from polluted sites have evolved, encompassing the feature of a higher resistance to Cd toxicity. Higher genetic diversity was observed to be more in contaminated populations than in uncontaminated populations. Heavy metal pollution can result in adverse effects on plant growth, soil microbial diversity and activity, and apparently has a stronger impact on the genetic structure. The results of this study provide new insights and a background to produce a genetic description of populations in a species that is suitable for use in phytoremediation practices.

Microorganisms and plants employ different mechanisms for the bioremediation of polluted soils. Using plants for the treatment of polluted soils is a more common approach in the bioremediation of heavy metal polluted soils. Combining both microorganisms and plants is an approach to bioremediation that ensures a more efficient clean-up of heavy metal polluted soils. However, success of this approach largely depends on the species of organisms involved in the process. Plants growing on these soils show a reduction in growth, performance, and yield. Bioremediation is an effective method of treating heavy metal polluted soils. It is a widely accepted method that is mostly carried out in situ; hence it is suitable for the establishment/reestablishment of crops on treated soils.

Soil pollution by heavy metals is a critical global environmental problem. Experts have estimated that more than 20 million hectares of farmland in China have been contaminated, accounting for 20% of the total landmass (Wei and Chen, 2001). Cd is considered to be one of the most phytotoxic metal pollutants due to its high mobility (especially in soil with low CEC and acidic pH), bioaccumulation in lower organisms and its easily being transferred to higher trophic levels in the food chain (Lin and Aarts, 2012). The toxicity of Cd pollution and its physical disturbance can influence plant survival, reproductive success and migration (Deng *et al.*, 2007). Plants are sedentary; they lack the ability to move actively to evade contaminated environment. Therefore, their only chance to survive in unfavorable conditions is the mobilization of defense mechanisms, and evolution of tolerate genotype (Chmielowska-B[1]k *et al.*, 2014).

Soil microorganisms, both free-living and symbiotic soil microbes in the rhizosphere of plants growing on metal contaminated soils, can increase plant biomass production and enhancing phytoremediation process. However, heavy metals affect the growth, morphology, and metabolism of soil microorganisms, through functional disturbance, protein denaturation or the destruction of the integrity of cell membranes (Leita *et al.*, 1995). Soil microorganisms are essential in the decomposition of soil organic matter; any decrease in the microbial diversity or abundance may adversely affect nutrient absorption from the soil for plant (Giller *et al.*, 1998a). The elevated levels of heavy metals in soils had significant impacts on the population size and overall activity of the soil microbial communities. Several studies, depending on the isolation-based techniques used, have revealed that heavy metal contamination gave rise to shifts in microbial populations (Gingell *et al.*, 1976; Barkay *et al.*, 1985; Roane and Kellogg, 1996). However, isolation-based techniques are limited because they only represent a small component of the microbial community. This limitation could be attributable to the fact that only a small percentage of soil microbes are culturable. A relatively improved procedure that may be useful in evaluating changes in microbial community structure is the determination of the metabolic profile of a particular system via the Biolog procedure (Garland, 1997). Biolog has been effective in characterizing the functional capability of soil organisms to utilize specific carbon substrates (Garland and Mills, 1991; Garland, 1996), and also has been widely used in assessing the functional diversity, associated with the microbial community in soil samples from farmland and grassland ecosystems (Sarathchandra *et al.*, 2001; Rutgers *et al.*, 2016).

Bioremediation is the use of organisms (microorganisms and/or plants) for the treatment of polluted soils. It is a widely accepted method of soil remediation because it is perceived to occur via natural processes. It is equally a cost effective method of soil remediation. Blaylock *et al.*, (1997) reported 50% to 65% saving when bioremediation was used for the treatment of 1 acre of Pb polluted soil compared with the case when a conventional method (excavation and landfill) was used for the same purpose. Although bioremediation is a non-disruptive method of soil remediation, it is usually time consuming and its use for the treatment of heavy metal polluted soils is sometimes affected by the climatic and geological conditions of the site to be remediated.

Effects of Phosphate Rock on Sequential Chemical Extraction of Lead in Contaminated Soils

Lead contamination is of great concern because of its adverse effects on human health, especially children. Ma *et al.*, (1997) evaluated the effects of phosphate rock on chemical associations of Pb in eight Pb-contaminated soils using a sequential extraction procedure. The chemical fractions are operationally defined by an extraction sequence in the order of increasing ability to dissolve Pb of lower solubilities. Additionally, more soluble forms of Pb are considered to be potentially more bioavailable than the less soluble forms. Lead in these soils was primarily associated with the carbonate and Fe-Mn oxide fractions (63–85%). Up to 21% of the Pb in these soils was associated with either the organic or the residual fraction and < 11% was associated with the water-soluble and the exchangeable fractions. Phosphate rocks effectively converted Pb from the water soluble, exchangeable, carbonate, Fe-Mn oxide, and organic fractions (collectively the nonresidual fraction) to the residual fraction, thus reducing Pb solubility and presumably bioavailability. Lead precipitation as a fluoropyromorphite-like mineral in these contaminated soils was suggested as the primary mechanism for reduced Pb solubility and Pb reduction in the nonresidual fraction. The effective conversion of Pb from potentially available fractions to the residual fraction suggests that phosphate rock has potential for in-situ immobilization in Pb contaminated soils.

Conclusion

Composting with phosphate is very cheap and reliable techniques for the solid waste containing organic matter. If the compost contains contaminants such as heavy metal then it is harm to environment. Heavy metals are toxic to soil, plants, aquatic life and human health if their concentration is high in the compost. Heavy metals exhibit toxic effects towards soil biota by affecting key microbial processes and decrease the number and activity of soil microorganisms. Even low concentration of heavy metals may inhibit the physiological metabolism of plant. Uptake of heavy metals by plants and subsequent accumulation along the food chain is a potential threat to animal and human health. The amendment of soil with rock phosphate is more favorable than other chemical fertilizers at contaminated sites. Hence, the use of rock phosphate as soil amendments should be encouraged.

REFERENCES

Barkay T., Tripp S. C., Olson B. H. (1985). Effect of Metal-rich Sewage Sludge Application on the Bacterial Communities of Grasslands. *Appl. Environ. Microbiol.* 49 333–337

Blaylock M. J., Salt D. E., Dushenkov S. Enhanced Accumulation of Pb in Indian Mustard by Soil-applied Chelating Agents, Environmental Science and Technology, Vol. 31, no. 3, pp. 860–865, 1997

Cao X, Ma LQ, Chen M, Singh SP, Harris WG. Impacts of Phosphate Amendments on Lead Biogeochemistry at a Contaminated Site. Environ Sci Technol. 2002. 15;36(24):5296-304.

Chmielowska-B¹k J., Gzyl J., Ruciñska-Sobkowiak R., Arasimowicz-Jelonek M., Deckert J. (2014). The New Insights into Cadmium Sensing. *Front. Plant Sci.* 5:245 10.3389/fpls.2014.00245

Deng J., Liao B., Ye M., Deng D., Lan C., Shu W. (2007). The Effects of Heavy Metal Pollution on Genetic Diversity in Zinc/Cadmium Hyperaccumulator *Sedum alfredii* Populations. *Plant Soil* 297 83–92. 10.1007/s11104-007-9322-5

Garland J. L. (1996). Analytical Approaches to the Characterization of Samples of Microbial Communities Using Patterns of Potential C Source Utilization. *Soil Biol. Biochem.* 28 213–221. 10.1016/0038-0717(95)00112-3

Garland J. L. (1997). Analysis and Interpretation of Community-level Physiological Profiles in Microbial Ecology. *FEMS Microbiol. Ecol.* 24 289–300. 10.1111/j.1574-6941.1997.tb00446.x

Garland J. L., Mills A. L. (1991). Classification and Characterization of Heterotrophic Microbial Communities on the Basis of Patterns of Community-level Sole-carbon-source Utilization. *Appl. Environ. Microbiol.* 57 2351–2359

Giller K. E., Witter E., Mcgrath S. P. (1998b). Toxicity of Heavy Metals to Microorganisms and Microbial Processes in Agricultural Soils: A Review. *Soil Biol. Biochem.* 30 1389–1414. 10.1016/j.envint.2008.06.009

Giller K., Amijee F., Brodrick S., Edje O. (1998a). Environmental Constraints to Nodulation and Nitrogen Fixation of *Phaseolus vulgaris* L in Tanzania II. Response to N and P Fertilizers and Inoculation with *Rhizobium*. *Afr. Crop Sci. J.* 6 171–178. 10.4314/acsj.v6i2.27813

Gingell R., Wallcave L., Nagel D., Kupper R., Pour P. (1976). Metabolism of the Pancreatic Carcinogens N-nitroso-bis (2-oxopropyl) Amine and N-nitroso-bis (2-hydroxypropyl) Amine in the Syrian Hamster. *J. Natl. Cancer Inst.* 57 1175–1178.

Leita L., De Nobili M., Muhlbachova G., Mondini C., Marchiol L., Zerbi G. (1995). Bioavailability and Effects of Heavy Metals on Soil Microbial Biomass Survival during Laboratory Incubation. *Biol. Fertil. Soils* 19 103–108. 10.1007/BF00336144

Lin Y. F., Aarts M. G. (2012). The Molecular Mechanism of Zinc and Cadmium Stress Response in Plants. *Cell. Mol. Life Sci.* 69 3187–3206. 10.1007/s00018-012-1089-z.

Ma L.Q.Rao G.N. Univ. of Florida, Gainesville, FL. (1997). Effects of Phosphate Rock on Sequential Chemical Extraction of Lead in Contaminated Soils. Journal of Environmental Quality. Online at http://agris.fao.org/agris-search/search.do?recordID=US19970128950

Roane T., Kellogg S. (1996). Characterization of Bacterial Communities in Heavy Metal Contaminated Soils. *Can. J. Microbiol.* 42 593–603. 10.1139/m96-080

Rutgers M., Wouterse M., Drost S. M., Breure A. M., Mulder C., Stone D., (2016). Monitoring Soil Bacteria with Community-Level Physiological Profiles Using Biolog ECO-Plates in the Netherlands and Europe. *Appl. Soil Ecol.* 97 23–35. 10.1016/j.apsoil. 2015.06.007

Ryan JA, Zhang P, Hesterberg D, Chou J, Sayers DE. (2001). Formation of Chloropyromorphite in a Lead-contaminated Soil Amended with Hydroxyapatite. Environ Sci Technol. 15;35(18):3798-803.

Sarathchandra S. U., Ghani A., Yeates G. W., Burch G., Cox N. R. (2001). Effect of Nitrogen and Phosphate Fertilisers on Microbial and Nematode Diversity in Pasture Soils. *Soil Biol. Biochem.* 33953–964. 10.1016/S0038-0717(00)00245-5

Wei C., Chen T. (2001). Hyperaccumulators and Phytoremediation of Heavy Metal Contaminated Soil: A Review of Studies in China and Abroad. *Acta Ecol. Sin.* 21 1196–1203.

Soil Environment and Conservation **Pages 102-117**
Edited by: **Dr. Ashok K. Rathoure; Dr. Pawan Kumar 'Bharti' and Dr. Alka Chauhan**
ISBN: 978-93-88854-10-8
Edition: **2019**
Published by: **Discovery Publishing House Pvt. Ltd., New Delhi (India)**

6

Soil and Sediment Quality Monitoring at Larsemann Hills, East Antarctica

Dr. Pawan Kumar Bharti[1]

ABSTRACT

Soil represents the loose and unconsolidated materials through the disintegration of rocks. The soil comprises of mineral and organic constituents differentiated into horizons of variable depth, which differs, from the materials underneath in morphology, physico-chemical properties and composition and biological characteristics. Soil serves as a reservoir of nutrients. The impact of pollutants on soil quality may be a rather slow process but it may be of greater concern in the long run.

Soil and sediment samples were collected from several locations of Bharti Island, Fisher Island, Mcleod Island, Broknes and Stornes peninsula by adopting established sampling procedures using auger. Detailed analysis of collected soils samples were carried out using the methodologies given in various relevant protocols as specified in IS: 2720. Chemical, titrimetric, gravimetric and instrumental methods were used for various analyses. Analytical grade Reagent (AR) and HPLC grade water was used in all analytical work, reagent preparation, samples dilution and blank corrections.

The result shows that quality of soil in this area is least affected by the activities of the surrounding research stations.

Keywords: Soil quality, sediment sampling, analysis, environmental monitoring

Introduction

Antarctica has more than 98% ice cover and only about 2% rocky area. Rocky area was selected for the constructions of India's third scientific research station 'Bharti' in east Antarctica. As in other parts of the world, Antarctica may also experience land use changes due to a number of activities - both man-made as well as natural.

Soil quality is simply defined as "the capacity of a specific kind of soil to function", i.e. mainly to provide nutrition to plants and absorb the drain water.

1 Antarctica Laboratory, R & D Division, Shriram Institute for Industrial Research, 19, University Road, Delhi-110 007, India

The different properties of soil are - texture, moisture, fertility (level of nitrogen, phosphorus, potassium) and pH level. The pH is the measure of a soil's acidity or alkalinity.

Each of these properties depends on different factors. For example, soil moisture depends on climate, topography and other soil characteristics. The temperatures of soils vary depending on their water holding capacity. Soils with low water holding capacity are warm.

Soil represents the loose and unconsolidated materials derived through the breaking down of rocks. The soil is a natural constituent of plants, animal, mineral and organic materials differentiated into horizons of variable depth. It also differs from the material below in morphology, physical make up, chemical properties, composition and biological characteristics. The comprehensive study of soil system in terms of its composition and contamination with a toxic chemical is of vital significance because it is an integral part of the bio-geographic system.

The soil comprises of mineral and organic constituents differentiated into horizons of variable depth, which differs, from the materials underneath in morphology, physical make up, chemical properties and composition and biological characteristics. The impact of pollutants and human activities on soil quality may be a rather slow process but it may be of greater concern in the long run. The percolation of pollutants may get accumulated in the soil and ultimately affect its quality.

Land environment study is an important study for prediction of various impacts due to construction and operational activities. The impacts on soil quality may be a rather slow process but it can sometimes cause concern in the long run. The fall out of heavy metals and other pollutants present in the smoke and dust emitted from construction site, local vehicular traffic and other sources may get accumulated in the soil and ultimately affect the trace metal concentration. Studies were carried out in the study area, for estimation of Physico – chemical characteristics of the soil.

Pollutant Migration Potential

Generally, the migration of pollutants released in an environment in the land occurs through the ground and when it interacts with the water table, it can pollute the ground making it unsuitable for domestic use and growth of plants. As no major regular polluting activities or industries were present in the study area and no land is required for domestic and agriculture uses, so the chances of soil pollution are very less.

Study Area Description

The Larsemann Hills is an ice-free area of approximately 50 km^2, located halfway between the Vestfold Hills and the Amery Ice Shelf on the southeastern coast of Prydz Bay, Princess Elizabeth Land, East Antarctica (69°30′00″ S, 76°19′58″E). The ice-free area consists of two major peninsulas (Stornes and Broknes), four minor peninsulas, and approximately 130 near shore islands. Nella Fjord further divides the eastern-most peninsula, Broknes, into western and eastern components. The closest significant ice-free areas are the Bolingen Islands (69°31′58″S, 75°42′E) 25 km to the south-west and the Rauer Islands (68 °50′59″S, 77°49′58″E) 60 km to the north-east[(11)].

India is presently carrying out scientific research programs on the Bharti Island between Quilty bay and Thala Fjord. The nearest Islands/peninsulas are Stornes and Broknes Peninsula, Fisher Island and Mcleod Island. Loose soil is found in the catchment area of these Islands/peninsulas. Larsemann Hill area was chosen to study existing soil characteristics.

Investigation and Soil Sampling

To investigate the existing soil and sediment quality of the study area, samples of soil from different locations were collected to cover important aspects of physical and chemical properties of soil quality therein. Samples were collected from several locations in Larsemann Hills by adopting established sampling procedures given in the IS: 2720 specifications. Undisturbed soils and sediments samples representative of the area was collected by means of auger.

Selection of Sampling Location

Soil samples collected from different locations in the study area have been assessed in the study area. All these sampling locations were chosen to represent the soil quality of the study area. Details of the soil sampling locations are given in the tabular form in this chapter.

Sampling and Analytical Methodology

A preliminary reconnaissance survey was made to get a general picture of the area's land use. The activities around the sampling sites were also taken into consideration to learn the sources of pollution if any or factors governing the Physico-chemical properties of the soil. The study was carried out to analyse the soil quality of the area and to assess the impact of constructional and operational activities on land environment.

Sampling

The team comprising of SIIR scientist and other members visited the site and identified the exact locations for soil and sediment sampling. At each location, the sample was collected with the help of hand-driven sampling augers from sub-surface region. Topsoil samples from all locations at depth of 15 cm. (sub surface) of the soil profile in the region were collected for Physico-chemical analysis. Sediment samples were collected from bottom of various lakes.

Analysis

Samples were collected from several locations of Bharti Island, Fisher Island, Mcleod Island, Broknes and Stornes peninsula by adopting established sampling procedures given in the IS: 2720 specifications. Undisturbed soils samples which are representatives of the area were collected by using auger. Detailed analysis of collected soils samples were carried out using the methodologies given in various relevant protocols as specified in IS: 2720. Chemical, titrimetric, gravimetric and instrumental methods were used for various analysis. HPLC grade water was used for reagent preparation, samples dilution and blank corrections. Analytical Reagent (AR) were used in analysis.

Attention was paid to collect adequate amount of composite samples for analysis with the standard methods. Samples were homogenised before testing. The samples were packed in dependable, waterproof containers. They were marked accurately and distinctly, brought to the SIIR laboratory for testing and analyzed as per ASTM, USEPA. Parameters and test protocols/methods for analysis of soil samples are given in the Annexure IV.

Soil

Soil represents the loose and unconsolidated materials through the disintegration of rocks. The soil comprises of mineral and organic constituents differentiated into horizons of variable depth, which differs, from the materials underneath in morphology, physical make up, chemical properties and composition and biological characteristics. Soil serves as a reservoir of nutrients. The impact of pollutants on soil quality may be a rather slow process but it may be of greater concern in the long run. The percolation of pollutants may get accumulated in the soil and ultimately affect its quality.

Sediment

The study site was visited and identified the exact locations for sediment sampling from the lake. At each location the sample was collected with the help of hand-driven sampling augers from sub-surface region. Sediment samples from all locations were collected from Lake Bottom for physico-chemical analysis. The other thing related to handling, storing, packing, transporting and analytical procedures were followed like the soil samples. Sediment samples from the Lake were collected from the bank area of lake, because the entire lake was in frozen condition.

Results and Discussion

Analytical results of all soil and sediment samples collected from Bharti Island, Fisher Island, Mcleod Island, Broknes peninsula and Stornes Peninsula are as follows:

Soil Quality at Bharti Island

The test results of soil samples from Bharti Island are given in Table 5.8.3A, 5.8.3B, 5.8.4A and 5.8.4B. pH value of all the samples was found to be in the range 6.8 to 8.5, which shows suitability of the soil for general fertility. Electrical conductivity (EC) is the indicator of soluble salts in the sample of soil. EC of collected soil samples varied in range of 120-311 µS/cm, when determined in the ratio of 1:5. The primary nutrient Phosphorous (as P_2O_5) was ranging between 57.37 – 1058.45 mg/kg. Secondary nutrients of the soil are mainly Calcium and Magnesium. Magnesium as (MgO) was found between 0.70 – 21.48% by mass, while Calcium as (CaO) was found varying between 0.5 – 15.40% by mass. Chloride (as Cl) was found varying between 0.05 – 1.01% by mass. Sulphate (as SO_4) was found between 0.01 – 0.06% in all soil samples. Cadmium was observed between 0.32 – 2.65 mg/kg in all samples. Iron (as Fe_2O_3) was found in the range of 3.0 – 16.11% by mass. Copper (as Cu) was found varying between 5.87 – 29.62 mg/kg. Chromium (as Cr) was found varying between 8.63 – 63.03 mg/kg. Zinc (as Zn) was found varying between 24.36 – 85.96 mg/kg. Manganese (as Mn) was found varying between 41.42 – 668.98 mg/kg. Sodium (as Na_2O) was found in the range of 1.32 – 9.61 % by mass. Potassium (as K_2O) was found in the range of 1.12 – 13.41% by mass. Aluminum (as Al_2O_3) was found in the range of 2.79 – 22.70% by mass. Gasparon and Matschullat gave similar trend of metals in soils at Larsemann Hills. Goldsworthy *et al.*, also investigated on the Soil and water contamination in Larsemann Hill area. Radiation contamination as (Cs-137) was found below Minimum Detection Limit (MDL) in all the samples.

Soil Quality at Fisher Island

The test results for soil sample from Fisher Island are given in Table 5.8.5A & 5.8.5B. pH value of the sample was found to be 7.3. EC of collected soil sample was 196 µS/cm, when determined in the ratio of 1:5. The primary nutrient Phosphorous (as P_2O_5) was found 100.65 mg/kg. Sodium (as Na_2O), Potassium (as K_2O), Calcium (as CaO), Magnesium (as MgO) Chloride (as Cl), Sulphate (as SO_4), Iron (as Fe_2O_3) & Aluminum (as Al_2O_3) were found to be 2.44%, 6.21%, 4.6%, 6.48%, 0.22%, 0.06 %, 4.56% & 11.35% by mass respectively.

Cadmium (as Cd), Chromium (as Cr), Zinc (as Zn), Manganese (as Mn) and Copper (as Cu) were observed to be 0.89, 12.97, 44.89, 302.31 and 4.18 mg/kg respectively in soil sample.

Soil Quality at Mcleod Island

The test results for soil samples from Mcleod Island are given in Table 5.8.5A & 5.8.5B. pH value of the samples was found to be in the range 7.7 to 7.9. EC of collected soil samples varied in range of 186 - 210 µS/cm, when determined in the ratio of 1:5. The primary nutrient Phosphorous (as P_2O_5) was ranging between 78.81 – 141.76 mg/kg. Magnesium as (MgO) was found between 4.67 – 9.31% by mass, while Calcium as (CaO) was found varying between 5.26 – 6.29% by mass. Chloride (as Cl) was found varying between 0.12 – 0.42% by mass. Sulphate (as SO_4) was found between 0.03 – 0.06% in all soil samples. Cadmium was observed between 0.07 – 0.49 mg/kg in soil samples. Iron (as Fe_2O_3) was found in the range of 6.32 – 7.79 % by mass. Copper (as Cu) was found varying between 6.20 – 9.23 mg/kg. Chromium (as Cr) was found varying between 11.35 – 41.60 mg/kg. Zinc (as Zn) was found varying between 42.01 – 68.08 mg/kg. Manganese (as Mn) was found varying between 214.96 - 386.37 mg/kg. Sodium (as Na_2O) was found in the range of 5.26 – 6.57% by mass. Potassium (as K_2O) was found in the range of 8.66 – 10.94% by mass. Aluminum (as Al_2O_3) was found in the range of 11.66 – 15.29% by mass.

Soil Quality at Broknes Peninsula

The test results for soil sample from Broknes peninsula are given in Table 5.8. 5A & 5.8.5B. pH value of the sample was found to be 6.9, while Electric Conductivity was found 241 μS/cm. Phosphorous (as P_2O_5) was found 378.07 mg/kg. Sodium (as Na_2O), Potassium (as K_2O), Calcium (as CaO), Magnesium (as MgO) Chloride (as Cl), Sulphate (as SO_4), Iron (as Fe_2O_3) & Aluminum (as Al_2O_3) were found to be 1.39%, 2.01%, 2.38%, 1.47%, 0.35%, 0.08%, 4.77% & 11.86% by mass respectively.

Cadmium (as Cd), Chromium (as Cr), Zinc (as Zn), Manganese (as Mn) and Copper (as Cu) were observed to be 0.99, 65.13, 78.83, 599.19 and 34.31 mg/kg respectively in soil sample.

Soil Quality at Stornes Peninsula

The test results for soil samples from Stornes peninsula are given in Table 5.8.5A & 5.8.5B. pH value of the samples was found to be in the range 6.8 to 7.2. EC of collected soil samples varied in range of 385 - 582 μS/cm, when determined in the ratio of 1:5. The primary nutrient Phosphorous (as P_2O_5) was ranging between 112.62 – 142.94 mg/kg. Magnesium as (MgO) was found between 1.50 – 2.16% by mass, while Calcium as (CaO) was found varying between 1.41 – 1.91% by mass. Chloride (as Cl) was found varying between 0.35 – 0.76% by mass. Sulphate (as SO_4) was found between 0.02 – 0.04% in all soil samples. Cadmium was observed between 0.21 – 0.24 mg/kg in soil samples. Iron (as Fe_2O_3) was found in the range of 2.49 – 3.49% by mass. Copper (as Cu) was found varying between 13.28 – 21.55 mg/kg. Chromium (as Cr) was found varying between 13.97 – 36.16 mg/kg. Zinc (as Zn) was found varying between 52.96 – 73.13 mg/kg. Manganese (as Mn) was found varying between 136.03 – 539.33 mg/kg. Sodium (as Na_2O) was found in the range of 2.36 – 3.17% by mass. Potassium (as K_2O) was found in the range of 1.66 – 2.43% by mass. Aluminum (as Al_2O_3) was found in the range of 1.27 – 5.27% by mass of soil.

Sediment Quality at Bharti Island

The test results for sediment samples from Bharti Island are given in Table 5.8.6A, 5.8.6B, 5.8.7A and 5.8.7B. pH value of all the samples was found to be in the range 6.6 to 7.6. Electrical conductivity (EC) of collected sediments samples varied in range of 113 – 278 µS/cm. Sodium (as Na_2O) was found in the range of 1.32 – 3.60% by mass. Potassium (as K_2O) was found in the range of 2.02 – 4.35% by mass. Calcium as (CaO) was found between 0.45 – 2.43% by mass, while Magnesium as (MgO) was found varying between 1.28 – 7.29% by mass. Iron (as Fe_2O_3) was found in the range of 5.02 – 9.81% by mass. Aluminum (as Al_2O_3) was found in the range of 4.18 – 8.83% by mass. Phosphorous (as P_2O_5) was ranging between 243.08 – 727.57 mg/kg. Chloride (as Cl) was found varying between 0.34 – 1.25% by mass. Sulphate (as SO_4) was found between 0.09 – 0.38 % in all samples.

Cadmium was observed between 0.63 – 1.72 mg/kg in all samples. Chromium (as Cr) was found varying between 63.04 – 167.67 mg/kg. Zinc (as Zn) was found varying between 56.65 – 212.99 mg/kg. Manganese (as Mn) was found varying between 125.03 – 353.20 mg/kg. Copper (as Cu) was found varying between 7.57 – 112.33 mg/kg.

Sediment quality at Fisher Island

The test results for sediment sample from Fisher Island are given in Table 5.8.7A & 5.8.7B. pH value of the sample was found to be 6.9. EC of collected sample was 179.0 µS/cm, when determined in the ratio of 1:5. Phosphorous (as P_2O_5) was found 385.28 mg/kg. Sodium (as Na_2O), Potassium (as K_2O), Calcium (as CaO), Magnesium (as MgO), Chloride (as Cl), Sulphate (as SO_4), Iron (as Fe_2O_3) & Aluminum (as Al_2O_3) were found to be 2.17%, 2.03%, 1.04%, 2.87%, 0.63%, 0.24%, 5.83% & 5.40% by mass respectively.

Cadmium (as Cd), Chromium (as Cr), Zinc (as Zn), Manganese (as Mn) and Copper (as Cu) were observed to be 0.87, 36.55, 112.22, 421.49 and 9.20 mg/kg respectively in sediment sample.

Sediment Quality at Mcleod Island

The test results for sediment sample from Mcleod Island are given in Table 5.8.7A & 5.8.7B. pH value of the sample was found to be 7.3. EC of collected sample was 189.0 µS/cm, when determined in the ratio of 1:5. Phosphorous (as P_2O_5) was found 265.98 mg/kg. Sodium (as Na_2O), Potassium (as K_2O), Calcium (as CaO), Magnesium (as MgO), Chloride (as Cl), Sulphate (as SO_4), Iron (as Fe_2O_3) & Aluminum (as Al_2O_3) were found to be 2.37%, 3.45%, 1.27%, 4.77%, 0.42%, 0.29%, 6.01% & 3.90% by mass respectively.

Cadmium (as Cd), Chromium (as Cr), Zinc (as Zn), Manganese (as Mn) and Copper (as Cu) were observed to be 0.73, 81.92, 71.86, 214.21 and 8.21 mg/kg respectively in sediment sample.

Sediment Quality at Broknes Peninsula

The test results for sediment sample from Broknes peninsula are given in Table 5.8.7A & 5.8.7B. pH value of the sample was found to be 6.7. EC of collected sample was 132.0 µS/cm, when determined in the ratio of 1:5. Phosphorous (as P_2O_5) was found 428.62 mg/kg. Sodium (as Na_2O), Potassium (as K_2O), Calcium (as CaO), Magnesium (as MgO), Chloride (as Cl), Sulphate (as SO_4), Iron (as Fe_2O_3) & Aluminum (as Al_2O_3) were found to be 1.84%, 2.17%, 1.06%, 1.43%, 0.85%, 0.38%, 3.25% & 3.98% by mass respectively.

Cadmium (as Cd), Chromium (as Cr), Zinc (as Zn), Manganese (as Mn) and Copper (as Cu) were observed to be 1.09, 86.29, 65.76, 157.21 and 20.12 mg/kg respectively in sediment sample.

Sediment Quality at Stornes Peninsula

The test results for sediment sample from Stornes peninsula are given in Table 5.8.7A & 5.8.7B. pH value of the sample was found to be 6.7. EC of collected sample was 125.0 µS/cm, when determined in the ratio of 1:5. Phosphorous (as P_2O_5) was found 385.76 mg/kg. Sodium (as Na_2O), Potassium (as K_2O), Calcium (as CaO), Magnesium (as MgO), Chloride (as Cl), Sulphate (as SO_4), Iron (as Fe_2O_3) & Aluminum (as Al_2O_3) were found to be 1.50%, 1.77%, 0.36 %, 0.42%, 0.31%, 0.11%, 2.85% & 3.57% by mass respectively.

Cadmium (as Cd), Chromium (as Cr), Zinc (as Zn), Manganese (as Mn) and Copper (as Cu) were observed to be 2.00, 54.0, 46.90, 187.45 and 12.10 mg/kg respectively in sediment sample. Wang *et al.*, [12] highlighted the weather processes and characteristics of soil at Stornes peninsula.

Radiation contamination as (Cs-137) was found below Minimum Detection Limit (MDL) in all soil and sediment samples collected from Bharti Island, Fisher Island, Mcleod Island, Broknes and Stornes peninsula at Larsemann Hills.

Sediment provides substratum and breeding ground for aquatic organisms especially to benthic communities. Sediment is also a source of nutrients and accumulated organic matter and it may help phytoplankton to uptake these in dissolved form from water. Sediment of a freshwater ecosystem plays very important role to regulate ecological balance.

Due to the less anthropogenic activities in Larsemann Hill area, any unwanted or foreign or toxic substance was not detected in any sediment sample. This condition is good for aquatic life. As most of the lakes have an oligotrophic status in Larsemann Hills, east Antarctica, so sediment has less organic load in comparison to eutrophic lakes. All the sediment samples have the basic constituents in different ratio. The chemical characteristic was also not found to be objectionable or outstanding or abnormal. Few heavy metals may arise in the surrounding by Geo-genic activities and soil is the probably one of the natural source of heavy metals.

Soil represents the loose and unconsolidated materials through the disintegration of rocks. The soil comprises of mineral and organic constituents differentiated into horizons of variable depth, which differs, from the materials underneath in morphology, physical make up, chemical properties and composition and biological characteristics. Soil serves as a reservoir of nutrients. The impact of pollutants on soil quality may be a rather slow process but it may be of greater concern in the long run. The percolation of pollutants may get accumulated in the soil and ultimately affect its quality. Goldsworthy *et al.,* also investigated on the Soil and water contamination in Larsemann Hill area. Tarnocai and Campbell(described the Physico-chemical characteristics of polar soils.

Larsemann Hill area is rocky and due to the weathering, loose particles from the rock reach the bank of low-lying area of lakes. Hall and Walton[(15)] described the rock weathering and soil formation process over a period of time. The soil samples have been collected from the locations where loose particles in form of soil have gathered. The major quality characteristics of polar soils may influence by the oil spillage. The result shows that existing quality of soil in this area is least affected by the activities of the surrounding research stations.

Table 6.1: Details of the Soil Sampling Locations

Sl.No.	Sampling Point	Point Code	Location	Latitude	Longitude
1	Near Lake L1	SQ – 1	Bharti Island	69° 24′ 18.5″	76° 11′ 32.2″
2	Near Lake L2	SQ – 2	Bharti Island	69° 24′ 25.4″	76° 11′ 27.4″
3	Near Lake L3	SQ – 3	Bharti Island	69° 24′ 21.9″	76° 11′ 13.8″
4	Near Lake L4	SQ – 4	Bharti Island	69° 24′ 32.1″	76° 11′ 46.7″
5	Near Lake L5	SQ – 5	Bharti Island	69° 24′ 26.0″	76° 10′ 59.0″
6	Near Lake L6	SQ – 6	Bharti Island	69° 24′ 33.2″	76° 10′ 32.8″
7	Near Lake L7	SQ – 7	Bharti Island	69° 24′ 31.9″	76° 11′ 23.0″
8	Near Lake L7A	SQ – 7A	Bharti Island	69° 24′ 29.4″	76° 11′ 45.2″
9	Near Lake L8	SQ – 8	Bharti Island	69° 24′ 55.7″	76° 12′ 43.7″
10	Near Lake L12	SQ – 12	Bharti Island	69° 25′ 03.1″	76° 11′ 32.4″
11	Near apple Hut	SQ – A	Bharti Island	69º 24′ 21.2″	76º 11′ 25.3″
12	Near melon Hut	SQ – M	Bharti Island	69º 24′ 28.7″	76º 11′ 05.3″
13	Near Lake ST1	SQ –ST1	Stornes Peninsula	69° 26′ 45.4″	76° 07′ 02.6″
14	Near Lake ST2	SQ –ST2	Stornes Peninsula	69° 26′ 18.8″	76° 07′ 36.0″
15	Near Lake ML1	SQ-ML1	Mcleod Island	69° 21′ 50.9″	76° 08′ 03.6″
16	Near Lake ML2	SQ–ML2	Mcleod Island	69° 22′ 10.2″	76° 08′ 35.1″
17	Near Lake BR	SQ –BR	Broknes Peninsula	69° 23′ 15.1″	76° 18′ 45.7″
18	Near Lake F	SQ – F	Fisher Island	69° 23′ 37.7″	76° 14′ 06.3″

Table 6.2: Details of the Sediment Sampling Locations

Sl.No.	Sampling Point	Location Code	Location	Latitude (S)	Longitude (E)	Altitude
1	Lake L1	SD – 1	Bharti Island	69° 24′ 18.5″	76° 11′ 32.2″	13 m
2	Lake L2	SD– 2	Bharti Island	69° 24′ 25.4″	76° 11′ 27.4″	38 m
3	Lake L3	SD– 3	Bharti Island	69° 24′ 21.9″	76° 11′ 13.8″	30 m
4	Lake L5	SD– 5	Bharti Island	69° 24′ 26.0″	76° 10′ 59.0″	52 m
5	Lake L7	SD – 7	Bharti Island	69° 24′ 31.9″	76° 11′ 23.0″	54 m
6	Lake L8	SD – 8	Bharti Island	69° 24′ 55.7″	76° 12′ 43.7″	06 m
7	Lake L12	SD-12	Bharti Island	69° 25′ 03.1″	76° 11′ 32.4″	33 m
8	Lake ST1	SD-ST1	Stornes Peninsula	69° 26′ 45.4″	76° 07′ 02.6″	29 m
9	Lake ML1	SD-ML1	Mcleod Island	69° 21′ 50.9″	76° 08′ 03.6″	34 m
10	Lake BR	SD-BR	Broknes Peninsula	69° 23′ 15.1″	76° 18′ 45.7″	37 m
11	Lake F	SD-F	Fisher Island	69° 23′ 37.7″	76° 14′ 06.3″	40 m

Table 6.3A: Texture of Soil Samples of Bharti Island

Sl. No.	Parameter	SQ-1	SQ-2	SQ-3	SQ-4	SQ-5	SQ-6
Soil Texture							
1	Sand* (%)	70	75	85	78	90	82
2	Silt (%)	22	15	10	14	7	10
3	Clay (%)	8	10	5	8	3	8

* including gravels and stones

Table 6.3B: Quality Characteristics of Soil Samples of Bharti Island

Sl.No.	Parameter	SQ-1	SQ-2	SQ-3	SQ-4	SQ-5	SQ-6
1	pH	7.8	7.6	8.0	7.3	7.5	7.1
2	Electrical Conductivityμs/cm	172.0	256.0	211.0	151.0	197.0	148.0
3	Sodium (as Na_2O)% by mass	4.35	2.33	3.84	5.46	2.63	1.53
4	Potassium(as K_2O)% by mass	7.96	6.35	13.41	2.82	3.02	3.01
5	Calcium (as CaO)% by mass	11.34	7.59	15.40	5.16	7.32	5.57

6	Magnesium (as MgO) %By mass	11.39	3.53	10.39	3.23	21.48	5.14
7	Iron (as Fe_2O_3)% by mass	16.11	9.35	11.06	11.30	9.87	6.98
8	Aluminum (as Al_2O_3)% by mass	15.95	9.24	12.27	12.34	21.46	8.68
9	Phosphorus (as P_2O_5)mg/kg	130.08	57.37	110.96	187.64	90.91	69.67
10	Cadmium (as Cd) mg/kg	1.53	0.49	1.84	0.95	0.83	0.32
11	Chromium (as Cr) mg/kg	21.23	31.82	19.31	63.03	9.13	11.35
12	Zinc (as Zn) mg/kg	85.96	69.14	24.86	57.04	24.36	36.17
13	Manganese (as Mn) mg/kg	186.55	92.16	102.04	142.58	50.54	41.42
14	Copper (as Cu) mg/kg	9.33	14.27	20.32	10.20	8.69	5.87
15	Chloride (as Cl) % by mass	0.45	0.77	0.05	0.86	0.21	0.46
16	Sulphate(as SO_4)% by mass	0.06	0.06	0.01	0.03	0.02	0.02
17	Radiation Contamination*(as Cs-137) Bq/kg	<MDL	<MDL	<MDL	<MDL	<MDL	<MDL

* MDL : < 1.9 bq / kg

Table 6.4A: Texture of Soil Samples of Bharti Island

Sl.No.	Parameter	SQ-7	SQ-7A	SQ-8	SQ-12	SQ-A	SQ-M
Soil Texture							
1	Sand* (%)	94	80	68	85	78	70
2	Silt (%)	4	14	22	12	12	22
3	Clay (%)	2	6	10	3	10	8

* including gravels and stones

Table 6.4B: Quality Characteristics of Soil Samples of Bharti Island

Sl.No.	Parameter	SQ-7	SQ-7A	SQ-8	SQ-12	SQ-A	SQ-M
1	pH	6.9	7.2	7.5	6.8	8.2	8.5
2	Electrical Conductivity µs/cm	130.0	162.0	290.0	120.0	311.0	174.0
3	Sodium (as Na_2O)% by mass	1.32	5.99	1.52	1.54	9.61	5.17
4	Potassium(as K_2O)% by mass	1.12	3.74	1.41	1.35	6.40	3.57
5	Calcium (as CaO)% by mass	2.29	2.20	1.21	0.50	11.59	6.49
6	Magnesium (as MgO)%By mass	1.31	1.21	0.70	0.49	12.14	14.17
7	Iron (as Fe_2O_3)% by mass	3.00	3.24	4.40	4.72	12.27	6.62
8	Aluminum (as Al_2O_3)% by mass	2.79	3.26	3.92	2.58	18.70	22.70

9	Phosphorus (as P_2O_5) mg/kg	317.65	124.12	508.64	1058.45	70.35	57.45
10	Cadmium (as Cd) mg/kg	0.88	0.42	1.07	0.62	2.65	1.17
11	Chromium (as Cr) mg/kg	36.94	45.47	45.60	58.58	16.82	8.63
12	Zinc (as Zn) mg/kg	46.35	65.71	71.77	83.39	54.00	35.45
13	Manganese (as Mn) mg/kg	152.05	139.25	600.90	668.98	114.43	82.02
14	Copper (as Cu) mg/kg	25.95	19.98	29.62	27.65	13.98	8.26
15	Chloride (as Cl) % by mass	0.45	0.78	0.50	0.30	1.01	0.62
16	Sulphate(as SO_4)% by mass	0.02	0.04	0.04	0.02	0.03	0.06
17	Radiation Contamination* (as Cs-137) Bq/kg	<MDL	<MDL	<MDL	<MDL	<MDL	<MDL

* MDL : < 1.9 bq / kg

Table 6.5A: Texture of Soil Samples of Various Islands/peninsula at Larsemann Hills

Sl.No.	Parameter	SQ-ST1	SQ-ST2	SQ-ML1	SQ-ML2	SQ-BR	SQ-F
Soil Texture							
1	Sand* (%)	83	80	90	85	90	85
2	Silt (%)	15	17	8	11	8	11
3	Clay (%)	2	3	2	4	2	4

*** including gravels and stones**

Table 6.5B: Soil Quality Characteristics of Various Islands/Peninsula at Larsemann Hills

Sl.No.	Parameter	SQ-ST1	SQ-ST2	SQ-ML1	SQ-ML2	SQ-BR	SQ-F
1	pH	6.8	7.2	7.9	7.7	6.9	7.3
2	Electrical Conductivityμs/cm	385.0	582.0	210.0	186.0	241.0	196.0
3	Sodium (as Na_2O)% by mass	2.36	3.17	6.57	5.26	1.39	2.44
4	Potassium(as K_2O)% by mass	1.66	2.43	8.66	10.94	2.01	6.21
5	Calcium (as CaO)% by mass	1.41	1.91	5.26	6.29	2.38	4.60
6	Magnesium (as MgO) %By mass	1.50	2.16	9.31	4.67	1.47	6.48
7	Iron (as Fe_2O_3)% by mass	3.49	2.49	6.32	7.79	4.77	4.56
8	Aluminum (as Al_2O_3)% by mass	1.27	5.27	11.66	15.29	11.86	11.35

9	Phosphorus (as P_2O_5) mg/kg	142.94	112.62	141.76	78.71	378.07	100.65
10	Cadmium (as Cd) mg/kg	0.21	0.24	0.49	0.07	0.99	0.89
11	Chromium (as Cr) mg/kg	36.16	13.97	11.35	41.60	65.13	12.97
12	Zinc (as Zn) mg/kg	73.13	52.96	42.01	68.08	78.83	44.89
13	Manganese (as Mn) mg/kg	539.33	136.03	214.96	386.37	599.19	302.31
14	Copper (as Cu) mg/kg	21.55	13.28	9.23	6.20	34.31	4.18
15	Chloride (as Cl) % by mass	0.35	0.76	0.42	0.12	0.35	0.22
16	Sulphate(as SO_4)% by mass	0.02	0.04	0.03	0.06	0.08	0.06
17	Radiation Contamination *(as Cs-137) Bq/kg	<MDL	<MDL	<MDL	<MDL	<MDL	<MDL

* MDL : < 1.9 bq / kg

Table 6.6A: Texture of Sediment Samples of Bharti Island

Sl.No.	Parameter	SD-1	SD-2	SD-3	SD-5	SD-7	SD-8
Soil Texture							
1	Sand* (%)	92	90	96	93	95	88
2	Silt (%)	6	9	3	5	4	8
3	Clay (%)	2	1	1	2	1	4

* including gravels and stones

Table 6.6B: Quality Characteristics of Sediment Samples of Bharti Island

Sl.No.	Parameter	SD-1	SD-2	SD-3	SD-5	SD-7	SD-8
1	pH	7.3	7.2	7.6	7.1	6.8	6.9
2	Electrical Conductivity µs/cm	165.0	136.0	197.0	181.0	116.0	278.0
3	Sodium (as Na_2O)% by mass	1.32	1.88	2.15	2.23	1.66	3.60
4	Potassium(as K_2O)% by mass	3.13	4.35	2.83	2.43	2.02	4.32
5	Calcium (as CaO)% by mass	0.74	0.86	1.15	1.34	0.45	2.43
6	Magnesium (as MgO) %By mass	3.93	5.17	6.35	3.27	1.28	7.29
7	Iron (as Fe_2O_3)% by mass	5.02	9.81	7.54	6.53	7.08	9.34

8	Aluminum (as Al_2O_3)% by mass	6.31	5.21	7.73	5.71	4.18	8.83
9	Phosphorus (as P_2O_5)mg/kg	317.20	727.57	586.27	424.68	387.28	340.90
10	Cadmium (as Cd) mg/kg	0.74	1.17	0.93	0.66	1.72	0.63
11	Chromium (as Cr) mg/kg	167.67	115.30	87.03	97.05	130.64	98.95
12	Zinc (as Zn) mg/kg	97.93	74.11	128.19	71.94	56.65	212.99
13	Manganese (as Mn) mg/kg	353.20	255.31	154.35	282.44	213.34	125.03
14	Copper (as Cu) mg/kg	53.92	25.03	34.56	21.09	12.81	112.33
15	Chloride (as Cl) % by mass	1.25	0.92	0.85	0.55	0.62	1.13
16	Sulphate(as SO_4)% by mass	0.22	0.12	0.09	0.35	0.15	0.38
17	Radiation Contamination *(as Cs-137) Bq/kg	<MDL	<MDL	<MDL	<MDL	<MDL	<MDL

* MDL : < 1.9 bq / kg

Table 6.7A: Texture of Sediment Samples of Various Islands/Peninsula at Larsemann Hills

Sl.No.	Parameter	SD-12	SD-ST1	SD-ML1	SD-BR	SD-F
Soil Texture						
1	Sand* (%)	94	97	96	95	92
2	Silt (%)	5	2	3	4	6
3	Clay (%)	1	1	1	1	2

* including gravels and stones

Table 6.7B: Sediment Quality Characteristics of Various Islands/peninsula at Larsemann Hills

Sl.No.	Parameter	SD-12	SD-ST1	SD-ML1	SD-BR	SD-F
1	pH	6.6	6.7	7.3	6.7	6.9
2	Electrical Conductivityµs/cm	113.0	125.0	189.0	132.0	179.0
3	Sodium (as Na_2O)% by mass	1.94	1.50	2.37	1.84	2.17
4	Potassium(as K_2O)% by mass	2.16	1.77	3.45	2.17	2.03
5	Calcium (as CaO)% by mass	0.66	0.36	1.27	1.06	1.04

6	Magnesium (as MgO)% By mass	1.63	0.42	4.77	1.43	2.87
7	Iron (as Fe_2O_3)% by mass	7.37	2.85	6.01	3.25	5.83
8	Aluminum (as Al_2O_3)% by mass	5.50	3.57	3.90	3.98	5.40
9	Phosphorus (as P_2O_5) mg/kg	243.04	385.76	265.98	428.62	385.28
10	Cadmium (as Cd) mg/kg	0.66	2.00	0.73	1.09	0.87
11	Chromium (as Cr) mg/kg	63.04	54.00	81.92	86.29	36.55
12	Zinc (as Zn) mg/kg	89.26	46.90	71.86	65.76	112.22
13	Manganese (as Mn) mg/kg	166.56	187.45	214.21	157.21	421.49
14	Copper (as Cu) mg/kg	7.57	12.10	8.21	20.12	9.20
15	Chloride (as Cl) % by mass	0.34	0.31	0.42	0.85	0.63
16	Sulphate(as SO_4)% by mass	0.18	0.11	0.29	0.38	0.24
17	Radiation Contamination *(as Cs-137) Bq/kg	<MDL	<MDL	<MDL	<MDL	<MDL

* MDL : < 1.9 bq / kg

Conclusion

In east Antarctica, Larsemann Hills is rocky area and due to weathering and harsh climate, particles from the rock reach to the bank of low-lying area of water bodies along with the katabatic winds. The soil samples have been collected from the locations where loose particles have accumulated and gathered in form of soil.

The result shows that quality of soil in this area is least affected by the activities of the surrounding research stations.

Composition of soil and sediment samples was analyzed to evaluate the quality and pollution load. This data may act as reference for further research.

REFERENCES

Everett, K.R. (1978): Some Effects of Oil on the Physical and Chemical Characteristics of Wet Tundra Soils. *Arctic*, 31: 260-276.

Goldsworthy P.M., Canning E.A. and Riddle M.J (2003): Soil and Water Contamination in the Larsemann Hills, East Antarctica, *Polar Record*, 39(211): 319-337.

Gasparon, M. and Matschullat, J. (2006): Trace Metals in Antarctic Ecosystems: Results from the Larsemann Hills, East Antarctica. *Applied Geochemistry*, 21: 1593-1612.

Gasparon, Massimo and Matschullat, Jörg (2004): Geogenic Sources and Sink of Trace Metals in the Larsemann Hills, East Antarctica: Natural Process and Human Impact, *Applied Geochemistry*, 21: 318-334.

Hall K.J. and Walton D.W.H. (1992): Rock Weathering, Soil Development and Colonization Under a Changing Climate. Philosophical Transactions of the Royal Society of London. Series B, Biological Sciences 338 (14) 269-277.

SIIR (2010): Long Term Environmental Monitoring and Impact Assessment Study at New Scientific Base at Larsemann Hills, 27th, 28th, 29th ISEA Combined Report to NCAOR, Submitted by Shriram Institute of Industrial Research, New Delhi.

Stüwe, K., Braun, H.M. and Peer, H (1989): Geology and Structure of The Larsemann Hills Area, Prydz Bay, East Antarctica, *Australian Journal of Earth Sciences*, Vol. 36: 219-241.

Tarnocai, C. and I.B. Campbell (2002): Soils of the Polar Regions, p. 1107-1115, *In:* R. Lal, ed. Encyclopedia of Soil Science. Marcel Dekker, New York, USA.

Wang Y.G., Zhao J., Chen C. S. (1997): Chemical Weathering at Stornes Peninsula, Larsemann Hills, East Antarctica. Jidi Yanjiu, Vol. 9(4), 273-282.

Soil Environment and Conservation **Pages 118-130**
Edited by: **Dr. Ashok K. Rathoure; Dr. Pawan Kumar 'Bharti' and Dr. Alka Chauhan**
ISBN: 978-93-88854-10-8
Edition: **2019**
Published by: **Discovery Publishing House Pvt. Ltd., New Delhi (India)**

7 Isolation of Bacteria From Oil Contaminated Soils Having Hydrocarbon Degrading and Nitrogen Fixing Ability

[1]Karishma Baishya

ABSTRACT

Contamination of soil by crude oil is a major concern in the present world, which represent severe hazardous effects on the ambient environment. In an effort at developing active microbial strains that could be of relevant in bioremediation of oil contaminated soil, a feasibility study was conducted to isolate bacteria from oil contaminated soil having both hydrocarbon degrading and nitrogen fixing ability. In the present investigation, four samples were collected from the refinery sites in Guwahati, Assam. From these samples, a total of six cultures were isolated having hydrocarbon degrading ability using enrichment media (M3 media), where paraffin oil was used as a sole carbon source. Out of these six hydrocarbon degrading bacterial isolates, three hydrocarbon degrading bacterial isolates were found to grow in nitrogen free medium. These bacterial isolates were subjected to colony morphology and microscopic study.

These hydrocarbon-degrading bacteria can be used to clean up oil-inundated soil and their nitrogen fixing ability can further enhance fertility of the contaminated sites.

Keywords: Bioremediation, Bacterial isolates, Hydrocarbon degraders, Nitrogen fixers, Oil pollution.

Introduction

As we dig deeper into the modern industrial age of technologies, several aspects of human life change. People benefit largely from life development and many live in prosperity, but prosperity has a price. Our environment that suffers daily from all kinds of pollutants and destruction pays this price. People now have to find ways to cure this destruction.

Oil contamination is one of the most dangerous pollution factors known today. It can cause a threat to the environment. It is very feared by environmentalists and it's very hard to control if it gets out of hand.

1 Research Scholar Deptt. of Environmental Sciences, Gauhati University, Guwahati, Assam, India

An oil spill is a release of a liquid petroleum hydrocarbon into the environment due to human activity, and is a form of pollution. Oil spills are an inevitable consequence of using petroleum. Spills can occur at the oil refinery due to leakage from joints of the oil pipelines, accidents of oil tankers during transportation, natural seeps, or during routine maintenance of infrastructure. Although pesticides are hydrocarbon pollutants of the soils, the main sources of hydrocarbon pollution are the spills and leaks of petroleum products (Potter, 1993). These spills have the largest immediate and economic impact as they harm, to a large extent, the ecosystem more than just the isolated location. These oil spills devastate the soil, surface and ground water and alter the microbial population at the polluted sites.

Soil contamination is slow and lethal. It acts over a long period of time by poisoning food crops, water supplies, etc. Oil contamination in soil results in an imbalance in the carbon-nitrogen ratio at the spill site, because crude oil is essentially a mixture of carbon and hydrogen. This causes a nitrogen deficiency in oil soaked soil, which retards the growth of bacteria and the utilization of carbon sources. Furthermore, large concentrations of biodegradable organics in the top layer deplete oxygen reserves in the soil and slow down the rates of oxygen diffusion into deeper layers.

Soil and ground water are often contaminated with gasoline or diesel fuel from leaking underground storage tanks and also due to accidental spills and leakage from pipelines. Due to their mobility, these compounds may cause considerable damage not only in soils but also in water intakes or ground water reservoirs (Gallego *et al.*, 2001). There are also many incidents in which significant quantities of oil were accidently released into the environment, causing environmental disasters. Exxon Valdez (1989), oil spills in South Central Alaska is an example, Pritchard *et al.*, (1992) and the Gulf war (1990) oil spills are possibly the most publicized and studied environmental tragedies in history. In Nigeria, the exploration and exploitation practices and the breaking of oil pipes lead to incessant pollution especially in the Nigar Delta area and the Southern part of Nigeria (Salu, 1999).

Petroleum and Diesel is a complex mixture of liquid and solid hydrocarbon, whose composition also varies with source. The components are paraffin hydrocarbon, saturated alicyclic hydrocarbon and aromatic hydrocarbon. Petroleum can be accidentally or deliberately released into the environment, leading to serious pollution problems. Still small release of petroleum hydrocarbon into aquifers can leads to concentration of dissolved hydrocarbon far in excess of regulatory limits.These pollution problems often results in huge disorder of both the biotic and abiotic components of the ecosystem more so that some hydrocarbon components have been known to belong to a family carcinogenic and neurotoxic organ pollutant. The process leading to the eventual removal of hydrocarbon pollutants from the environment has been extensively documented and involves physical, chemical and biological alternatives.

Polycyclic aromatic hydrocarbons (PAHs) are persistent organic pollutants that are widely distributed in soils (Wilcke, 2007).Different State and Central Pollution Control Boards have classified PAHs as hazardous chemicals, because of their toxic, carcinogenic and tetra genic effects on living body. At present, hydrocarbon fuels (mainly diesel) contain an excessive quantity of PAHs causing abundant distribution of the same in the ecosphere.

Petroleum oil both in crude form and its various refined products cause pollution problem of varying magnitudes. Assam in the Northeast region of India has rich petroleum hydrocarbon deposits on which the renowned oil industry has come up in the state. Pollution caused by petroleum hydrocarbons during the various processes of exploration, transportation, refining and downstream processing have resulted in considerable pollution of the soil and water. Environmental problems caused by petroleum hydrocarbons have emerged a major concern for general public, government and the oil industries.

Oil refineries generate a huge amount of oily sludge, annually. The cumulative sludge, generated over the decades of existence of these refineries, is life threatening in its ecological impact, since it takes years for even a few hundred tones of waste to degenerate naturally. Moreover, this waste is supposed to be dumped in identified locations in secured pits. However, the oil refineries in Indiado not find it a viable proposition to construct such storage pits. Moreover, storing the waste is not a sustainable approach to manage oily sludge, since it exposes the local habitats to dangerous levels of toxicity through air and water pollution.

Crude oil of North - East regions contains about 11-18.8% of waxy substances (IOC Ltd., QC: TR/F-034, Repot No. 101.4/10, 2004) mainly paraffin wax of C_{18} to C_{30}. This huge amount of waxy substance creates considerable problems to the oil industry with respect to the followings:

(*a*) Paraffin wax deposits adjacent to production wells greatly reduce productivity by plugging fluid flow channels.

(*b*) Deposition of waxy crude oil also takes place in the perforations and production tubing effecting crude oil productive.

(*c*) Deposition of waxy substances inside the pipeline is also a major problem that occurs during transportation of crude oil from drilling station to oil refinery.

A number of strategies based on mechanical and chemical approaches are being followed to overcome these problems arising out of the occurrences of wax in higher proportions in the crude oil. Some of these approaches are-removal of the waxy deposits from the production tubing by scrapping; hot oil washing to dissolve paraffin waxes on the perforations; washing with organic solvents such as xylene or toluene to remove paraffin from perforations and the formations; addition of amines to these solvents can aid solubilization of asphaltene deposits. These modes of removal of paraffin wax are very costly and at the same time these often create environmental pollutions.

Life in our planet is sustained in a fragile biological balance; microorganisms play an important role in nutritional chains that are an important part of this biological balance. Adapting several abilities, microorganisms have become an important influence on the ecological systems, making them necessary for superior organisms' life in this planet. Ability of the microorganisms to transform and degrade many types of pollutants in different matrixes (soil, water, sediments and air) has been widely recognized during the last decades. Microbial remediation has become a promising approach to remediate oil-contaminated soils. There are two commonly used approach of treatment, namely bioaugmentation by inoculation with oil degrading strains and biostimulation by supplementation with carbon sources or other nutrients to stimulate indigenous microbial activity and to increase microbial activity during bioremediation (Hamdi *et al.,* 2007; Mohan *et al.,* 2009). Bioaugmentation by introduced microorganisms with high degradation capability plays an important role in oil-contaminated soils (Dejonghe *et al.,* 2001; Van Herwijnen *et al.,* 2006; Jacques *et al.,* 2008; Silva *et al.,* 2009).

Nitrogen- fixing capability of such organisms has environmental significance in soils, which commonly have very low levels of fixed nitrogen. Spills of diesel and jet fuels on such soils result in extremely high soil carbon/nitrogen ratios, which may limit microbial degradation of the hydrocarbons. In addition, spilled oils usually penetrate to a depth such that surficial photosynthetic nitrogen fixation would be of limited benefit in ameliorating the carbon/nitrogen ratios below the surface. Therefore, heterotrophic nitrogen- fixing activity in contaminated soils may be important for natural attenuation of oil spills by providing combined nitrogen to hydrocarbon- degrading microbes, indirectly enhancing bioremediation at oil contaminated sites.

Rehabilitation of Oil-inundated Soil

Leaks, spillages and accidental Fallouts of petroleum products and crude petroleum itself are of common occurrences nowadays in the world. In Assam, the second biggest blowout of crude petroleum and natural gas occurred recently in the month of February (Feb 1996). Natural gas along with crude gushed out of the well No 109 of Rudrasagar oil fields and all the low lying areas with waist-deep layer of crude oil. The nearby people were evacuated. The first biggest blow out occurred in 1967.

An estimated 1.9 million liters of kerosene (No 1 grade fuel oil) spilled out of an underground pipeline when it broke on Nov 22, 1975 near Crosswicks,

New Jersey. An oil fountain gushed from the rapture for about 15 minutes, sprayed kerosene over approximately 1.5 ha of wheat field.

In case of such an accident, it has been noticed that, the moisture content of the soil influences the nature and extent of the damage done by the oil considerably when the break or overflow occurs. In case of a wet soil, the oil tends not to soak downwards but to flow over the surface and to collect in pools at depression places. In such instances collected oil can be pumped out and can be recovered mostly by oil field crews. The small amount of oil that one left gradually disappears as a result of biodegradation. On the other hand, in case of dry soil, overflow oil tends rapidly to soak downward and saturate the soil to a greater or lesser and topography.

Nature has the capacity to get itself clean from the pollutants. Depending on the nature of pollutants and the extent of pollution it takes a course of time. A variety of techniques have been successfully used to clean up soil and ground water contaminated with oil. Mechanical method to reduce hydrocarbon pollution is expensive and time consuming. Biological treatment, on the other hand, has developed as one of the most promising treatment technologies for petroleum hydrocarbons. The persistence of petroleum pollution depends on the quantity and quality of the hydrocarbon mixture and the properties of the affected ecosystem. Although light petroleum products, like gasoline are efficiently removed by many physico-chemical methods, in case of pollution from heavy hydrocarbons like those present in Diesel or Kerosene the process of biodegradation is of significant importance. Hydrocarbons including PAHs have been long recognized as substrates supporting microbial growth (Bushnell and Haas, 1941; Speight, 1991; Ehrlich, 1995). Bioremediation makes use of indigenous oil-consuming microorganisms, called petrophiles, by enhancing and fertilizing them in their natural habitats. Petrophiles are very unique organisms that can naturally degrade large petroleum hydrocarbons and utilize them as a food source. (Harder, 2004). Microorganism degrades these compounds by using enzymes in their metabolism and can be useful in cleaning up oil-contaminated sites (Alexander, 1999).

Microbial remediation of a hydrocarbon-contaminated site is accomplished with the help of a diverse group of microorganisms, particularly the indigenous bacteria present in soil. These microorganisms can degrade a wide range of target constituents present in oily sludge (Barathi and Vasudevan, 2001; Mishra *et al.*, 2001; Eriksson *et al.*, 1999). Biodegradation of individual hydrocarbon compounds by pure bacterial strains has been studied extensively and metabolic pathways have been described (Heitkamp and Cerniglia, 1988; Gibson and Subramanium, 1984; Rehm and Reif, 1981; Stirling and Watkinson, 1977). Notable among them were the bacterial species of *Arthrobacter* (Edgehill and

Finn, 1982), *Flavobacterium* (Saber and Crawford,1985), *Sphingomonas* (a novel *Pseudomonas* sp) (Radehaus and Schimidt, 1992), *Pseudomonas* spp. (Leung *et al.*, 1977),*Acinetobacter*(George-Okafor *et al.*, 2005). Other organisms such as fungi can also degrade the hydrocarbons in engine oil to an extent. Davies, T.S. and Westlaki, W.S. Pointed out those 28 out of 34 types of fungi are capable to grow on crude oils. In total, 40 fungal types are capable to grow on crude oil and species of many of the fungi can grow on n-hydrocarbons. Fungi and yeasts use pure aliphatic hydrocarbons as sole carbon and energy sources. Thus, bioremediation has long been applied as a treatment technology that is cost effective, ecologically friendly, and for the decontamination of hydrocarbon-polluted soils.

However, without allowing the nature to slowly restore a soil sample, the process may be accelerated by adopting some measures, emergency cleanup operation being the first step. A rehabilitation program may be consisted of liming, fertilizer addition, frequent tilling etc. these measures are designed to promote the microbial degradation of the residual oil. These are based on general principles of hydrocarbon degradation in soil. Dry microorganisms contain 14% N, 3% P and 1%S in the form proteins, nucleic acids, polysaccharides and low molecular weight compounds. On the other hand, hydrocarbons (petroleum products) comprise hydrogen and carbon with small amounts of nitrogen and sulphur and essentially no phosphorous. Thus microorganisms must find utilizable sources of N, S and P in their environment if they are growing to grow on hydrocarbons as their carbon and energy source.

In the present investigation, a preliminary work has been carried out to isolate the bacterial strains from oil-contaminated soils to assess their potentials for bioremediation. When few or no indigenous degradative microorganisms exist in a contaminated area and practically does not allow time for the natural enrichment of suitable population, inoculation may be a convenient option.

The main objectives considered for the present study include:

1. To isolate bacterial strains capable of degrading hydrocarbons from oil contaminated soils e.g., oily sludge
2. To screen the same bacterial strains for their nitrogen fixing ability.

Methods and Materials

Sampling

About 10 g soil samples were aseptically collected with a sterile spatula from soils at the refinery site. All samples were placed into sterile polythene bags and stored at 4°C immediately they were brought to the laboratory.

Isolation of Hydrocarbon Degrading Bacteria

Isolation was performed using an enrichment medium (M_3 Medium) containing the following composition.

Salts	Quantity (g/l)
Macronutrients	
NH_4NO_3	4.0
$NaNO_3$	2.0
K_2HPO_4	4.0
Na_2HPO_4	4.0
$MgSO_4$	0.5
$CaCl_2$	0.1
$FeSO_4$	0.01
$ZnSO_4$	0.007
Micronutrients	**(μg/l)**
$CuSO_4$	7.5
$H3BO_4$	15
MoO_3	15

The pH was adjusted to 6.8-7. To the above medium 0.2% paraffin oil was added. The medium was dispensed in 50 ml volumes into 150 ml Erlenmeyer flasks and autoclaved. Subsequently, 1.0 g of each soil sample was added into each flask of the medium and incubated at 30 °C in a shaker (120 rpm) for 7 days. After that, 1.0 ml sample was taken from each culture and transferred into fresh enrichment medium, followed by incubation as described above for one week. The enrichment procedure was repeated for the third time, before their bacterial contents was isolated using a solid medium containing the enrichment medium and 15.0 g/l of pure agar. Inoculated plates were purified by repeatedly sub-culturing. Pure cultures obtained by this procedure were stored in slants of enrichment medium with 15.0g/ l pure agar.

Screening for Nitrogen Fixing Bacteria

The pure cultures obtained were screened for nitrogen fixing ability in a nitrogen free medium containing the following composition.

Salts	Quantity (g/l)
Mannitol	2
K_2HPO_4	0.5
$MgSO_4 . 7H_2O$	0.2
$FeSO_4 . 7H_2O$	0.1
DistilledH_2O 1000 ml	1000

The pH of the medium was adjusted to 6.3 to 6.7. The pure bacterial cultures were inoculated into the autoclaved nitrogen free broth and incubated at 30 °C for 2 days. The cultures after incubation were again inoculated onto the same medium containing 15g/l agar. The isolated colonies obtained were observed for their colony morphology and other microscopic examination.

Microscopic Study of the Bacterial Cultures

The bacterial isolates showing both hydrocarbon degrading and nitrogen fixing ability were studied for their various microscopic characters such as:

- ***Colony morphology***: Study of colony morphology includes colour, size, margin, opacity, elevation, etc.
- ***Gram's staining***: Gram's staining of the cultures was performed by the method as described by **Cappucino.**
- ***Motility test***: Motility test was performed by hanging drop method as described by **Cappucino.**
- ***Spore staining***: Spore staining was performed by the method as described by **Cappucino**.

Results and Discussion

Isolation of Hydrocarbon Degrading Bacteria

A total of six bacterial cultures were isolated based on colony morphology. The isolates were designated as HD1, HD2, HD3, HD4, HD5 and HD6.

Fig. 7.1: Enrichment of Bacterial Cultures in M3 Medium.

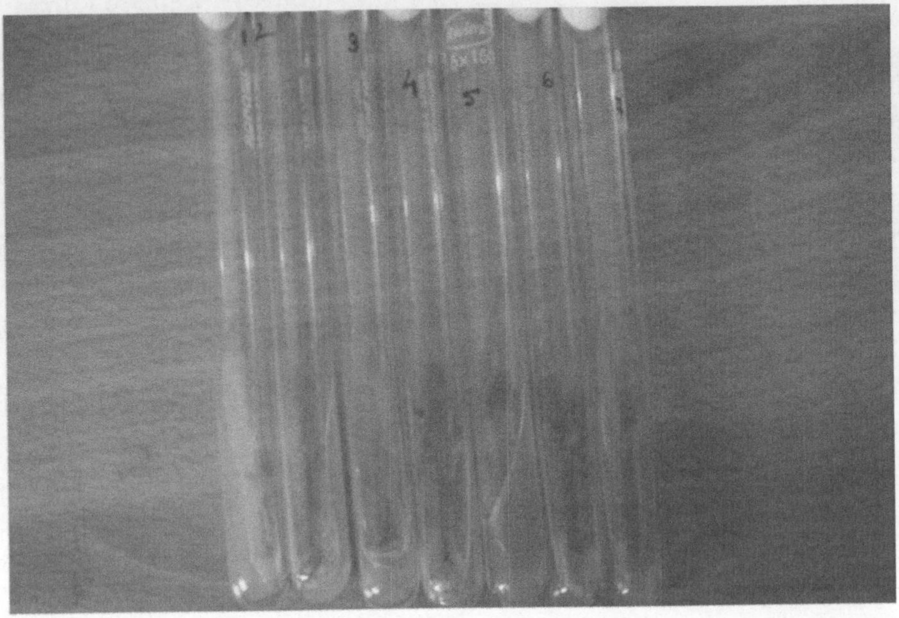

Fig. 7.2: Pure Cultures of Hydrocarbon degrading Bacteria preserved in agar slants.

Screening for Nitrogen Fixing Bacteria

Out of six hydrocarbon degrading bacterial isolates three bacterial isolates were found to grow in the nitrogen free medium. The isolates were HD1, HD2 and HD4.

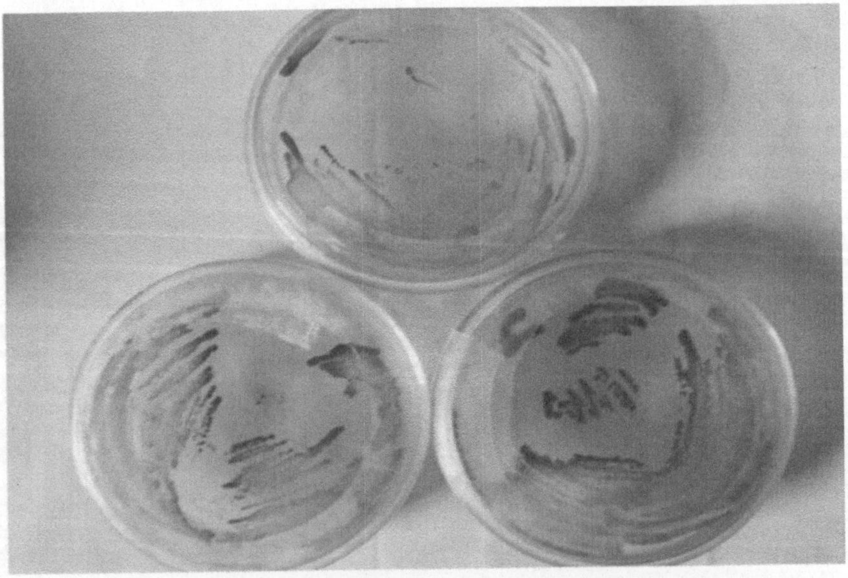

Fig. 7.3: Isolation of Nitrogen-Fixing Bacteria in Agar Plates.

Fig. 7.4: Pure Culture of Hydrocarbon Degrading and Nitrogen Fixing Bacteria.3.3 Microscopic study of the bacterial cultures

Colony Morphology

The colony morphology of the six bacterial isolates was recorded in the table 7.1.

Table 7.1: Colony Morphology of Hydrocarbon Degrading Bacteria

Sl.No.	Isolate No.	Colony Morphology
1.	HD1	**Colour:** off white; **Size:** 1.5mm; **Margin:** irregular; **Opacity:** opaque; **Elevation:** flat
2.	HD2	**Colour:** greenish and shiny; **Size:** 1.0mm; **Margin:** irregular; **Opacity:** opaque; **Elevation:** concave
3.	HD3	**Colour:** off white; **Size:** 0.5 mm; **Margin:** ovate; **Opacity:** opaque; **Elevation:** flat
4.	HD 4	**Colour:** greenish; **Size:** 1.3 mm; **Margin:** round; **Opacity:** opaque; **Elevation:** concave
5.	HD5	**Colour:** creamy; **Size:** 1.0 mm; **Margin:** round; **Opacity:** opaque; Elevation: raised
6.	HD6	**Colour:** greenish; **Size:** 0.5 mm; **Margin:** round; **Opacity:** opaque; Elevation: raised

Gram's Staining

The result of gram's reactions was recorded in the table 7.2.

Table 7.2: Gram's Reaction of the Bacterial Isolates having Hydrocarbon Degrading and Nitrogen Fixing Ability.

Sl. No.	Isolate No.	Gram's Reaction
1.	HD1	Gr +ve, coccus, Occurred singly
2.	HD2	Gr +ve rod,Occurred singly
3.	HD4	Gr +ve rod Occurred singly

Motility Test

The result of the motility test is recorded in the table 7.3.

Table 7.3: Motility Test of the Bacterial Isolates having Hydrocarbon Degrading and Nitrogen Fixing Ability

Sl. No.	Isolate No.	Motility
1.	HD1	Non-motile.
2.	HD2	Motile, movement is Unidirectional
3.	HD4	Highly motile, movement is Zigzag.

Spore Staining

The result of spore staining is recorded in the table 7.4.

Table 7.4: Spore Test of the Bacterial Isolates Having Hydrocarbon Degrading and Nitrogen Fixing Ability

Sl. No.	Isolate No.	Spore staining
1.	HD1	Non-spore former
2.	HD2	Non-spore former
3.	HD4	Non-spore former

The ability to isolate high numbers of certain oil degrading microorganisms from oil-polluted environment is commonly taken as evidence that these microorganisms are the active degraders in the environment. Although, hydrocarbon degraders may be expected to be readily isolated from oil associated environment, the same degree of isolated from a total related environment such as soil.

In the present investigation, four samples were collected from the refinery site in Guwahati, Assam. From these samples, a total of six cultures viz. HD1, HD2, HD3, HD4, HD5 and HD6 were isolated having hydrocarbon degrading ability where paraffin oil was used as the sole carbon source. On the other hand three bacterial isolates viz. HD1, HD2 and HD4 were also found to grow in the nitrogen free medium thereby indicating the potent nitrogen fixer. This preliminary study helps in screening of bacterial isolates, which can be used for bioremediation of oil contaminated agricultural field where such contamination has made a huge loss in the agricultural products. Using an environmental friendly approach, like use of potent bacterial isolate as screened in the study and application of proper consortia as well is expected to greatly reduce this burning issue.

The significance of the study lies in enrichment of consortia capable of hydrocarbon degrading under N_2 – limited conditions. However, further works have to be carried out towards proper screening of efficient bacterial isolates such as the rate of degradation of various poly aromatic hydrocarbons and the reduction of acetylene to determine hydrocarbon degrading and nitrogen fixing ability respectively so that these isolates can be applied commercially.

REFERENCES

Alexander, M., 1999, Biodegradation and Bioremediation (2nd edition) Academic Press, San Diego.

Bushnell, L.D., Haas, H.F., 1941, The Utilization of Hydrocarbons by Microorganisms. *J. Bacterial.* 41:653-673.

Barathi, S., Vasudevan, N., 2001, Utilization of Petroleum Hydrocarbons by *Pseudomonas flourescens* Isolated from a Petroleum-Contaminated Soil. *Environ.Int.* 26:413-416.

Dejonghe. W., Boon. N., Seghers. D., Top. F.M., Verstracte. W., 2001 Bioaugmentation of Soils by Increasing Microbial Richness: Missing Links. *Environ. Microbial.* 3, pp. 649-657.

Davies, T.S. and Westlaki, W.S., Crude Oil Utilization by Fungi. 146-156 pp.

Exxon. Valdez.,1989 Oil Spills in South Central Alaska. Alaska Resources Library and Information Services.

Ehrlich, H.L., 1995,*Geomicrobiology,* Marcel Dekker, Inc., New York, N.Y.

Edgehill, R.U., Finn, R.K., 1982, Isolation, Characterization and Growth Kinetics of Bacteria Metabolizing Pentachlorophenol. *European Journal of Applied Microbiology and Biotechnology,* 16, 179-184pp.

Eriksson, M., Dalhammer, G., Borg-Karlson, A.K.,1999, Aerobic Degradation of a Hydrocarbon Mixture in Natural Uncontaminated Potting Soil by Indigenous Microorganism at 20 C and 6 C. *Appl. Microbial, Biotechol.* 51:532-535.

Gallego. Jose. L.R., Lordedo.J., Llamas. J.F., Vazquez. F., Sanchez. J., 2001, Bioremediation of Diesel-contaminated Soils: Evaluation of Potential in situ Techniques by Study of Bacterial Degradation. *Biodegradation,* 12(5), pp. 325-335.

George-Okafor, U.O., Tasie, F.O., Nwankwo, J.I., 2005, Degradation Activities of Bacteria Flora Resident at Remote and Recent Hydrocarbon Contaminated Soils Located within Enugu Metropolies. *Journal of Applied Sciences,* 8(2), 4780-4791.

Gibson, D.T., Subramanium, V., 1984, Microbial Degradation of Aromatic Hydrocarbons. In: Gibson, D.T. (Ed), *Microbial Degradation of Organic Compounds,* Marcel Dekkar., New York, 181-252.

Heitkamp, M.A; Cerniglia, C.E., 1988, Mineralization of Polycyclic Aromatic Hydrocarbons by a Bacterium Isolated from Sediment Below an Oil Field. *Appl. Environ. Microbial.* 54(6), 1612-1614.

Harder, H., 2004,*Bioremediation of Engine Oil.* Little Flower Academy. Dallas, Texas.

Hamdi. H., Benzerti. S., Manusadzianas. L., Aoyama. I., Jedidi. N., 2007,Bioaugmentation and Biostimulation Effects on PAHs Dissipation and Soil Ecotoxicity under Controlled Conditions. Soil Biol.*Biochem.,* 39, pp. 1926-1935.

Jacques. R.J.S., Okeka. B.C., Bento. F.M., Teixeira. A.S., Perabla. M.C.R., Camargo.F.A.O., 2008, Microbial Consortium Bioaugmentation of a Polycyclic Aromatic Hydrocarbons Contaminated Soil. *Bioresour. Technol* 1:99, pp. 2637-2643.

Leung, S.T., Cassidy, M.B., Shaw, K.W., Lee, H., Trevors, J.T., Lohmeler-Vogel, E.M., Vogel, H.J., 1997, Pentachlorophenol Biodegradation by *Pseudomonous* spp. UG25 and UG30. *World Journal of Microbiology*, 13, 305-313.

Mishra. S., Jyot, J., Kuhad, R.C., Lal, B., 2001, Evaluation of Inoculam Addition to Stimulate Insitu Bioremediation of Oily Sludge Contaminated Soils. *Appl. Environ. Microbial.* 67(4):1675-1681.

Mohan. S.V., Falkentoft. C., Nancharaiah. Y.V., Mc. Swain. Sturm. B.S, Wattaiu. P., Wildwrer. P.A., Wuertz. S., Hausner. M., 2009, Bioaugmentation of Microbial Communities in Laboratory and Pilot Scale Sequencing Batch Biofilm Reactors using the TOL Plasmid. *Bioresour. Technol.* 100, pp. 1746-1753.

Potter. J.L., 1993, Analysis of Petroleum Contaminated Soil and Water: An Overview, in: Calabrese, E.J., Kostecki, P.T. (Eds), *Principles and Practices for Petroleum Contaminated Soils.* Lewis Publishers, Chelsea, pp. 11-14.

Pritchard. P.H., Muller. J.G., Rogers. J.C., Kremer. F.V., Glaser. J.A., 1992, Oil spill bioremediation: Experiences, Lessons and Results from the Exxon Valdez Oil Spill in Alaska. *Biodegradation* 3, pp. 315-335.

Rehm, H.J., Reif, I., 1981, Mechanism and Occurrence of Microbial Oxidation of Long-chain Alkanes. 1st Ed. Springer Berlin/Heidelberg, 175-215.

Radehaus, R.M., Schimidt, S.K., 1992, Characterization of a Novel *Pseudomonas* sp. that Mineralizes High Concentration of Pentachlorophenol. *Appl. and Env. Microbiol.*, 58, 2879-2885.

Salu. A.D., 1999, Securing Environmental Protection in the Nigeria Oil Industry. *Modern Practice Journal of Finance and Law,* 3, pp 31-39.

Silva. I.S., Das Santos. E., de Menezes. C.R, de Faria. A.F., Franciscon. E., Grossman. M., Dorrant. L.R., 2009, Bioremediation of a Poly Aromatic Hydrocarbon Contaminated Soil by Native Soil Micro Biota and Bioaugmentation with Isolated Microbial Consortia. *Bioresour. Technol.* 100, pp. 4669-4675.

Speight, J.G., 1991, *The Chemistry and Technology of Petroleum.* Harcel Dekker, New York, N.Y.

Stirling, L.A., Watkinson, R.J., 1977, Microbial Metabolism of Alicyclic Hydrocarbons: Isolation and Properties of a Cyclohexane-Degrading Bacterium. *J. Gen. Microbial.*, 99(1), 119-125.

Saber, D.L., Crawford, R.I., 1885, Isolation and Characterization of *Flavobacterium* Strains that Degrade Pentachlorophenol. *Appl. Environ. Microbial.*, 50, 1512-1518.

Van Herwijnen. R., Joffee. B., Ryngaert. A., Hausner. M., Springael. D., Govers. H.A.J, Wuertz. S., Parsons. J.R., 2006, Effects of Bioaugmentation and Supplementary Carbon Sources on Degradation of Polycyclic Aromatic Hydrocarbon by a Soil Derived Culture. *FEMS Microbiol.* Ecol. 55, pp. 122-135.

Wilcke. W., 2007, Global Patterns of Polycyclic Aromatic Hydrocarbons (PAHs) in Soil. *Geoderma,* 141, pp. 157-166.

Soil Environment and Conservation **Pages 131-146**
Edited by: **Dr. Ashok K. Rathoure; Dr. Pawan Kumar 'Bharti' and Dr. Alka Chauhan**
ISBN: 978-93-88854-10-8
Edition: **2019**
Published by: **Discovery Publishing House Pvt. Ltd., New Delhi (India)**

8

Soil Amendments with Bio-Char

[1]Dr. Ashok K. Rathoure

Introduction

Agricultural efficiency depends significantly on the quality of soils, the main source of agricultural productivity. Land improvement (amelioration) became the most important component of peasant labor at the dawn of agricultural development. Amelioration differs from the common annual agricultural practices in that the effects on the soil can be radical and long lasting. It can be defined as a system of measures for radical improvement of unfavorable hydrologic, soil, and agro-climatic conditions, with a view to the most efficient use of land resources. Along with the effect on land productivity, amelioration allows us to bring poor and unused land into agricultural production, to improve the sanitary state of soils and the environment, and, hence, to raise the living standards and quality of life for people. The main amelioration practices are engineering reclamation (irrigation, drainage, filling up, flood walls, etc.), chemical, anti-erosion and agronomic amelioration. Specific methods of land reclamation include the agricultural use of sea and lake bottoms, the development of desert soils, and the improvement of the heat regime of soils (thermal amelioration). Soil amelioration was indispensable over vast areas, with agriculturally unfavorable conditions found in almost all countries. Over thousands of years of the history of land amelioration, experience has been accumulated, the theory of amelioration has been developed, and its methods have been improved. Today, all developed countries have special laws regulating land reclamation policy. The efficiency of amelioration depends on the level of field management.

Efficient and sustainable agriculture is impossible without special measures aimed at improving land quality. Historically, the most significant and wide-scale measures for creation of sustainable agricultural systems were related to irrigation and drainage practices. It is interesting to trace the progress of irrigation and drainage technologies from earth to stone and then to high

[1] Eco Chem Sales & Services, Surat (GJ), India

ferroconcrete dams; from a water bucket to windmills and electric pump stations; from spades to powerful machines and sprinklers; from open ditches to closed tile and plastic pipe drainage systems. The problems of ecological safety of land amelioration and the creation of highly productive and sustainable agro-landscapes, ensuring the sustainable development of modern civilization, are the focus of attention of scientists and specialists in agriculture and land management. There is no doubt that their significance in the twenty-first century will increase even more.

Background

Soil amendment with biochar can be proposed as a means to sequester C and improve soil fertility. Application of charcoal to soils is hypothesized to increase bio-available water, build soil organic matter, enhance nutrient cycling, lower bulk density, act as a liming agent and reduce leaching of pesticides and nutrients to surface and ground water. Leach *et al.,* (2010) also documented that application of biochar to the soil enabling increases in agricultural productivity without, or with much reduced, applications of inorganic fertilizer. Furthermore, Harley (2010) indicted that biochar is a promising amendment for ameliorating drastically disturbed soils due to its micro-chemical, nutrient, and biological properties. Biochar-based strategies are thus being seen to offer valuable routes to building sustainable agricultural futures, particularly for resource poor farmers for whom soil fertility and water availability are seen as key constraints on crop production and food security. The extent of the effect of biochar on crop productivity and soil carbon sequestration is, however, variable due mainly to the different biophysical interactions and processes that occur when biochar is applied to soil, which are not yet fully understood (Sohi *et al.,* 2009). For instance, in nitrogen limited soils, application of high rates of biochar may affect growth negatively due to immobilization effect (Lehmann *et al.,* 2006). Moreover, feedstock and pyrolysis conditions (temperature, holding time, etc.) may affect both stability and nutrient content and availability of biochar (Novak *et al.,* 2009).

Need of Amelioration technology

Driven by climate change and population growth, increasing human pressure on land forces conversion of natural landscapes to agricultural fields and pastures while simultaneously depleting land currently under agricultural use (Lal, 2009). Consequently, a vicious circle develops; further aggravating climate change, soil degradation, erosion, loss of soil organic matter (SOM) and leaching of nutrients. Therefore, sustainable concepts for increased food production are urgently needed to lower pressure on soils, in order to reduce or prevent the negative environmental impacts of intensive agriculture. A key for such strategies is the maintenance or increase of SOM level inducing positive ecosystem services such as increased productivity, nutrient and water storage, intact filter capacity, rooting, aeration and habitat for soil organism etc. One efficient way to increase SOM level is compost application, produced especially from biomass wastes. During the last decades, attention was paid at the professionalization of composting due to several trends in today's society. On the one hand, growth of livestock breeding and intensification of crop production has occurred while an increasing shortage of other hand, urbanization and growing population interconnected with an increased amount of waste output is responsible for environmental hazards and pollution. Therefore,composting became an efficient means of waste processing, soil amelioration and general environmental improvement. However, up to now reported C sequestration potential due to compost management is limited in terms of C use efficiency and long-term C preservation even combined with organic farming and no till management. Therefore, new concepts for C sequestration combating against further raise of atmospheric CO_2 emissions are urgently needed.

Compost

Composting is the biological de-composition and stabilization of organic matter derived from plants, animals or humans through the action of diverse microorganisms under aerobic conditions (Smith and Collins, 2007). The final product of this biological process is a humus-like, stable substrate, being free of pathogens and plant seeds which can be beneficially applied to land as an agent for soil amelioration or as an organic fertilizer. Although historical traditions such as those of Ancient Egyptians or Pre-Columbian Indians of Amazonia suggest that composting is an ancient method for soil amelioration, fundamental scientific studies of this biological process were published only in the past four decades. Process engineering and the knowledge about the dependence and interaction of numerous competing forces and factors within a composting matrix have been just recently established. Multiple composting methods and systems have been developed, varying from small,home-made reactors used by individual households, over medium-sized, on-site reactors operated by farmers, to large, high-tech reactors used by professional compost producers. In spite of different process techniques, the fundamental biological, chemical and physical aspects of composting remain always the same. This concerns for example the suitability of different input materials and amendments as well as their appropriate composition,substrate degradability, moisture control, porosity, free air space, energy balance as well as decomposition and stabilization (Bidlingmaier *et al.*, 2000).

All proper composting processes go through four stages:

(*a*) Mesophilic,

(*b*) Thermophilic,

(*c*) Cooling,

(*d*) Compost maturation.

The duration of each stage depends on the initial composition of the mixture, its water content, aeration and quantity and composition of microbial populations (Neklyudov *et al.*, 2006; Smith and Collins, 2007).

Numerous publications provide evidence on the multiple benefits of compost application to soil. Effects range from soil stabilization and amelioration to phyto-sanitary impacts of mature compost. Feedstock, compost maturity and compost quality can influence intensity and degree of effects on soil physical, chemical and biological properties. Application may trigger short-term improvements such as increasing microbial activity. Long-term effects on soil properties could be achieved by preservation and increase of the stable SOM pool (Amlinger *et al.*, 2007). Soil organic matter is of essential importance for maintaining soil quality by improving biological, physical and chemical soil conditions. It consists of a variety of simple and complex carbon compounds. While the stable SOM pool is characterized by hardly decomposable organic compounds with several beneficial, long-term effects for soil amelioration and conservation, the labile pool of SOM provides easily accessible food for soil organisms and nutrients for plant growth (Termorshuizen *et al.*, 2005). Soil fauna, notably earthworms (*Lumbricidae*), in turn, positively influence a wide variety of different physico-chemical properties. These positive effects are especially caused by their feeding behaviour, bioturbation and the production of droppings consisting of organo-mineral complexes. The latter is of main importance for the formation of stable SOM pools in soils.

Impact on Soil

Reduction of Bulk Density

Compost application generally influences soil structure in a beneficial way by lowering soil density due to the admixture of low density OM into the mineral soil fraction. This positive effect has been detected in most cases and it is typically associated with an increase in porosity because of the interactions between organic and inorganic fractions (Amlinger *et al.*, 2007).

Increase of Aggregate Stability

In general, soil structure is defined by size and spatial distributions of particles, aggregates and pores in soils. The volume of solid soil particles and the pore volume influences air balance and root penetration ability. As a general fact the more soil structure is compacted, the more unfavorable are the soil conditions for plant growth. By incorporation of compost into the soil, aggregate stability increases most effectively in clayey and sandy soils. Positive effects can be expected by well humified, as well as fresh, low-molecular OM. Macro-aggregates are mainly stabilized by fungal hyphen, fine roots, root hair and microorganisms with a high portion of easily degradable polysaccharides. Subsequently, the importance of stronger degraded organic compounds for the stabilization of smaller aggregates increases with time of transformation periods ranging from some few to several thousand years. In this respect, the aromatic structure of inert organic compounds seems to play an important role in stabilizing micro-aggregates in the range of 2-20 μm as well as 20-250 μm by polyvalent cation bridges with clay minerals. Besides clay minerals and oxides, fine roots, hyphen networks as well as glue-like polysaccharides originated from root and microbial exudates significantly contribute to the formation of micro-aggregates. Furthermore, aggregate and pore properties of soils are associated with specific active surface area influencing several storage and exchange processes in soil. The higher the specific surface area, the more intensive interactions can occur between soil fauna, microorganisms and root hairs under optimum conditions e.g. sufficient humidity.

Improvement of Pore Volume and Hydraulic Conductivity

Hydraulic conductivity is the percolation rate in soils per area and time unit depending on

- Actual soil moisture tension,
- Number, size and form of soil pores (pore size distribution).

Organic matter applied by compost improves water conductivity of soils by providing a food source for soil organisms which contribute to the formation of macro-pores, in turn. Additionally, it has a direct structure-stabilizing effect for soil. A resulting increase of hydraulic conductivity is of main importance, especially for clayey soils.

Increase of Field Capacity, Secondary Pore Structures and Improved Water Retention

Field capacity (FC) is defined as the amount of water which a water-saturated soil can retain against gravity after 2-3 days. It is mainly influenced by pore volume and pore size distribution because only pores below a pore diameter of 50 μm can retain water against gravity due to higher capillary force. However, adhesive force of pores with a diameter below 0.2 μm is so high that this water is not available for plants. Field capacity and available water holding capacity are generally influenced by the particle size,structure and content of OM. Several studies confirm a significant, positive impact of OM amendment to soils on FC. Amongst others, this effect results from the improved formation of secondary pore structures which can be mainly ascribed to root and animal tubes. This is important for soils with low portions of primary meso-pores. In this respect, compost increases the portion of meso and macro-pores because of an improved aggregation and stabilization of soil significantly initiated by various soil organisms.

Improved Air Balance

The portion of air in soils results from the difference between total pore volume and the pores filled with water. Air permeability and air exchange in soils predominantly depends on pores > 50 μm. While sandy soils are characterized by a high portion of primary macro pores resulting in a proper aeration,clayey or compacted soils have few macro pores which may cause lack of oxygen availability. For these latter soils, OM applied by compost has a significant ameliorating effect by improving porous soil structure and its stabilization, stimulating the formation of secondary macro pores especially by roots and animals tubes.

Reduction of Soil Erosion and Run-off

Reduced erosion is mainly related to the improved soil structure by the addition of compost which, in turn, is pointed out by better infiltration rate, pore volume and enhanced stability through aggregation. According to Amlinger *et al.*, (2007), experimental trials showed a clear correlation between increases of SOM, reductions of soil density, soil loss and water run-off. Five years long compost application resulted in 67% reduced soil erosion, 60% reduced run-off, 8% lower bulk density and 21% higher OM content compared to control plots.

Improved Heat Balance of Soils

Soil temperature influences the reaction rate of chemical,metabolic and biological growth processes of organisms. While temperature fluctuations mainly depend on climate, radiation absorption can be influenced by color. Composts are dark-colored resulting in higher light absorption and thus reflection rate of light from a light source. Therefore, higher light absorption will warm up soils supplied with compost faster than light-colored soils. It will promote germination of seeds, especially during spring. However, as temperature increases in summer, uncovered dark soils can heat up extremely. As a result, soil can dry out due to a higher evaporation which, in turn, affects plant growth and soil biology negatively. In such case, compost mulching systems offer a good solution because they obtain reduced fluctuations of soil temperature which results from the shading effect of mulch loosely covering the soil surface.

Enhancement of Nutrient Level

Compost contains significant amounts of valuable plant nutrients including N, P, K, Ca, Mg and S as well as a variety of essential trace elements (Smith and Collins, 2007). Thus, compost can be defined as an organic multi nutrient fertilizer. Its nutrient content as well as other important chemical properties like C/N ratio, pH and electrical conductivity (EC) depends on the used organic feed-stocks and compost processing conditions. By an appropriate mixture of these organic input materials humus and nutrient-rich compost substrates can be produced serving as a substitute for commercial mineral fertilizers in agriculture. However, their diverse beneficial properties for amelioration outreach their nutrient content.

Increase of Cation Exchange Capacity (CEC)

The CEC is one of the most important indicators for evaluating soil fertility, more specifically for nutrient retention and thus it prevents cations from leaching into the groundwater. According to Amlinger *et al.,* (2007), SOM contributes about 20 – 70% to the CEC of many soils.

Increase of pH Value, Liming Effect and Improved Buffering Capacity

Soil pH is an indicator for soil acidity or soil alkalinity and is defined as the negative logarithm of hydrogen ions activity in a soil suspension. It is important for crop cultivation because many plants and soil organisms have a preference for slight alkaline or acidic conditions and thus it influences their vitality. In addition, pH affects availability of nutrients in the soil. Compost application has a liming effect due to its richness in alkaline cations such as Ca, Mg and K which were liberated from OM due to mineralization. Consequently, regularly applied compost material maintains or enhances soil pH. Only insome few cases a pH decrease was observed after compost application.

Reduction and Immobilization of Pesticides and Persistent Organic Pollutants (POPs)

A contamination of soils or composts with pesticides and POPs can occur in consequence of environmental pollution, conventional farming practice by using chemicals and pesticides and by incorporation of contaminated materials into compost or soil. Therefore, unpolluted feed-stocks should be generally preferred for composting in order to avoid critical concentrations of pollutants. However, pesticides and POPs can be degraded orim mobilized during compost processing or by the properties of the final compost product. Based on temperature and oxidative microbial and biochemical processes, composting contributes to an effective reduction of organic pollutants. Polychlorinatedbiphenyls (PCB) were degraded up to 45% during composting. Linearalkyl benzene sulphonates (LAS), Nonylphenols (NPE) and Di (2-ethylhexyl) phthalate (DEHP) which are mainly found in sewage sludge are degraded almost completely under oxidative conditions. Additionally, the degradation rate of halogenated organic compounds and pesticides is much higher than in soils, especially during the thermophilic stage. Mineralization rate of pollutants is reported to be more effective in compost soil mixtures if mature compost is applied. This concerns especially the degradation of polycyclic aromatic hydrocarbons (PAH) and other hydrocarbons. Due to the high level of humified OM, particularly mature composts contribute to sorption and immobilization of POPs resulting in a lower availability of POPs and reduced toxicity.

Immobilization of Heavy Metals

Similar to pesticides and POPs, there are several sources for heavy metal input. To a limited extent, heavy metals or trace elements serve as plant nutrients while their accumulation can cause toxicity. In this respect, OM applied by compost is able to adsorb heavy metals and reduce their solubility resulting in immobilization. Apart from some non-crystalline minerals with very high surface areas SOM has probably the greatest capacity to bond most heavy metals. The sorption strength of heavy metals to SOM generally decrease in the following order: Cr(III) >Pb(II) > Cu(II) > Ag (I) > Cd (II) = Co(II) = Li(II). On the other hand, significant correlations between the solubility of Cd, Cu, Zn, Pb and Ni and SOM content have been reported by Holmgren *et al.*, (1993) for a range of soils from the USA. Organic matter applied by compost even effectively prevents mobilization of heavy metals for a long time after the cessation of compost addition. In order to guarantee the lowest possible pollutant input over time, raw materials for composting have to be separated and preferably unpolluted feedstock should be used. However, the prevention of environmental pollution and thus the contamination with heavy metals is basically a general matter for the society and for politics.

Biological Soil Properties

One of the most important effects of compost use is the promotion of soil biology. In this respect, the following three aspects seem essential:

(*a*) Food supply for soil heterotrophic organisms by adding degradable carbon compounds with OM,

(*b*) Optimization of habitat and niche properties in soil *e.g.* water and air balances, increase of specific surfaces, retreat areas etc.,

(*c*) Introducing compost biota into soil as an inoculant,

Compost has a stimulation effect on both the microbial community in the compost substrate as well as the soil-born microbiota of soils.

Two fractions of OM are responsible for the level of microbial activity in general:

(*a*) Easily degradable organic compounds may increase microbial activity and biomass temporarily while

(*b*) A persisting increase of microbial biomass depends on a constant enhancement of stable OM which is particularly promoted by mature compost addition.

Microorganisms perform several ecological and environmental functions. With regard to compost, the following microbial effects seem of main importance:

- *Degradation and humification*: A gradual breakdown of organic compounds is performed by a succession of different soil organisms over time. While at the beginning easily degradable organic substances are decomposed, further decomposition and transformation of the remaining by-products occur, finally resulting in a stable humus like compost product which is subjected to only slow decomposition rates.
- *Mineralization, biological immobilization and nutrient cycling:* On the one hand,microorganisms convert complex organic substances to low-molecular, inorganic substance. By this mineralization process, nutrients are released for plant growth so that the plant nutrients can cycle within the ecosystem. On the other hand, soil organisms immobilize nutrients into their own biomass. By this way, e. g. N is protected from leaching.
- *Aggregation:* Microorganisms contribute to the formation and stabilization of aggregates by the synthesis of biofilms and exudates as well as by their living or dead biomass.
- *Degradation or reduction of pesticides, POPs and phytotoxic compounds:* By microbial metabolism, several chemical compounds which are harmful for plants, can bede composed, transformed or immobilized.
- *Suppression of pathogens and diseases:* The diversity of microorganisms in mature composts exhibit suppressive effects on several pathogens and diseases which could harm plant life or human health.

Growth and Health of Plant

The compost creates a favorable environment for plant and root growth especially by

(*i*) Promoting a porous soil structure for optimized root penetration,

(*ii*) Decreasing soil erodibility due to the formation of stable aggregates. Consequently, plant roots are less exposed to direct damage caused by eroded topsoil and water can better infiltrate into soil,

(*iii*) Intensifying essential interactions between root hairs, soil fauna and microorganisms due to an enhancement of specific surface area,

(*iv*) Improving percolation,

(*v*) Enhancing water storage capacity and improving water retention which helps plants better overcome critical climate conditions like droughts,

(*vi*) Providing valuable macro- and micro-nutrients in the long term due to slow mineralization rates, better nutrient adsorption as well as enhanced storage capacity which prevents from leaching,

(*vii*) Improving buffering capacity which helps to maintain uniform reactions and conditions for better plant growth, (*viii*) Promoting the degradation, reduction or immobilization of harmful substances like pesticides, POPs, heavy metals and phyto-toxic compounds which can interfere plant life and health,

(*ix*) Providing microbial symbionts and beneficial soil organisms a habitat which has a positive influence on vitality and growth of plants,

(*x*) Protecting plants from pathogens and diseases due to anti-phyto-pathogenic potential of compost.

Due to its multiple positive effects on the physical, chemical and biological soil properties,compost contributes to the stabilization and increase of crop productivity and crop quality. Long-term field trials proved that compost has an equalizing effect of annual/seasonal fluctuations regarding water, air and heat balance of soils, the availability of plant nutrients and thus the final crop yields. For that reason, a higher yield safety can be expected compared to pure mineral fertilization. Better crop results were often obtained if during the first years higher amounts of compost were applied every 2ndto 3rdyear than by applying compost in lower quantities of <10 Mg(DM) ha^{-1} every year. However, crop yields after pure compost application were mostly lower when compared to mineral fertilization (Amlinger *et al.*,2007), at least during the first years. This can be explained by the slow release of nutrients(especially nitrogen) during mineralization of compost.

Compost use does not only improve the growth and productivity of crops in terms of quantity but it could be also proved that quality of agricultural products is influenced in a positive way. By examination of several crops in situ, an increase of beneficial and healthy ingredients and a decrease of harmful substances in the final crop product after compost use compared to a treatment with mineral fertilizer application can be observed.

Biochar

Biochar has a high specific surface area (400-800 m^2 g^{-1}), it provides a habitat for soil microorganisms which can degrade more labile SOM. In addition, higher microbial activity accelerates soil stabilization as outlined in the previous section. Furthermore, higher mineralization of labile SOM and biochar itself provided important nutrients for plant growth. Biochar is produced by thermal treatment at oxygen deficiency *e.g.* by pyrolysis orgasification, resulting in three products: char, gas and tarry oils. The relative amounts and characteristics of each are controlled by the process conditions such as temperature, residence time, pressure, and feedstock type. Biochar production can be chemically described by water elimination followed by increasing aromatic condensation, which can be expressed as decreasing atomic ratios of O/C and H/C along the combustion continuum. However, biochar is no clearly defined chemical compound. Instead, it is a class of compounds along the combustion continuum and we need to define thresholds for materials which are claimed to be biochar. Recently, on the basis of about 100biochar samples differing in feedstock and production process, the following elemental ratio thresholds were suggested for biochar, O/C<0.4 and H/C<0.6 (Schimmelpfennig and Glaser, 2012). The second important ecological property of biochar is presence of functional groups on the edges of the polyaromatic backbone which are formed by partial oxidation.

Due to its recalcitrance against microbial degradation, biochar is very stable in soil compared to other OM additions, making its application to soils a suitable approach for the build-up of SOM and thus, for C sequestration. The prevailing scientific understanding of biochar degradation in soil is that some portions of it are quite readily decomposable (labile), while the core structure of the material is highly resistant to degradation. C sequestration with biochar addition to soils could be quite significant since the technology could potentially be applied in many areas including croplands, grasslands and also a fraction of forestlands. The maximum capacity of carbon sequestration through biochar soil amendment in croplands alone was estimated to be about 428 Gt C for the world. This capacity is estimated according to the maximal biochar amount that could be cumulatively placed into soil while still beneficial to soil properties and plant growth; and the arable land area that the technology could potentially be applied through biochar agricultural practice. If using also grassland soils and 30% of forest soils, a worldwide biochar sequestration potential of 1,126 Gt C would be possible.

Climate Change

Photosynthesis captures more CO_2 from the atmosphere than any other process on Earth. Each year, terrestrial plants photo-synthetically fix about 440 Gt CO_2 being equivalent to 120 Gt C per year from the atmosphere into biomass. This corresponds to about one-seventh of the CO_2 stock in the atmosphere (820 Gt C). However, biomass is not a stable form of carbon material with nearly all returning to the atmosphere in a relatively short time as CO2 because of respiration and biomass decomposition. As a result, using biomass for carbon sequestration is no good option. Any technology that could significantly prolong the lifetime of biomass materials would be helpful to global carbon sequestration. A conversion of only about 7% of the annual terrestrial gross photosynthetic products into a stable biomasscarbon material such as biochar would be sufficient to offset the entire amount (nearly 9.7 Gt Ca^{-1}) of CO_2 emitted into the atmosphere annually from the use of fossil fuels. More realistic estimates are that annual net CO_2, CH_4 and N_2O emissions could be reduced by a maximum of 1.8 Pg C a^{-1} without endangering world food security and soil fertility (Woolf *et al.*, 2010) corresponding to 16% of current anthropogenic CO_2 emissions. Therefore, biochar can significantly contribute to climate change mitigation but additional technologies are required to quantitatively offset fossil fuel-derived CO_2 emissions. The substitution of fossil fuels by developing and extending renewable energies is another essential key factor for greenhouse gas emission reduction or avoidance while still meeting the basic requirements of electrical or thermic energy consumption demands of society.

Soil Fertility

Biochar application to soil influences various soil physico-chemical properties. Due to the high specific surface area of biochar and because of direct nutrient additions via ash ororganic fertilizer amendments, nutrient retention and nutrient availability were reported being enhanced after biochar application. Higher nutrient retention ability, in turn, improves fertilizer use efficiency and reduces leaching. Most benefits for soil fertility were obtained in highly weathered tropical soils but also higher crop yields of about 30% were obtained uponbiochar addition in temperate soils. Furthermore, enhanced water-holding capacity can also cause a higher nutrient retention because of a reduced percolation of water and the herein dissolved nutrients. However, since biochar has only low nutrients contents in general, plant nutrients must be supplied externally (Glaser and Birk, 2011). With respect to potential nutrient sources, only C and N can be produced in situ via photosynthetic organisms and biological N fixation, respectively. All other elements, such as P, K, Ca and Mg must be added for nutrient accumulation which can be best achieved by adding organic fertilizers such as manure or compost.

Combined Effect of Compost and Biochar

Compared to compost and biochar mixing, an increased decomposition of biochar can be expected during composting although biochar is much more stable than other organic materials. As observed by Kuzyakov *et al.*, (2009), biochar decomposition rates increase as long as easily degradable C-rich substrate is available. Additionally, Nguyen *et al.*, (2010) reported that higher temperature increased biochar oxidation and thus decomposition. However, these effects are much lower for biochar than for compost feedstock. On the other hand, surface oxidation will enhance the capacity of biochar to chemisorb nutrients,minerals and dissolved OM. The overall reactivity of biochar surfaces therefore probably increases with composting. From the compost point of view, there is evidence that biochar as a bulking agent improves oxygen availability and hence stimulates microbial growth and respiration rates. Pyrolysis condensates adsorbed to biochar initially provoked increased respirationrates in soils which most likely occur also during composting. Biochar incompost provides habitats for microbes, thereby enhancing microbial activity. Steiner *et al.*, (2011) reported increased moisture absorption of biochar-amended composts with beneficial effects on the composting process.

Biochar could cause a positive priming effect due to its high surface area providing habitat for microorganisms and due to input of partly labile C substrate. On the other hand, biochar is a stable compound which could stabilize labile compost OM thus providinga negative priming effect. Composting of biochar could be successfully conducted over a wide biochar/organic material ratio covering up to 50% biochar by weight. During composting, a relative enrichment of biochar was observed which is obvious as biochar is much more stable than organic waste materials (Erben, 2011). However, biochar caused a significant positive priming effect on non-biochar composting materials at low (1%) biochar concentrations while at high (50%) biochar concentrations a significantly negative priming effect could be observed. Therefore, a synergistic benefit for overall C sequestration could be observed when biochar was composted together with organic waste material. Further co-benefits might arise for soil microbial biomass and community structure composition and for biochar surface oxidation which still has to be proven scientifically. Combining biochar addition and fermentation resulted in negative priming, but the effect was weaker here than that of non-fermented treatments and hence ascribed rather to biochar alone than to its reinforcement of fermentation-induced negative priming.

Agricultural Efficiency

Combination of biochar with inorganic and organic fertilizers is clearly advantageous over the sole biochar or fertilizer amendments. Plant growth significantly increased after biochar addition. Although pure compost application showed highest absolute yield during two growth periods, biochar compost mixture revealed highest relative performance. It should be mentioned here that biochar compost mixture received only 50% of pure biochar and 50% of pure compost treatments, thus providing evidence for biochar compost synergism. In addition, it can be expected that in the long-term, compost will be mineralized more quickly than biochar or compost biochar mixtures. Mineral fertilizer retention was significantly more efficient when biochar was present although biochar did not increase cation exchange capacity at least after the first harvest. In comparison to mere mineral fertilizer there were clear advantages of plant growth and soil quality of the biochar-amended soils, especially when combining fertilizer (both inorganic and organic) with biochar. The importance of biochar incorporation, additional amendments like clay minerals can add further value to the final compost product *e.g.* by promoting an enhanced CEC due to their high adsorption or swelling capacity. Their incorporation into organic substrates promotes the formation of organo-mineral complexes initiated by the biological activity of soil fauna after subsequent soil application. Other amendments like ash, excrements or urine contribute to the nutrients stock of the final composting product and can enhance microbial activity by their nutrient supply. Moreover, for providing adequate moisture conditions during composting urine can be added instead of water for preventing the dehydration of composting piles while adding nutrients at the same time. After compost maturation, the final compost substrate can be beneficially applied to soils. In this respect, the soil biota contribute to a further transformation of the applied material and provide essential ecological services, for instance by promoting aggregation and further OM stabilization. By enhancing the specific biological, physical and chemical properties of soils amended with the biochar composting substrates, plant growth is generally promoted.

Conclusion

The agriculture is the most important economic activity in the world which provides the food as raw material essential to human life. Soil, as a control on the biogeochemical and hydrological cycles of the Earth system and a provider of vital goods and services to sustain life, is one of our most important natural resources. Access, efficiency and afford ability of agricultural information continue to be a major impediment for raising agricultural productivity. The amelioration technology is in its early stages of development, there are many concerns about the applicability of the technology in the tropics. Efficient and sustainable agriculture is impossible without special measures aimed at improving land quality. It is recommended to amend the soil for better agricultural efficiency and sustainability.

REFERENCES

Amlinger, F.; Peyr, S.; Geszti, J.; Dreher, P.; Karlheinz, W. & Nortcliff, S. (2007). *Beneficial Effects of Compost Application on Fertility and Productivity of Soils. Literature Study,* Federal Ministry for Agriculture and Forestry, Environment and Water Management, Austria.

Amlinger, F.; Peyr, S.; Geszti, J.; Dreher, P.; Karlheinz, W. & Nortcliff, S. (2007). *Beneficial Effects of Compost Application on fertility and productivity of soils. Literature Study,* Federal Ministry for Agriculture and Forestry, Environment and Water Management, Austria, Retrieved from www.umweltnet.at/filemanager/download/20558/

Bidlingmaier, W. & Gottschall, R. (2000). *Biologische Abfallverwertung,* Ulmer, ISBN 3800132087, Stuttgart (Hohenheim).

Erben, G. A. (2011). Carbon Dynamics and Stability of Biochar Compost. An Evaluation of Three Successive Composting Experiments, Bachelor Thesis, University of Bayreuth, Bayreuth.

Glaser, B. &Birk, J. J. (2011). State of the Scientific Knowledge on Properties and Genesis of Anthropogenic Dark Earths in Central Amazonia (terra preta de Índio). *GeochimicaEt Cosmochimica Acta*doi:10.1016/j.gca.2010.11.029.

Harley A. (2010). Biochar for Reclamation in the Role of Biochar in the Carbon Dynamics in Drastically Disturbed Soils. US-Focused Biochar Report, US Biochar Initiative, 2010.

Hartmann, R. (2003). Studienzurstandortgerechten Kompostanwendung auf dreipedologis-chunterschiedlichen, landwirtschaftlichgenutzten Flächen der Wildesauer Geest, Niedersachsen. Bremen, Germany, Universität Bremen, Institutfür Geographie.

Holmgren, G.G.S., Meyer, M.W., Chaney, R.L., Daniel, D.B. (1993). Cadmium, Lead, Zinc, Copper and Nickel in Agricultural Soils of the United States of America. Journal of Environmental Quality, 22: 335-348.

Kuzyakov, Y.; Subbotina, I.; Chen, H. Q.; Bogomolova, I. &Xu, X. L. (2009). Black Carbon Decomposition and Incorporation into Soil Microbial Biomass Estimated by C-14 labeling. *Soil Biology & Biochemistry* 41, 210-219.

Lal, R. (2009). Soils and Food Sufficiency. A Review. *Agronomy for Sustainable Development* 29, 113-133.

Leach M., Fairhead J., Fraser J., and Lehner E., (2010). Biocharred Pathways to Sustainability? Triple Wins, Livelihoods and the Politics of Technological Promise, STEPS Working Paper 41, STEPS Centre, Brighton, UK.

Lehmann J., Gaunt J., and Rondon M., (2006). Bio-char Sequestration in Terrestrial Ecosystems—A Review, Mitigation and Adaptation Strategies for Global Change, 11(2):403–427,

Liu, B.; Gumpertz, M. L.; Hu, S. & Ristaino, J. B. (2007). Long-term Effects of Organic and Synthetic Soil Fertility Amendments on Soil Microbial Communities and the Development of Southern Blight. *Soil Biology and Biochemistry* 39, 2302-2316.

Lutzow, M. von; Kögel Knabner, I.; Ludwig, B.; Matzner, E.; Flessa, H.; Ekschmitt, K.; Guggenberger, G.; Marschner, B. & Kalbitz, K. (2008). Stabilization Mechanisms of Organic Matter in Four Temperate Soils: Development and Application of a Conceptual Model. *Journal of Plant Nutrition and Soil Science,* Vol. 171, No. 1, pp. 111–124.

Neklyudov, A. D.; Fedotov, G. N. & Ivankin, A. N. (2006): Aerobic Processing of Organic Waste into Composts. In: *Applied Biochemistry & Microbiology 42 (4),* pp. 341–353.

Nguyen B.T., Lehmann J., Hockaday W.C., Joseph S., Masiello C. (2010). Temperature Sensitivity of Black Carbon Decomposition and Oxidation, *Environ. Sci. Technol.*, Vol. 44, No. 9, pp. 3324-3331.

Novak J. M., Busscher W. J., Laird D. L., Ahmedna M., Watts D. W., and Niandou M. A. S., (2009). Impact of Biochar Amendment on Fertility of a Southeastern Coastal Plain Soil, Soil Science, 174(2):105–112.

Ouedraogo, E.; Mando, A. & Zombre, N. P. (2001). Use of Compost to Improve Soil Properties and Crop Productivity Under Low Input Agricultural System in West Africa. *Agriculture Ecosystems & Environment* 84, 259-266.

Schimmelpfennig, S. & Glaser, B. (2012). Material Properties of Biochars from Different Feedstock Material and Different Processes. *Journal of Environmental Quality* in Press. doi:10.2134/jeq2011.0146

Smith J.L.; Collins, H.P.; Bailey V.L. (2010). The Effect of Young Biochar on Soil Respiration, *Soil Biology and Biochemistry*, Vol. 42, Issue 12, pp. 2345-2347.

Smith, J.L. & Collins, H.P. (2007). Composting. In: *Soil Microbiology, Ecology, and Biochemistry* (3rd edition), Paul, E.A., (Ed)., pp. 483-486. Academic Press, ISBN 0125468075, 9780125468077, Burlington.

Smith, J.L. & Collins, H.P. (2007). Composting. In: *Soil Microbiology, Ecology, and Biochemistry* (3rd edition), Paul, E.A., (Ed)., pp. 483-486. Academic Press, ISBN 0125468075, 9780125468077, Burlington.

Sohi S., Lopez-Capel E., Krull E., and Bol R., (2009). Biochar, Climate Change and Soil: A Review to Guide Future Research, CSIRO Land and Water Science Report 05/09, CSIRO, Highett, Australia.

Steiner, C; Melear, N.; Harris, K. & Das, K.C. (2011). Biochar as Bulking Agent for Poultry Litter Composting, *Carbon Management*, June 2011, Vol. 2, No. 3, pp. 227-230.

Termorshuizen, A. J.; van Rijn, E. & Blok, W. J. (2005). Phytosanitary Risk Assessment of Composts. *Compost Science & Utilization* 13, 108-115.

Woolf, D.; Amonette, J. E.; Street-Perrott, F. A.; Lehmann, J. & Joseph, S. (2010). Sustainable biochar to Mitigate Global Climate Change. *Nature Communications* 1, 56.

Soil Environment and Conservation Pages 147-186
Edited by: Dr. Ashok K. Rathoure; Dr. Pawan Kumar 'Bharti' and Dr. Alka Chauhan
ISBN: 978-93-88854-10-8
Edition: 2019
Published by: Discovery Publishing House Pvt. Ltd., New Delhi (India)

9 Phytoremediation of Arsenic-Contaminated Soils

Dr. Prasann Kumar[1] and Shweta Pathak[2]

ABSTRACT

Arsenic is a common n-type dopant in semiconductor electronic devices, and the optoelectronic compound gallium arsenide is the second most commonly used semiconductor after doped silicon. Arsenic and its compounds, especially the trioxide, are used in the production of pesticides, treated wood products, herbicides, and insecticides. These applications are declining, however. A few species of bacteria are able to use arsenic compounds as respiratory metabolites. Trace quantities of arsenic are an essential dietary element in rats, hamsters, goats, chickens, and presumably many other species, including humans. However, arsenic poisoning occurs in multicellular life if quantities are larger than needed. Arsenic contamination of groundwater is a problem that affects millions of people across the world. One of the simplest arsenic compounds is the trihydride, the highly toxic, flammable, pyrophoric arsine (AsH_3). This compound is generally regarded as stable, since at room temperature, it decomposes only slowly. At temperatures of 250–300°C decomposition to arsenic and hydrogen is rapid. Several factors, such as humidity, presence of light and certain catalysts (namely aluminium) facilitate the rate of decomposition.

Keywords: Arsenic, Bacteria, Crop, Decline, Essential, Forage.

Introduction

Arsenic (As) toxicity has been recognized for centuries. In the last few decades a large number of articles have been published with regard to As. Arsenic has become a great concern because of its chronic and epidemic effects on human, plant and animal health (Hughes *et al.,* 2011). Presenting in the terrestrial, marine and freshwater environments in various chemical forms, As may cause substantial damages to the plant and animal kingdoms (Meharg and Hartley-Whitaker, 2002). Arsenic contamination in the groundwater is becoming more

[1] Department of Agronomy, School of Agriculture Lovely Professional University, Jalandhar, Punjab, 144411, India
[2] Department of Plant Physiology, I.Ag. Sci., BHU., Varanasi, 221005, U.P., India

of a threat day by day due to its hazardous effects. Both human and plant species are affected by groundwater As contamination. Worldwide, nearly 150 million people spanning over 70 countries are affected by As contamination (Brammer and Ravenscroft, 2009). Countries of South and South-East Asia are mainly affected by As and over 110 million people of these areas are affected by As. Environmental exposure of As through contaminated drinking water severely affects human health. In recent decades, large-scale groundwater pollution by geogenic As in Bangladesh and India (West Bengal) has been detected, which has largely promoted this element into the environment and largely contaminated water, soils and crops. Evoked by the risk of As entering the food chain, the detection of As-contaminated agricultural soils has renewed interest in studying the dynamics of As in the soil environment. The primary use of metallic arsenic is in alloys of lead (for example, in car batteries and ammunition). It oxidizes readily in air to form arsenic trioxide and water, and analogous reactions take place with sulfur and selenium instead of oxygen. Compounds of arsenic resemble in some respects those of phosphorus, which occupies the same group (column) of the periodic table. The most common oxidation states for arsenic are: –3 in the arsenides, which are alloy-like intermetallic compounds, +3 in the arsenites, and +5 in the arsenates and most organoarsenic compounds. Arsenic also bonds readily to itself as seen in the square As_3^{-4} ions in the mineral skutterudite. In the +3 oxidation state, arsenic is typically pyramidal owing to the influence of the lone pair of electrons. After entering the human body, As creates complex problems: it may cause severe chronic diseases that damage the liver, lungs, kidneys, bladder, prostate and so on; even As-induced cancer is not uncommon (Benbrahim-Tallaa and Waalkes, 2008). Arsenic is non-essential and toxic for plants, especially in higher concentrations. Roots are usually the first tissue to be exposed to As; root extension and proliferation are inhibited by As. Translocating through shoots, As can severely inhibit plant growth by slowing or arresting cell expansion or biomass accumulation. Arsenic can reduce plants' reproductive capacity through losses in fertility, reducing development of reproductive organs. Thus, the yield components of plants are also hampered and the result is reduced yield or fruit production (Garg and Singla, 2011). Arsenic can actively react with enzymes and proteins, and thus disrupts biochemical functions of cells; and thus photosynthesis, respiration, transpiration and plant metabolism processes are seriously hampered in other aspects by As toxicity (Meharg and Hartley-Whitaker, 2002). Arsenic is responsible for reactive oxygen species (ROS) generation within the cell that may cause lipid peroxidation and protein oxidation, thus severely affecting cellular and subcellular organelles, and it can even damage the DNA. Sufficiently high concentrations of As may cause plant death by interfering with metabolic processes (Finnegan and Chen, 2012). Considering its damaging effects, remediation of As toxicity has become a great concern and is highly complex. Various approaches have been developed for the remediation of As toxicity. Plants have genetic potential to remove, degrade and metabolize heavy metals including As (Hasanuzzaman and Fujita, 2012). Soil microbes also play a large role in reducing As toxicity. Moreover, remediations of As by employing different agronomic practices are also important. This chapter reviews sources, status and hazards of As; it also reviews some As-detoxifying mechanisms within plants. This chapter sheds light on the effects of As toxicity on rice and various approaches for remediation of As from the soil or the environment.

Environmental Chemistry of Arsenic

Arsenic is a naturally occurring element widely distributed in the Earth's crust. Arsenic is a metalloid and it occurs in many minerals, either in conjunction with other elements or as a pure elemental crystal. It is the most common cause of acute toxic metal poisoning (Hasanuzzaman and Fujita, 2012). It is one of the toxic metals / metalloids in the environment having diverse chemical behaviour. Arsenic, with atomic number 33, and situated in Group 15 of the periodic table, exists in four different oxidation states, namely, (–III), (0), (III) and (V); however, oxidized As(III) and As(V) are the most widespread forms in nature (Goessler and Kuehnelt, 2002). Since As is a metalloid and it is seated under nitrogen (N) and phosphorus (P) in the periodic table, it has an excess of electrons and unfilled orbitals that stabilize formal oxidation states (+5 to –3). Thus, As has a greater oxidation potential (i.e. the ability to lose electrons) than N and P, which increase its cationic character (O'Day 2006). There are many forms, or species, of As in the environment, including: (1) inorganic arsenate (AsO_4^{3-}) and arsenite (AsO_3^{3-}), (2) methylated anionic species, (3) volatile As hydrides and (4) organoarsenic species in food. Under moderately reducing conditions, arsenite (+3) may be the dominant form. Under normal environmental conditions, the most stable forms and thus most readily detected forms, are in oxidation state +5. They are the most common mobile species in water, soil and sediment. Arsenic also has the capacity. To bind to a variety of organic ligands with different coordination geometries and its greater redox potential than P helps to explain why mechanisms of As toxicity in living organisms still remain unclear. Important factors affecting As chemistry, and its mobility in soils, are soil solution chemistry (pH and redox conditions), solid composition, As bearing phases, adsorption and desorption and biological transformations, volatilization and cycling of As in soil (Sadiq, 1997). In general, inorganic As species are more mobile and toxic than organic forms to living organisms, including plants, animals and humans (Meharg and Hartley-Whitaker, 2002). In general, arsenite is known to be more toxic and mobile than arsenate (Panstar-Kallio and Manninen, 1997; Stronach, *et al.*, 1997).

Sources of Arsenic Contamination in Soil and Environment

Arsenic ranks 52nd in crustal abundance and it is a major constituent in more than 245 minerals and that is why it is widely distributed worldwide (O'Neill, 1995). However, the concentration is variable depending on the parent materials. For instance, the mean concentrations of As in igneous rocks range from 1.5 to 3.0 mg kg^{-1}, whereas in sedimentary rocks they range from 1.7 to 400 mg kg^{-1} (Smith *et al.*, 1998). The alluvial and deltaic sediments containing pyrite have favoured the As contamination of groundwater in Bangladesh. Most regions of Bangladesh are composed of a vast thickness of alluvial and deltaic sediments, which can be divided into two major parts—the recent flood plain and the terrace areas.

Arsenic can be introduced into the environment from various sources; mainly categorized as geological (geogenic) and anthropogenic (human activities) sources. In addition, small amounts of As also enter the soil and water through various biological sources (biogenic) that are rich in As (Mahimairaja *et al.*, 2005). Anthropogenic sources of As contamination are the predominant sources of As contamination in industrialized countries. However, unlike other toxic metals, geological reasons for As contamination are more prominent than anthropogenic sources in some areas of the world. In Bangladesh, for instance, the recent episode of extensive As contamination in groundwaters is mostly of geological origin, transported by rivers from sedimentary rocks over many years (Mahimairaja *et al.*, 2005). Although many are anthropogenic, their capacity to release As greatly depends on their bioavailability in nature as well as the chemical nature (speciation). The major anthropogenic sources of As include: mining, ore dressing and smelting of non-ferrous metals; production of As and As compounds; petroleum and chemical industries; pesticides, beer, table salt, tap water, paints, pigments, cosmetics, glass and mirror manufacture; fungicides, insecticides, treated wood and contaminated food; dyestuff and the tanning industry (Hasanuzzaman and Fujita, 2012. For centuries, humans have utilized As compounds [especially, realgar (As_4S_4), or piment (As_2S_3) and arsenolite (As_2O_3)] in a wide variety of products, which include: pigments, medicines, alloys, pesticides, herbicides, glassware, embalming fluids and as a depilatory in leather manufacturing (Eisler, 2004).

The involvement of As with agricultural practices began after the green revolution when the use of pesticides and fertilizers increased rapidly. Some pesticides, herbicides and fertilizers contain As in their formulation, and thus the industries that manufacture As-containing pesticides and herbicides release As into soil and water. The chemical compounds which are released in soil through pesticides are mainly calcium arsenate $Ca_3(AsO_4)_2$, magnesium arsenate ($Mg_3(As_2O_4)_2$), zinc arsenate $Zn_3(As_2O_4)_2$, zinc arsenite $Zn_3(AsO_3)_2$, lead arsenate $PbHAsO_4$ and Paris Green $Cu(C_2H_3O_2)_2{\cdot}3Cu(AsO_2)_2$ (Mahimairaja *et al.*, 2005). Chatterjee and Mukherjee (1999) reported that indiscriminate dis-charge of industrial effluents from the manufacturing of Paris Green (an arsenical pesticide) caused As contamination in soil and groundwater in the residential area of Kolkata, India. The two other herbicides, monosodium methanearsonate and disodium methanearsonate, were reported to release significant amounts of As into the soil (Smith *et al.*, 1998). In the United States, Adriano (2001) reported that the use of sodium arsenite ($NaAsO_2$) to control aquatic weeds has contaminated small fish ponds and lakes in many regions. As reported by Bolan and Thiyagarajan (2001) timber treatment effluent is considered to be the major source of As contamination in aquatic and terrestrial environments in New Zealand. A large portion of As is released during mining and smelting processes of different metals like Au, Cu, Pb and Zn because As is extensively distributed in the sulphide ores of these metals (Mahimairaja *et al.*, 2005). In addition, the flue gases and particulate from smelters can contaminate nearby ecosystems down-wind from the operation with a range of toxic metals, including As (Adriano, 2001). Coal combustion also emits As to the atmosphere in a gaseous form.

Some plants and micro- and macroorganisms affect the redistribution of As through their bioaccumulation (e.g. biosorption), biotransformation (e.g. biomethylation) and transfer (e.g. volatilization). However, the biological sources contribute only small amounts of As into soil and water ecosystems. Sometimes, As can be transferred from soil to plants and then to animals and humans, involving terrestrial and aquatic food chains. For example, poultry manure addition is considered to be one of the major sources of As input to soils. Both inorganic and organic species of As undergo various biological and chemical transformations in soils, including adsorption, desorption, precipitation, complexation, volatilization and methylation.

Status of Arsenic Toxicity in the World

Arsenic is not a new hazard in the world. It is one of the oldest poisons in the world and an important global environmental contaminant (Vaughan, 2006). In the Middle Ages, As was used as an efficient suicidal agent and also used in many high-profile murders, and thus it was often known as the 'king of poisons' and the 'poison of kings' (Hughes *et al.*, 2011). In the last century, As was found to be highly abundant in soils, sediments and waters because of intensive mining and metallurgical activities or the alteration of geothermal systems (Vaughan 2006). In nature, As ranks 20th, 14th and 12th in order of abundance in the Earth's crust, seawater and the human body, respectively (Mandal and Suzuki, 2002). Considerable increase in metal mining and combustion of fossil fuel in the last century resulted in the release of significant amounts of toxic metals including As (Callender, 2003). In the 1990s, the high levels of As in well water came to light – outbreaks of skin disease and cancers in many parts of Bangladesh and part of West Bengal, India showed the 'worst mass poisoning in history'. Later, As contamination in drinking water and agricultural soil has been studied and their adverse effects are observed in crop and human health. In several reports, As was assumed to be an ubiquitous element and to be the twentieth most abundant element in the biosphere (Woolson, 1977; Mandal and Suzuki, 2002) because of its presence in soil, water, air and all living matter in any of the forms of solid, liquid and gas. Although the average concentration of As (in the inorganic form) in the earth's crust is 2–5 mg kg^{-1} (Tamaki and Frankenberger, 1992), it has become a widespread problem in many parts of the world. Toxic levels of As have been reported in many countries such as Argentina, Bangladesh, Cambodia, Chile, China, Ghana, Hungary, do still occur'. Their statement was based on a report where As poisoning made headlines in 2003 when As was detected in the coffee served at a church meeting in Maine (Zernike, 2003; Health, 2013). In agricultural practices As-based pesticides started to be used in 1867 with the introduction of Paris Green to control Colorado potato beetles and mosquitoes (Cullen, 2008). Later, another As-based pesticide, lead arsenate, came to be extensively used in late 1800s as a pesticide for apple and cherry orchards which was less toxic to plants and more effective than Paris Green (Peryea, 1998a). However, the use of these pesticides became limited as they have toxic effects for human and plant health.

The National Academy of Sciences, Medical and Biological Effects of Environmental Pollutants (NAS, 2000), established that the average As content of the Earth's crust is 2.5 mg kg^{-1}; however, it may exceed the limit, ranging from 45 to 3275 mg kg^{-1} (Nagy *et al.*, 2005). In soil, As is present in differing amounts ranging from 0.1 to 50 mg kg^{-1} (mean 5–6 mg kg^{-1}) which varies considerably between various regions in the world (Mandal and Suzuki, 2002). Arsenic is present in soils in higher concentrations than those in rocks (Mandal and Suzuki, 2002). When rocks weather, As may mobilize as salts of arsenous and As acid (H_3AsO_4) (Irgolic *et al.*, 1995). The variation of As concentration in soil also depends on several factors, where soil characteristics are important. Several reports indicated that As content is 10.3–8.5 mg kg^{-1} in Japanese paddy soils, 4.6–2 mg kg^{-1} in Korean soils and 9.1–6.7 mg kg^{-1} in soils from Thailand (Mandal and Suzuki, 2002).

Arsenic contamination in agricultural crops has gained more attention in recent years. However, the presence of As greatly varies with soil types and crop species, and even cultivars. The As concentrations in agricultural plants varied from 0.007 to about 7.50 mg kg^{-1} as reported in different studies (Mandal and Suzuki, 2002; Roychowdhury *et al.*, 2002; Liao *et al.*, 2005; Dahal *et al.*, 2008). Mandal and Suzuki (2002) found that As concentration in plants varied from less than 0.01 to about 5.0 mg kg^{-1}. However, the exact information on the current status of As in soil, water and plants is still a matter of survey or research.

Arsenic Hazard: A Bangladesh Perspective

The problem of As contamination in the groundwater of Bangladesh is the worst in the world. In Bangladesh, arsenopyrite has been identified as the prime source of As pollution (Fazal *et al.*, 2001a) and in the groundwater As is found to be present in all four important forms, namely, $H_2AsO_3^-$, $H_2AsO_4^-$, methyl As acid [$CH_3AsO(OH)_2$] and dimethyl As acid [$(CH_3)_2As(OH)$] (Fazal *et al.*, 2001b). In 1990s, the As problems came to the attention of researchers. The problem of As is currently a national concern with vital consequences on human lives and crop productivity.

Arsenic in tube well water was first identified in 1993 by Department of Public Health and Engineering (DPHE) (BGS, 1999). The prevalence of As in drinking water has been identified in 61 out of 64 districts of the country. However, the degree of contamination varies from 1% to over 90% with an average contamination of 29% (DPHE, 2013). In some parts of Bangladesh where the concentration of As is high, As in drinking water is a major cause of chronic health effects and its reduction is considered a high-priority. In a survey jointly conducted by DPHE-UNICEF, it was revealed that 271 of 463 upazilas of the country suffered (more or less) from the As problem (DPHE, 2013). According to BGS/DPHE (2001), more than 35 million people in Bangladesh are exposed to As contamination in drinking water exceeding the national standard of 50 $\mu g\ l^{-1}$, and an estimated 57 million people are at the risk of exposure to As contamination where underground water is used mainly for drinking, cooking and other household activities (Rabbani *et al.*, 2002; Das *et al.*, 2004; Huq, 2008). As a result, at least 1 million people are likely to be affected by arsenicosis, which has been termed as the 'greatest mass poisoning in human history'. Among 64 districts of Bangladesh, the worst districts affected with As contamination are Chandpur (90%), Munsiganj (83%), Gopalganj (79%), Noakhali (69%), Madaripur (69%), Satkhira (67%), Comilla (65%), Shriatpur (65%), Faridpur. The number of polluted wells is insignificant at depths greater than 100–150 m, while the maximum contamination has been suggested to be between 15 and 30 m which could be associated with a zone of mixing between shallower and deeper groundwaters induced by pumping for drinking water and irrigation (Harvey *et al.*, 2005; Smedley, 2005; Klump *et al.*, 2006). A UNICEF (2008) report reveals that of the total 4.7 million tube wells in Bangladesh, as many as 1.4 million had traces of As more than that delineated by the Bangladesh government. In case of Bangladesh, deep tube wells (> 150 m depth) are generally safe. Some studies reported As concentration in uncontaminated land of Bangladesh, which varies from 3–9 mg As kg^{-1} (Ullah, 1998; Alam and Sattar, 2000). Conversely, elevated As concentrations were observed in many studies in agricultural land irrigated with As-contaminated water, which is in some cases found to be about 10- to 20-times higher than As concentrations in non-irrigated land. Ullah (1998) reported As concentrations in top agricultural land soil (up to 0–30 cm depth) up to 83 mg As kg^{-1}. However, this finding is not identical in agreement with other studies, such as Islam *et al.*, (2005) (up to 80.9 mg As kg^{-1}), Alam and Sattar (2000) (up to 57 mg As kg^{-1}) of soil samples collected from different districts of Bangladesh.

Arsenic contamination in crop land has been identified recently and came to the attention of researchers in the last decade (Ali *et al.*, 2003). The problem of As is very prominent in rice cultivation as many rice fields are dependent on groundwater irrigation, which is often contaminated by As because the area irrigated is increasing day by day. In practice, ordinary crop plants do not accumulate enough As to be toxic to humans; growth reductions and crop failure are likely to be the main consequences. It is likely that because of the soil / plant barrier effect, increased As concentrations in soils will reduce crop production substantially before enhanced food-chain accumulation occurs. Long-term use of As-contaminated underground water in irrigation has resulted in an increase of its concentration in agricultural soil and eventually in crop plants (Ullah, 1998; Huq *et al.*, 2003; Rahman *et al.*, 2007a, c). Surveys on paddy soil throughout Bangladesh showed that As concentrations were higher in agricultural soils of those areas where shallow tube wells (STWs) have been in operation for longer periods of time, and As-contaminated underground water from those STWs have been irrigated to the crop fields (Meharg and Rahman, 2003).

Most of the research on the As toxicity in agriculture is carried out in rice-farming systems because it is the main food crop of Bangladesh and most of the rice is grown with irrigation water. In their survey, Ross *et al.*, (2005) calculated that 76% of the boro rice is grown in areas where shallow tube wells have less than 0.050 mg l^{-1}, 17% in areas with 0.050–0.100 mg l^{-1} and 7% in areas with more than 0.100 mg l^{-1}. In a report, Ali *et al.*, (2003) observed clear differences in As accumulation in rice soil grown with or without irrigation. High levels of As were detected in the irrigated field (3.2–27.5 mg kg^{-1}), whereas in areas where irrigation water does not contain As, the soil As level was very low (0.10–2.75 mg kg^{-1}). However, the higher levels of As were found in the top 7.5–15 cm (i.e. the plough zone) and they decreased with soil depth. Based on the results of 71 soil samples in rice fields, Meharg and Rahman (2003) found that the highest soil concentration (46 mg kg^{-1}) was obtained in soils irrigated with high As-content water, while the minimum concentration (< 10 mg kg^{-1}) was observed in soils irrigated with low-As water.

Huq and Naidu (2003) concluded that the As loading in crop field depends on the amount of irrigation water per season. For instance, in irrigated boro (winter) rice irrigated with 1000 mm of water per season, the As loading was calculated to be 1.36–5.5 kg ha^{-1} yr^{-1}. Conversely, spring wheat (*Triticum aestivum*) irrigated with 150 mm of irrigation water per season, the loading of As was only 0.12–0.82 kg ha^{-1} yr^{-1}. More importantly, Meharg and Rahman (2003) reported that the soil irrigated with water having only 0.1 mg l^{-1} may increase top soil (10 cm depth) As levels as much as 1 mg kg^{-1} As in a year. Similarly, Duxbury and Zavala (2005) estimated that rice fields irrigated with As-contaminated water for 10 years may add 5–10 mg of As per kg of soil. Arsenic accumulation in plants due to irrigation water application also differs significantly in different cultivars. For instance, between two boro rice cultivars, BRRI dhan28 was found to accumulate more As than BRRI dhan29 grown in a pot with the same soil (Huq *et al.,* 2006). They also noted that in either variety, As(III) was more prominent than As(V). In another study, Rabbi *et al.,* (2007) found that the high-yielding variety (HYV) of rice accumulated more As than the local variety. In a study, Huq and Naidu (2003) found almost similar amounts of As (< 1.0 mg kg^{-1} dry weight) in wheat grain compared to rice grain, but the amount of As was much lower in wheat roots and other parts compared to rice. An extensive study with 330 rice samples grown in aman and boro seasons were studied by Williams *et al.,* (2006). The study area was throughout Bangladesh. They found a positive correlation between As in the groundwater and in the rice plant which was much stronger in boro rice than aman. The As concentration in rice also differed significantly in different locations with southwestern parts contaminated with higher concentration of As following the pattern: Faridpur > Satkhira > Chuadanga > Meherpur. This was due to the higher levels of As in irrigated soils compared to nearby non-irrigated soils. Conversely, other parts of the country did not show differences in As concentrations either in irrigated or non-irrigated soils. Several other reports indicated that the soils in the western and southwestern parts of the country have the highest concentration of As (FAO, 2006). Apart from Williams *et al.,* (2006), Islam *et al.,* (2005) also conducted an extensive study on the levels of As in water, soil and crops at 456 locations in five upazilas. They found that the classified the upazilas according to soil concentrations were: Faridpur > Tala > Brahmanbaria > Paba > Senbag. Most of the studied soil samples (53%) contained less than 10 mg As kg^{-1}, 26% soil contained 10.1– 20 mg As kg^{-1} and the rest soil samples (18%) contained more than 20 mg As kg^{-1}. There was also a seasonal variation of As concentration in water where boro season allowed more As in boro than in aman season. Yamazaki *et al.,* (2003) showed that As concentration in Bangladesh soil also varied depending on the types of sediment. They studied five soil profiles collected from 15 depths from southwest Bangladesh. They reported that clay sediment contained the high concentration of As (20–111 mg kg^{-1}) followed by clay (4–18 mg kg^{-1}) and sand (3–7 mg kg^{-1}).

In last few decades, rice has extensively been studied to determine its level of contamination in relation to health risk. A group of studies analyzed a total of 788 rice samples (USAID, 2003; Duxbury *et al.,* 2003; Hironaka and Ahmad, 2003; Meharg and Rahman, 2003; Shah *et al.,* 2004) that indicated that the daily As intakes from 84% of the Bangladeshi rice samples exceed daily As intake from water at a standard of 10 mg l^{-1}. This provides an indication that rice alone may be an important source of exposure in the Bangladeshi food system. Rahman *et al.*, (2007a) investigated the accumulation and distribution of As in different fractions of rice cv. BRRI dhan28 and BRRI hybrid dhan1 collected from an As-affected area of Bangladesh (Sathkhira, Bangladesh) which was irrigated with As-contaminated groundwater (0.07 mg l^{-1}). They found that As content was about 28- and 75-fold higher in root than in shoots and raw rice grain, respectively. The order of As concentrations in different parts was: rice hull > bran-polish > brown rice > raw rice > polished rice. Laizu (2007) also analyzed a total of 400 vegetable samples under 20 varieties and found a large range of As concentrations, indicating the risk of potential hazard of the affected crops to the health of the people in Bangladesh. Ullah *et al.*, (2009) analyzed 330 soil samples taken from 11 districts and they observed the As level to be above permissible limits in 10 districts. They found the highest contamination of 54.74 mg kg^{-1} dry soil in Jessore district which was more than double than the permissible limit (20 mg kg^{-1} dry soil) indicating the severity of the problem. However, in Bangladesh huge attempts have been made to raise awareness of As problems among the people. Many Government and NGOs are working in this area. The DPHE has measured As levels of shallow tubules of the country and identified the As-contaminated and the safe ones. Although lots of effort have been made to find safe drinking water there, no suitable measure has been established yet. In addition to the drinking water problem, continued irrigation with As-contaminated water increases the extent of As contamination in agricultural land soil in Bangladesh (Ullah, 1998; Alam and Sattar, 2000; Ali *et al.*, 2003; Islam *et al.*, 2004)

Arsenic Uptake and Transportation in Plants

Whether from anthropogenic or geogenic sources, As has accumulated in the soils and groundwater, and even the atmosphere. Soil is the primary medium for plant growth and water is a basic need for plants; so As accumulated in those is easily uptaken by plants. However, the rate of uptake or accumulation of As greatly depends on several factors such as soil type, plant species and mechanisms of uptake. The capacity of As uptake by plants also varied with the speciation of As. Arsenite, is known to be more toxic and mobile than arsenate (Stronach, *et al.*, 1997). Roots are the first point of entry of As from where it moves to different plant parts of terrestrial and emergent plants. However, submerged plants may also take up As through leaves from the water column (Wolterbeek and van der Meer, 2002). In general, As is primarily found in the roots rather than in the shoots of plants. In rice, Rahman *et al.*, (2007c) observed 28- to 75-times-higher As concentration in roots than in shoots. Later, Rofkar and Dwyer (2011) obtained a more than 15-times higher As may make a significant contribution to the total amount of As in a plant. In their report Bravin *et al.*, (2008) observed that about 60% of the total As (173 mg As kg^{-1}) was accumulated in rice root which was grown under reducing conditions and separated into an apoplastic fraction, while only 39% (112 mg As kg^{-1}) of the total As was retained in the non-apoplastic fraction. Compared to roots, the shoot tissue contained only 1% (2.3 mg As kg^{-1}) of total As. Chen *et al.*, (2005) found 17% of the total As in the apoplast of As-hyper accumulating fern, *Pteris vittata*. From the apoplast As can enter into the plant cytosol. This movement is governed by sevaral factors. Uptake of AsO_4^{3-} into the cell cytoplasm has been suggested to occur by high-affinity phosphate transporters, while AsO_3^{3-} has been suggested to be taken up by aquaglyceroporins (Meharg and Macnair, 1992; Meharg and Jardine, 2003), which are also responsible for the uptake of other As compounds such as momethylarsonic acid (MMA) and dimethylarsinic acid (DMA) (Rahman *et al.*, 2011).

In some cases, large amounts of As were locked up in plant roots and only relatively small amounts of As (as AsO_4^{3-} and AsO_3^{3-}) were exported via the xylem to above-ground tissues, as observed by Pickering *et al.*, (2000). Arsenic in soil is found mainly in the oxidized form (AsO_4^{3-}). Later, a portion of the AsO_4^{3-} taken up into plant roots may be held in cell walls (possibly as $FeAsO_4$). Some portion of As passes through root membranes, most likely via transporters that facilitate the uptake of phosphate (Pickering *et al.*, 2000), which is chemically similar to AsO_4^{3-}. Inside the root cells, some $AsO_4^{3''}$ is reduced to AsO_3^{3-}. A small fraction of the AsO_4^{3-} and AsO_3^{3-} move from root to leaf via the xylem (Pickering *et al.*, 2000). Arsenate is then reduced to $AsO_3^{3''}$ by the activity of the enzyme *arsenate* reductase (ArsC), which combines with thiol (–SH) compounds to form As–thiolates. In this form, As is probably shuttled irreversibly into the vacuoles, where it can no longer damage the plant. For the long-distance movement of As, little or no information is available on the nature of the transporter involved. As described by Tripathi *et al.*, (2007), plants take up AsO_4^{3-} and AsO_3^{3-} through phosphate transporters and aquaglycero-porins (NIP), respectively. Small amounts of organic As MMA and DMA can also be taken up through unknown transporters (Tripathi *et al.*, 2007). Long-distance transport of As from root-to-shoot takes place in the form As(V) and As(III). Plants assimilate sulphate (SO_4^{2-}) to form cysteine (Cys) for the synthesis of glutathione (GSH) in two adenosine triphosphate (ATP)-dependent steps: in the first, rate-limiting step, γ-glutamylcysteine (γEC) is synthesized by γ-glutamylcysteine synthetase (γ-ECS) using Cys and γ-glutamic acid (γ-Glu) as substrates; and in the second step, GSH is synthesized by glutathione synthetase (GS), using glycine (Gly) as a substrate (Tripathi *et al.*, 2007). In response to As, plants induce synthesis of phytochelatins (PC), through the action of phytochelatin synthase (PCS) which can be transported through the vascular tissues. As a process of detoxification, AsO_4^{3-} is reduced to AsO_3^{3-} by arsenate reductase (AR) using GSH as a reducing agent. Phytochelatins and GSH coordinate with As(III) to form a variety of complexes. These complexes can be sequestered in the vacuole by ABC-type transporter. However, there is no clear evidence so far in this regard. Apart from this, large amounts of unbound AsO_3^{3-} are found in vacuoles, but whether these are transported as free As(III) is still unknown (Tripathi *et al.*, 2007; Verbruggen *et al.*, 2009). The uptake of As from root to shoot and its accumulation and sequestration broadly depends on the transporters involved in As uptake which are also mediated by the constitutive expression of genes that encode the various transporters. Generally, the expression of those genes is greater in hyper accumulator plants compared with non-accumulators (Krämer, 2005). For instance, Lei *et al.*, (2012) reported that P transportere has a large role in As translocation in As hyper accumulator *P. vittata*. Geng *et al.*, (2006) found different capacities of As uptake and distribution by two cultivars of winter wheat (*T. aestivum*) (Jing 411 and Lovrin 10) grown with or without P supply. Between the two cultivars, Lovrin 10 invested more biomass production to roots than Jing 411, which might be partly responsible for higher shoot P and As concentrations and higher shoot-to-root ratios of As concentrations. In addition, Lovrin 10 allocated less As to roots than Jing 411 and the difference disappeared with decreasing P supply. Sharma and Travlos (2012) reported that a concentration of 100 μM phosphate was able to protect the test plant from As (100 μM)-mediated oxidative stress in pearl millet (*Pennisetum typhoides*).

Plant Responses to Arsenic Toxicity

Recently As toxicity in plants has come into light as a number of studies indicated its negative impact on plants. Arsenic has different forms which can be frequently taken up by roots, transported from the root to shoots via the xylem, further accumulated to the aerial parts of plants, including the seeds (Pickering *et al.*, 2006). Several research findings indicated the adverse effects of As on the growth physiology and the ultimate yield of crops.

Seed Germination

Marked decreases in germination percentage and shoot and root elongation were recorded with As treatments in rice seedlings. The germination decreased significantly with the increase in As concentration. Root length, shoot length, root and shoot fresh weight of rice seedlings were greatly inhibited at 50 mM As (III) and 500 mM As (V) (Shri *et al.*, 2009). In *Vigna mungo,* control treatment resulted in germination percentage over 97%, while it was only 83 and 70% when exposed to 100 and 200 μM As, respectively. Shoot and root length, and fresh weight of seedling also decreased (Srivastava and Sharma, 2013). In wheat seedlings, the effects of As were determined on seed germination, root and shoot length and biomass production under different concentrations. However, low concentrations of As (0–1 mg kg^{-1}) stimulated seed germination and the growth of root and shoot. Treatment of *Phaseolus aureus Roxb* with different concentrations of As decreased the percentage of germination, germination index and vigour index. More inhibitory effects were observed at higher doses of As. Compared to untreated control, the As treatments of 1, 25, 50 and 100 mg l^{-1} reduced the germination percentage by 13, 43, 52, 74; 14, 44, 56 and 74%; the seedling vigour reduced by 14, 44, 56 and 74%, respectively (Patel *et al.*, 2013). In *Vigna mungo* seed placed in As-free conditions resulted in 100% seed germination, whereas in 100 μM As treatment germination percentage was as low as 67%. Apart from a reduction in germination percentage, the root and shoot length of germinated seedlings were also reduced by As toxicity (Srivastava and Sharma, 2013). While studying the effects of As (0, 0.5, 1, 5, 15, 20 mg kg^{-1}) on *T. aestivum* cv. Zhengzhou-9023, Li *et al.*, (2007) observed that germination performance of the plant was better in lower concentrations and with the increase of concentration germination was adversely affected. At an As concentration of 0.5 mg kg^{-1} the germination energy and germination index increased by 104.33% and 101.97%, respectively. The vitality index increased by 6.56% at an As concentration of 1 mg kg^{-1}. Germination energy, germination percentage, germination index and vitality index reduced significantly, by 9.60%, 4.04%, 10.73% and 46.61%, respectively, with higher As concentration of 20 mg kg^{-1} (Li *et al.*, 2007).

Growth

Higher As concentration can inhibit growth because of interference with plant metabolic processes that often leads to death. Several reports described the morphological changes, reduced fresh and dry biomass of roots and shoots under As-rich growing medium (Mokgalaka-Matlala *et al.*, 2008; Shaibur *et al.*, 2008; Srivastava *et al.*, 2009). Plant height of *Lens culinaris* decreased with increasing concentrations of As in irrigation water. As also decreased leaf number, root length and biomass production (Ahmed *et al.*, 2006). Accumulation of As in in *Ceratophyllum demersum* L. increased linearly (13–15% each day) depending on both As concentration (AsV, 0, 10, 50, 250 μM Na_2HAsO_4) and duration (1, 2, 4 and 7 days) of exposure. At 50 μM, plants accumulated about 76 μg As g^{-1} dry weight after 4 days but no visible symptoms of toxicity were found. After 7 days, the same treatment resulted in an As level of 201 μg g^{-1} dry weight and biomass production decreased significantly. Plant exposure to 250 μM As(V) resulted in a sharp increase in As accumulation (525 μg As g^{-1} dry weight) after 7 days of exposure with a great decrease in biomass (Mishra *et al.*, 2008). In rice plants, height and shoot biomass production were reduced to a great extent with the increase of soil As concentrations. The highest number of tiller (15.51 pot^{-1}) was recorded for control As treatment in BRRI hybrid dhan 1. The same treatment produced 12.34, 10.24, 9.14 and 8.43 tillers in BRRI dhan29, BRRI dhan35, BRRI dhan28 and BRRI dhan36, respectively. In *Lactuca sativa* L. cv. Hanson, As accumulation in leaves and roots increased with the increase of As(V) and As(III) concentration (6.6, 13.2, 26.4 and 52.8 μM As). The highest As concentration has been found in roots. Highest As transported to the leaves occurred when plants were exposed to As(III). Relative growth rate (RGR) of leaves and roots were decreased with the accumulation of As. When exposed to 52.8 μM As(V) and As(III), reduction of leaf growth was recorded as 39 and 29%, respectively. With exposure to As(V), root growth reduced by 50%; it reduced to 33% by As(III). At 52.8 μM As(V) the roots relative growth reduced by 50% (Gusman *et al.*, 2013).

Arsenic accumulation increased in *Ceratophyllum demersum* L. with increased concentrations and durations of As, which was correlated with PC content. The percentage of As chelated by PCs dropped by 19% at 50 μM and by 14% at 100 μM, after 4 days that increased As accumulation (Mishra *et al.*, 2008). Root length of rice seedlings decreased by 23 and 37%, respectively, after exposure at 25 and 50 μM As for 24 h. The reduction in coleoptiles length was only in the range from 8 to 15% with the same As dose. Without decreasing the root length significantly, increase of As accumulation was evident due to As exposure. Roots accumulated 21.2- and 35.0-fold higher As at 25 and 50 μM As exposure compared to control. Coleoptiles accumulated only 8.5- and 15.5-fold greater As at 25 and 50 μM As-exposure compared to control (Singh *et al.*, 2009). Arsenic treatments of 5 and 10 mg kg^{-1} irrigation water reduced *Vigna radiata* plant growth. Different growth parameters like root length, fresh and dry weight and shoot length, fresh and dry weight were significantly reduced compared to those in plants treated with irrigation water without As treatment. Moreover, As irrigation water reduced different nutrient accumulation in the shoot including P, K, S, Ca and Mg. With the increase of As concentration this trend was more severe. In case of iron accumulation in the shoot, this trend was inverted and with the increase of As concentration, iron accumulation increased (Sultana *et al.*, 2012). Number of plants per pot, stem length, number of leaves per plant, fresh yield *Amaranthus retroflexus* L. decreased drastically and gradually from lower to higher concentrations of As (5, 10, 15, 20, 25, 30, 35, 40, 45, 50, 55, 60 mg l^{-1}). Arsenic application also increases the As uptake of this plant and thus resulted in increased As concentration in root, stem and leaf (Choudhury *et al.*, 2009). The biomass and height of wheat plant increased by 24.1 and 7.8% separately at 60 mg As kg^{-1} soil. Under exposure to high levels of As, the wheat height and biomass decreased significantly (Liu *et al.*, 2012).

Water Relations

Under toxic metal stress, plant organs show a wide-range of secondary stresses; water or osmotic stresses are common among them (Requejo and Tena, 2005; Zhao *et al.*, 2009). Plants respond in various ways to maintain the water status to cope with these kinds of stresses. Osmotic adjustment, regulation of water content or water potential are adapted by plants in response to As exposure (Grasielle *et al.*, 2013). In response to As stress, accumulation of proline, glycine betaine or osmotic adjustment by Na^+ within plants have been reported to maintain water balance (Ben Hassine *et al.*, 2008; Grasielle *et al.*, 2013). Among different doses of As (6.6, 13.2, 26.4 and 52.8 μM As) water use efficiency of *Lactuca sativa* L. cv. Hanson did not change up to 26.4 μM concentration. Significant reduction of water use efficiency was recorded at the highest concentration of (52.8 μM) As(V) and As(III) application. As(V) and As(III) reduced plant transpiration. But compared As(V), As(III) exposure affected more plant transpiration and reduced by 81% at 52.8 μM As(III). Stomatal conductance in lettuce was reduced by 61% at 52.8 μM As(V). The same concentration of As(III) caused a higher reduction (78%) of stomatal conductance (Grasielle *et al.*, 2013).

Exposure of As for 96 h at 500 μM concentration reduced water use efficiency, increased transpiration rate and did not affect stomatal conductance in *Hydrilla verticillata* (L.f.) Royle (Srivastava *et al.*, 2013). As (0.25 and 0.5 mM $Na_2HAsO_4 \bullet 7H_2O$) reduced the leaf relative water content (RWC) of wheat seedlings. The leaf RWC reduced by 15 and 17% with 0.25 and 0.5 mM As, respectively, as compared to control plants (Hasanuzzaman and Fujita, 2013). A decrease in RWC due to As treatment was also reported in bean plants (Stoeva *et al.*, 2005). In xerohalophyte plant species *Atriplex atacamensis* after 14 days of As treatment (100 μM), root or leaf water contents did not change, but stem water content increased. Root water potential was decreased when exposed to 1000 μM As after 14 days. Root water potential decreased more after 28 days with both the As doses. Leaf water potential remain unchanged with the As doses. Shoot water potential decreased in As in a dose- and day-dependent manner. Stomatal conductance remained unaltered at 100 μM As and decreased at 1000 μM As (Vromman *et al.*, 2011). In pea leaf compared to the control treatment, the RWC declined with increasing concentration of As(V) (60–90 mg kg^{-1}) (Garg and Singla, 2012). Osmolytes were also increased significantly. Exposure of plants to varying As (V) doses improved the protein and soluble sugar synthesis and accumulation. Protein increased by 48% and soluble sugar increased by 172%; increase in As also caused significant increase in the accumulation of proline and glycine betaine (Garg and Singla, 2012). In *Spartina densiflora* Brongn, as compared to the control plant, the water use efficiency, leaf water content and stomatal conductance decreased with increasing As concentrations (0.7, 2.7, 6.7 and 13.4 mM As) (Mateos-Naranjo *et al.*, 2012).

Photosynthesis

Different forms and concentrations of As application were recorded to slow down net photosynthesis (Stoeva and Bineva, 2003). Light-harvesting apparatus can be affected by As stress. Decreases in chlorophyll (Chl) content and / or decreased photosystem II activity are some common effects of As toxicity (Singh *et al.*, 2006; Rahman *et al.*, 2007c; Duman *et al.*, 2010). Photosynthetic electron flow through thylakoid membranes may be reduced under As stress. In the carbon fixation reactions centre, As reduces the potential to produce ATP and nicotinamide adenine dinucleotide phosphate (NADPH). Replacement of P by As(V) in photophosphorylation may cause uncoupling of thylakoid electron transport from ATP synthesis (Avron and Jagendorf, 1959; Watling- Payne and Selwyn, 1974). Decreased activity or availability of enzyme of Chl biosyntehsis [β-aminolevulinic acid (ALA) dehydratase] or Chl degradation by chlorophyllase may reduce Chl content (Jain and Gadre, 2004). As exposure in many plant species also reduced photosynthetic pigment (Rahman *et al.*, 2007c; Duman *et al.*, 2010). Under As stress, limitation of photosynthesis might be due to chlorophyll degradation. As is also supposed to limit the supply of photosynthetic carbon that may trigger Chl degradation (Finnegan and Chen, 2012). Arsenic negatively affected the photosynthetic process of *Lactuca sativa* L. cv. Hanson by impairing the photochemical and biochemical steps of photosynthesis. Chl *a* fluorescence results indicate that the photosynthetic apparatus and chloroplastic pigments were not damaged by the As(V) and As(III) concentrations used (6.6, 13.2, 26.4 and 52.8 μM As). But liquid-phase photosynthesis of lettuce plants were reduced by different As(V) and As(III) concentrations. Stomatal conductance (gs) showed a similar trend like liquid-phase photosynthesis (Grasielle *et al.*, 2013). A decrease of the ribulose-1,5-bisphosphate carboxylase / oxygenase (RuBisCO) large subunit was investigated under As stress in rice leaves (arsenate, 50 or 100 μM) that resulted in downregulation of RuBisCO and chloroplast 29 kDa. These were responsible for decreased levels of photosynthesis. Protein expression profile investigation of rice leaves revealed that As increased expression of several proteins associated with energy production and metabolism (Ahsan *et al.*, 2010).

Arsenic interferes with carbon fixation capacity. The RuBisCO large subunit content in the carbon fixation side of photosynthesis of rice leaves decreased with As(V) treatment (Ahsan *et al.*, 2010). As RuBisCO large subunit is encoded by the plastid DNA, it is supposed that As also interferes with chloroplast DNA gene expression that may decrease this protein (Bock, 2007). In As(V)-treated *Arabidopsis* RuBisCO small subunit transcripts increased (Abercrombie *et al.*, 2008). In isolated pea chloroplasts, As(III) inhibits the light activation of photosynthetic CO_2 fixation (Marques and Anderson, 1986). As has been attributed to an impairment of electron transport activity that inhibits photosynthesis (Nwugo and Huerta, 2008). As at 500 μM concentration and 96 h exposure led to a significant decline in Chl *a* content, Chl *b* and carotenoids after 96 h in *Hydrilla verticillata* (L.f.) Royle. Net photosynthetic rate, electron transport rate and PS II efficiency also declined (Srivastava *et al.*, 2013). In lettuce the photosynthetic electron transport values were reduced by 62 and 47% at 52.8 μM for As(V) and As(III), respectively, compared to control values. But non-photochemical quenching values increased significantly with As(V) and As(III) exposure, especially at the highest concentrations. The electron transport rate values reduced gradually with the increase of As concentration, The highest reduction values are 47 and 37% compared to control for As(V) and As(III), respectively (at 52.8 μM) (Grasielle *et al.*, 2013). Under As stress when carbohydrate availability is low, Chl can be used as a source of metabolic carbon that may reduce the Chl content (Araújo *et al.*, 2011). The Chl contents in the leaves of wheat plants showed the opposite trend, with lower and higher dose of As where As concentration ranged from 0–20 mg kg^{-1}. An As concentration up to 0.5 mg kg^{-1} increased Chl a, Chl b and total Chl contents by 18.46, 20.98 and 19.20%, respectively. At the highest concentration of As (20 mg kg^{-1}) they reduced by 32, 35 and 33%, respectively (Li *et al.*, 2007). Different As treatments (10, 20 and 30 mg kg^{-1}) reduced Chl a content up to 59% and decreased Chl b content up to 75% in different rice varieties (BRRI dhan28, BRRI dhan29 , BRRI dhan35, BRRI dhan36, BRRI hybrid dhan 1) (Rahman *et al.*, 2007b).

Yield

Several reports indicated a huge decline in crop yield under As toxicity. By reducing plant reproductive capacity through losses in fertility As resulted in reduced fruit production and yield (Garg and Singla, 2011). Irrigation water containing 1, 2, 5 and 10 mg l^{-1} As concentration were applied on *Vigna radiata* plant. With negative effects on different growth parameters, As also affected its number of pods and seed numbers per pod. Reduction of these yield components resulted in significant reduction of yield (Sultana *et al.*, 2012). Arsenic treatment resulted in a marked decrease in effective tillers per pot, filled grains per panicle and 1000-grain weight; these together contributed reduced grain yield. Rice grain yield of rice was reduced by 20.6% for 15 mg kg^{-1} As treatment and 63.8% due to 30 mg kg^{-1} As. Conversely, straw yield was reduced by 21.0 and 65.2 % with the same dose of As treatments (Islam and Jahiruddin 2010). Different As levels 5, 10, 15, 20, 25, 30, 35, 40, 45, 50, 55, 60 mg l^{-1} were applied on *Amaranthus retroflexus* L. and their effects were studied as compared to control. Compared to control only 9% yield reduction was recorded for 5 mg l^{-1}. This reduction increased with the increase of As concentration, 30 mg l^{-1} As resulted 63% yield reduction, whereas 55 mg l^{-1} or higher concentration resulted in 100% yield reduction (Choudhury *et al.*, 2009).

Impairment of reproductive development was suggested to reduce yield under severe As stress. Anomalous reproductive structures morphogenesis, fertilization, abortion of female gametophyte, abnormal anther, disruption of sporo- and gametogenesis processes induced by As might reduce the yield (Ghanem *et al.*, 2009; Vromman *et al.*, 2013). Even if after successful completion of the above-mentioned processes, As may interfere with grain filling or assimilate transfer process together with other physiological processes that might lead to reduced grain yield (Vromman *et al.*, 2013). Arsenic application in rice significantly reduced yield and different yield-contributing parameters including the number of panicles per plant, panicle dry weight, the number of spikelets and full grains per plant and 1000-grain weight (Vromman *et al.*, 2013). Varietal difference of rice plant performance was evident under As stress. Yield was measured considering panicle number, filled grain production and weight of total grain. Number of panicles and filled grain in BRRI hybrid dhan 1 were 12 and 101, respectively, under As stress. Conversely, in BRRI dhan36 they were 7 and 53; in BRRI dhan35: 9 and 77; in BRRI dhan29: 9 and 83; in BRRI dhan28: 7 and 54, respectively. Grain yield was 42, 11, 14, 16 and 10 g per pot for BRRI hybrid dhan 1, BRRI dhan36, BRRI dhan35, BRRI dhan29 and BRRI dhan28, respectively (Rahman *et al.*, 2007a). Lower levels of As (< 60 mg kg^{-1}) resulted in slight increase of wheat grain yield. The inverse result was found for higher As doses. Length of spike and 1000- grain weight also showed similar trends. The yield reduction by 80 mg kg^{-1} and 100 mg kg^{-1} were 20 and 36%, respectively (Liu *et al.*, 2012).

Oxidative Stress

Plant exposure to As leads to production of ROS: these may include superoxide ($O_2{\bullet}^-$), hydroxylradical (•OH) and hydrogen peroxide (H_2O_2) (Ahsan *et al.*, 2008; Mallick *et al.*, 2011). ROS are capable of peroxidating membrane lipids, readily damaging the proteins, amino acids, nucleotides and nucleic acids (Møller *et al.*, 2007). Membrane damage resulted in a product of lipid peroxidation, malondial-dehyde (MDA) that is considered as an indicator of oxidative stress (Shri *et al.*, 2009). Lipid peroxidation, besides impairing the cellular function, generates lipid-derived radicals which also have detrimental effects (Van Breusegem and Dat, 2006; Møller *et al.*, 2007). Arsenic treatment resulted in increases of As accumulation, H_2O_2 accumulation and lipid peroxidation in rice roots (Ahsan *et al.*, 2008). Another study with rice roots reveled that As exposure at 25 and 50 μM for 4 h, $O_2{\bullet}^-$ content increased significantly by 20 and 53%, respectively, over untreated controls. Further, at 8 and 24 h, 50 μM As-exposure, $O_2{\bullet}^-$ content increased by 72 and 79%, respectively. In response to 25 μM As, H_2O_2 content increased by 7, 6 and 5.5 times after 4, 8 and 24 h. As at 50 μM showed similar trends in increase of H_2O_2 but its content increased many fold higher than corresponding lower doses (Singh *et al.*, 2009). At 25 μM As-treatment, root oxidizability (RO) of rice roots increased by 1.2- to 5.3-fold after 4–24 h and at 50 μM As the RO increased 2.6- and 8.1-fold at the same time duration (Singh *et al.*, 2009). Shri *et al.*, (2009) also found that As treatment accumulated As within the rice seedlings and increased malondialdehyde (MDA) content. The wheat seedlings exposed to 0.25 and 0.5 mM As increased the MDA level by 58 and 180%, respectively, compared to the control. Treatment with 0.25 and 0.5 mM As increased the H_2O_2 content by 41 and 95% compared to control (Hasanuzzaman and Fujita, 2013). Compared to control, the wheat seedlings treated with 0.25 and 0.5 mM As treatment increased the oxidized glutathione and GSSG content (increased by 50 and 101%) (Hasanuzzaman and Fujita, 2013). From fur-ther study, Hasanuzzaman and Fujita (2013) observed that significant reduction of the antioxidant-scavenging system and the glyoxalase system were down regulated which might increase the oxidative stress. As (100 and 500 μM) exposure for 24 and 96 h in *Hydrilla verticillata* (L.f.) Royle increased the rate of $O_2{\bullet}^-$ production. The increase in rate was higher in higher and longer periods of As concentration. The higher increase in $O_2{\bullet}^-$ production is supposed to be associated with decreased content of ASC at 500 μM As (Srivastava *et al.*, 2013). Higher and longer duration of As exposure increased oxidative stress by decreasing activities of antioxidant enzymes. Activity of superoxide dismutase (SOD) increased up to 50 μM As(V) until 4 days, then its activity declined. Ascorbate peroxidase (APX) activity decreased at 250 μM As exposure of 2 days. Glutathione peroxidase (GPX) decreased after 4 days exposure to 50 μM As(V). Catalase (CAT) activity decreased at the lower dose of 10 μM As(V) concentration after 2 days in *Ceratophyllum demersum* L. While studying the oxidative stress level the opposite trend was observed. That is, with increasing dose and duration of As exposure, the oxidative stress was reduced. Seven days' exposure to 250 μM As resulted in significant increases in the levels of $O_2{\bullet}^-$, H_2O_2, MDA and ion leakage by 40, 23, 64 and 80%, respectively (Mishra *et al.*, 2008). With increasing concentrations of As, $O_2{\bullet}^-$ content in leaves of wheat seedlings increased. It was amplified by 3, 28, 42, 50 and 57% at 0.5, 1, 5, 15, 20 mg kg^{-1} of As, respectively. Slight increase of MDA level was observed when the concentration was lower than 1 mg kg^{-1}. Conversely, at higher As concentrations (5–20 mg kg^{-1}) the extent of increase was higher. MDA content increased by 22.68% under As concentration of 20 mg kg^{-1} (Li *et al.*, 2007). Under stronger As concentrations, ROS generation increases so high that the antioxidant defence mechanisms may be overwhelmed, leading to cellular damage. This damage can lead to cell death (Van Breusegem and Dat, 2006). Thus, the mechanism of ROS production under As should be known. The mechanism of the As-induced production of ROS is not well understood. One of the proposed ideas is that ROS might be generated from As detoxification processes like reduction of As(V) to As(III), the induction of PC synthesis and so on (Meharg and Hartley-Whitaker, 2002). Besides generation of ROS under As stress (Ahsan *et al.*, 2008; Mishra *et al.*, 2008; Shri *et al.*, 2009), As can upregulate those genes which regulate antioxidant enzymes (Abercrombie *et al.*, 2008; Norton *et al.*, 2008; Chakrabarty *et al.*, 2009), proteins (Requejo and Tena, 2005; Ahsan *et al.*, 2008) and enzymatic activities as well (Srivastaba *et al.*, 2005; Shri *et al.*, 2009); these effects might be considered very important for reducing the oxidative stress within the plant.

Antioxidant Defence in Plants in Response to Arsenic Stress

Plants are equipped with various enzymes and other components which are distributed in chloroplast, cytoplasm, apoplast, mitochondria, peroxisome, membranes and those components composed an effectual antioxidant system to fight against different ROS. Chief non-enzymatic compounds are ascorbate (AsA), glutathione (GSH), carotenoids, tocopherols and some other phenolic compounds. The common enzymes of antioxidant systems are SOD, catalase (CAT), ascorbate peroxidase (APX), monodehydroascorbate reductase (MDHAR), dehydroascorbate reductase (DHAR), glutathione reductase (GR), glutathione *S*-transferase (GST), glutathione peroxidase (GPX) and peroxidases (POX) (Mittler *et al.*, 2004; Ashraf, 2009; Gill and Tuteja, 2010; Hasanuzzaman and Fujita, 2013). Content of non-enzymatic components and activities of antioxidant enzymes have been documented to modulate under different stress conditions including As stress.

In *O. sativa* seedlings, As treatment accumulated As within the plant and MDA in seedlings were increased significantly with increasing As concentration. At the same time compared to control, upregulation of antioxidant enzyme activities and the isozymes of SOD, APX, POD and GR substantiated under As stress (Shri *et al.*, 2009). As treatment resulted in increases of As accumulation, H_2O_2 accumulation and lipid peroxidation in rice roots. GSH has been suggested to play a central role in protecting rice roots from these damages by upregulating SAMS (*S*-adenosyl-methionine synthetase), CS (cysteine synthase), GST and GR. However, roles of GSH or activation of these enzymes largely depends on the dose of As together with many other factors (Ahsan *et al.*, 2008). Accumulation or generation of thiol compounds has been correlated with a reduction of oxidative stress. Thiol compounds increased up to a certain dose and duration of As exposure and then they declined. Arsenate exposure significantly increased the synthesis of NP-SH (non-protein thiol), cysteine and GSH in a concentration- and duration-dependent manner. Maximum increase in the levels of NP-SH (107%), cysteine (41%) and GSH (60%) was noticed when plants were exposed to 50 μM As(V) for 2 days. Beyond these exposure their levels started declining and oxidative stress started to increase in *Ceratophyllum demersum* L. The activities of SOD, APX, GPX and CAT played important roles in keeping ROS lower in lower doses and duration of As exposure (Mishra *et al.*, 2008). Activation of antioxidant enzymes has also been reported in gene expression levels. *Arabidopsis*, encoding genes for different SOD (FeSOD, MnSOD, Cu / ZnSOD) showed different responses under As(V) stress. Cu / ZnSOD were induced twofold by As(V) exposure in the transcripts; these encoded a chloroplastic and a cytosolic gene. The transcripts for an FeSOD showed fivefold down regulation (Abercrombie *et al.*, 2008). In response to As exposure, catalase, GST, GRX and peroxidase transcript and enzymatic activity often increase (Ahsan *et al.*, 2008; Norton *et al.*, 2008; Chakrabarty *et al.*, 2009). In rice As(V) exposure at least 10 GST genes were upregulated and two GST genes were downregulated (Norton *et al.*, 2008; Chakrabarty *et al.*, 2009).

Responses of low-As-accumulating (LARG) and high-As-accumulating (HARG) rice (*Oryza sativa*) genotypes were studied under different forms and doses of As [As(III) ($NaAsO_2$; 0, 10 and 25 μM) and As(V) (Na_2HAsO_4; 0, 10 and 50 μM) for 1, 4 and 7 days]. As compared to LARG, the HARG genotypes accumulated up to 23 times higher As in the root and 15 times higher As in the shoot. Antioxidant enzymes APX, GPX and SOD played major roles in reducing the oxidative stress induced by As. In roots, compared to control, the highest APX activity of 227% was recorded on 7 days exposure to 50 μM As(V) in LARG, while HARG displayed the highest induction of 309% at the same exposure. Shoots of LARG at 50 μM As(V) exposure led to a significant enhancement of SOD by 512%, and in HARG its activity increased by 208% (as compared to control). For GPX activity, in all durations HARG genotypes showed higher activity as compared to LARG shoots. Higher induction of anti-oxidant enzymes in HARG genotypes (compared to LARG) was correlated to MDA content (Dave *et al.*, 2012). Application of sodium arsenite (50 and 150 μM and 300 μM; 2 and 4 days) in two varieties (Varuna and Pusa Bold) of *Brassica juncea* showed differential accumulation of As. Increased As tolerance in Pusa Bold was due to the defensive roles of antioxidant enzymes including SOD, CAT and GPX, induction of mitogen-activated protein kinase (MAPK) and upregulation of PCS transcript that produces metal-binding peptides (Gupta *et al.*, 2009).

Modulation of non-enzymatic and enzymatic components was documented in many other plant species. As resulted in elevation of GSH and phytochelatin contents in *Hydrilla verticillata* (Srivastava *et al.*, 2007). Exogenous GSH and cystine supplementation under As stress reduced oxidative stress and restored the growth of rice seedlings (Shri *et al.*, 2009). Exposure of cucumber plant to As increased AsA concentration in hypocotyls and decreased its content in roots (Czech *et al.*, 2008). A marked increase in AsA level and AsA / DHA (ratio of reduced ascorbate, AsA and oxidized ascorbate, DHA) was recorded during As exposure in the fronds of As-hyperaccumulator *Pteris vittata* compared to As-sensitive *P. ensiformis* (Singh *et al.*, 2006). Light harvesting and membrane-associated anti-oxidant activity are important functions of carotenoid. Carotenoids are able to protect from harmful free radicals and ROS produced naturally during photosynthesis (Collins 2001). As (133 μM , 10 days) increased carotenoid content in hyperaccumulator *P. Vitteta* and decreased in *P. ensiformis* (Singh *et al.*, 2006). Carotenoid levels reduced in oat, bean and red clover plants grown in As-contaminated soil (Stoeva *et al.*, 2005). Increase of APX activity has been reported in many crops by other researchers including in mung bean (Singh *et al.*, 2007), bean (Stoeva *et al.*, 2005) and maize (Miteva and Peycheva 1999) exposed to As. As(V) stress caused induction of chloroplast Cu / Zn SOD, Cu / Zn SOD and SOD copper chaperone and resulted in reduction of

Fe SOD (Abercrombie *et al.*, 2008). Stimulation of GR activity in rice seedlings was correlated with higher GSH content in the As-induced oxidatively stressed rice seedlings (Shri *et al.*, 2009). Enhanced GR activity has also been observed in roots of *Pteris vittata, Ptries ensiformis, Nephrolepis exaltata* (Srivastava *et al.*, 2005). Guaiacol per-oxidase activity increased As-induced oxidative stress in mung bean plant (Singh *et al.*, 2007). The GST activity in mesquite and maize plant were also increased by As stress (Mylona *et al.*, 1998; Mokgalaka-Matlala *et al.*, 2009).

In our recent study, we observed that As at different doses (0.25 and 0.5 mM) created oxidative stress which is revealed by the As-induced elevated H_2O_2 and MDA levels. Moreover application of SNP or sodium nitroprusside as a source of NO improved non-enzymatic antioxidan and the enzymatic components of antioxidant systems. Enhanced activities of antioxidant enzymes and improved levels of non-enzymatic components. together acted to reduce the oxidative damage induced by As stress (i.e. H_2O_2 and MDA levels)

Remediation of Arsenic Hazards

Since As pollution in soil and water is becoming a serious threat for crop production worldwide, it is necessary to find suitable mechanisms to cope with As problems. Like other toxic metals, remediation of As toxicity is complex. However, the possible ways to mitigate As problems may include genetic improvement, antioxidant defence, alteration of metabolism and synthesis of PC. Phytoremediation would be an excellent way to remediate As from soils which may limit the As toxicity as plants get a safe environment in which to grow. Different agronomic management, especially water and nutrient management are also found to be somehow effective in mitigating As toxicity. Genetic variation in the response of plants to As in terms of uptake and metabolism provides the potential to devise agronomic cultivars better suited to As-enriched soils.

Agronomic Management

Since irrigation water is one of the most important sources of As contamination in crop fields, the proper management of irrigation may be a strategy to mitigate As toxicity. Farmers often use more irrigation water than needed. Optimizing water input would be a sound option to reduce As input while saving water. Furthermore, aerobic growth conditions in paddy fields may reduce the bio-availability and uptake of As in rice. Breeding of crops plants tolerant to As or low accumulation of As in harvestable parts, cultivation of crops other than rice when water is scarce, etc., may be other options (Shahariar and Huq 2012). Based on a study conducted by Shahariar and Huq (2012), it was reported that growing rice at reduced moisture levels could reduce As toxicity without com-promising the yield. Reduced moisture may also minimize As uptake due to the reduction in phytoavailability, thereby preventing the exposure of

As to food chain as well. Huq *et al.*, (2006) investigated the role of water regime management in mitigation of As in Bangladeshi rice (cv. BRRI dhan28 and BRRI dhan29 grown with added As (0, 10, 20 and 40 mg As kg^{-1} soil). They examined two different water regimes (100 and 75% of field capacity). In roots of BRRRI dhan 28, the maximum As accumulation from As(III)-treated soil was 17.6 mg kg^{-1} dry weight at saturated soil (100% field capacity), whereas at 75% field capacity it was 15.4 mg kg^{-1}. In the case of BRRI dhan29, As accumulation was a bit higher which was determined as 31.04 and 22.65 mg kg^{-1} at irrigation regimes 100 and 75% of field capacity, respectively. Thus it was concluded that As accumulation can be minimized even when rice is grown at 75% field capacity without hampering the yield (Huq *et al.*, 2006). However, it is not suitable where irrigation cut-off has adverse effects on crops' productivity. For instance, in the United States, growing rice in the field with completely dry conditions for 10–14 days just before panicle initiation, significantly reduced As accumulation but the yield was reduced drastically (Brammer, 2007). In such a case, proper timing of irrigation cut-off is an important concern.

Both irrigation and tillage practices can be managed towards the mitigation of As from soil. Talukder *et al.*, (2011) reported that As content of rice straw and grain grown under permanent raised bed (PRB) was six- and three-times, respectively, lower over the As content of rice grown in flat bed conditions. Later, Sarkar *et al.*, (2012) recommended deficit irrigation as an option to mitigate As load of rice grain in West Bengal, India. They observed that addition of As through irrigation water had a direct impact on total As load of the soil. For instance, application of 690 mm of water up to 45 days after transplanting (DAT) under continuous ponding (CP) resulted in the highest concentration (18.18 mg kg^{-1}) of total As in surface soil (0–150 mm). A reduction in the amount of irrigation to 200 and 390 mm, respectively, under intermittent ponding (IP) and aerobic (AER) conditions during 16–45 DAT decreased the As load by 2.98 and 11.22%. Arsenic content in soil, rice root, rice shoot, rice leaf and rice grain was 18.74, 22.14, 2.48, 4.20, 0.56 mg kg^{-1}, respectively, with CP, whereas the As content was 16.22, 20.54, 1.86, 3.51, 0.46 mg kg^{-1}, respectively, with adoption of aerobic conditions. At harvest stage (80 DAT) the differences were 3.06 and 13.43%, respectively. However, they concluded that imposition of IP only during the vegetative stage was found to be optimum in terms of reduction of As content in straw and grain, respectively, by 23 and 33%, over farmers' irrigation practices with insignificant decrease in grain yields (Sarkar *et al.*, 2012).

Fertilizer management was also found to be beneficial in mitigation of As toxicity. Since, phosphorus (P) is a chemical analogue of As (Adriano, 2001) and competes with As in plant uptake (Meharg and Macnair, 1992), the effect of P on the sorption / desorption of As in soil environments has received great attention, especially when P is used as a crop fertilizer (Peryea, 1998b). In a study, shown in this work, the role of P fertilization in preventing As uptake and translocation in wheat plants is highlighted. According to Li *et al.*, (2009) S played important roles in As detoxification and accumulation in As hyperaccumulator *Pteris vittata* and the As-hypertolerant plant *Adiantum capillusveneris* (A. capillusveneris). Under As exposure, sulphydryl groups (–SH) increased in both plants, indicating that arsenate enhanced sulphur assimilation and S then played different roles in the two plants (Li *et al.*, 2009). While studying with *Vigna mungo*, Srivastava and Sharma (2013) found that As-treated plants showed reduction in their growth and pigment content. Arsenic significantly enhanced lipid peroxidation, electrolyte leakage and level of proline and also significantly altered the antioxidant metabolism. However, application of phosphate with As resulted in significant alterations in most of the traits and led to better growth in black gram (*Vigna mungo*). In a recent study, Tripathi *et al.*, (2013) found a beneficial effect of Si on the mitigation of As toxicity in rice. They found that rice plants treated with 1 mM Si reduced As content in rice exposed to 25 μM As. However, in tolerant rice cultivar (Triguna), the effect of cultivar (IET-4786). Reduction of As content in tolerant and sensitive cultivar was 24 and 18% on addition of 1 mM Si. This might be due to the reduction in As(III) uptake by rice because of the direct competition between Si and As(III) during uptake (Ma *et al.*, 2008; Guo *et al.*, 2009).

Alternative farming may be a possible way to mitigate As problems. Substituting dry-land crops such as wheat or maize for rice, or growing rice as a dry-land crop, could reduce the problem of As contamination of soils and food crops. In some countries, research is in progress to breed As-tolerant rice varieties, but the use of such varieties would not reduce the accumulation of As in soils, so it might provide only a short-term, interim measure until an alternative safe irrigation supply could be provided.

Phytoremediation of Arsenic-Contaminated Soils

Phytoremediation or plant-based remediation technology has recently come to the fore as a strategy to clean up contaminated soils and water. Suthersan (2002) defined it as 'the engineered use of plants in situ and ex situ for environmental remediation'. It refers to the use of higher plants and their associated microbiota for the clarification of soil, sediment and groundwater; selected plant species acquire the genetic potential to remove, degrade, metabolize or immobilize a number of contaminants including metals and metalloids. Phytoremediation is a cost-effective 'green' technology which is non-intrusive, aesthetically pleasing, socially accepted technology to remediate polluted soils (Garbisu *et al.*, 2002; Kachout *et al.*, 2010; Hasanuzzaman and Fujita, 2012). There are differ-ent processes of phytoremediation such as phytoextraction / phytoaccumulation, phytostabilization, phytodegradation / phytotransformation, rhizofiltration, rhizodegradation, phytovolatilization and phytorestauration (Hasanuzzaman and Fujita, 2012).

Although there are several processes of phytoremediation, phytoextraction is the most important and has been extensively studied. This remediation technique is employed to recover metals from contaminated soils using non-food crops where metals are absorbed by roots and subsequently translocated within the above-ground parts of plants. Genetic and physiological potential of some plants species making them effective to accumulate, translocate and tolerate high concentration of metals and are used for phytoextraction. According to Chaney *et al.*, (1997), naturally occurring plants called 'metal hyperaccumulators' can accumulate 10- to 500-times higher levels of toxic metals than cultivated crops. The efficiency of phytoextraction is determined by the accumulation factor, indicating the ratio of toxic metal concentrations in the plant organs (shoots, roots) and in the soil and the seasonally harvestable plant biomass (Kvesitadze *et al.*, 2006). There are three processes that regulate the movement of toxic metals from root tips to xylem (root symplasm). The sequestration of toxic metals occurs inside cells; they are then subjected to symplastic transport to the stele, and subsequent release into the xylem). Generally, the toxic metal such as As content in a plant body decreases in the following sequence: root > leaves > stems > inflorescence > seed (Lal, 2010). However, the metal-accumulating capacity greatly varies with plant species.

To date, more than 400 hyperaccumulating species have been reported, but only a few species belong to As hyperaccumulators such as *Pteris vittata, P. cretica, P. longifolia, P. umbrosa, Pityrogramma calomelanos, Dryopteris jux-taposita and Nephrodium molle* are able to hyper accumulate As when grown in soils added with As (Ma *et al.*, 2001; Visoottiviseth *et al.*, 2002; Zhao *et al.*, 2002; Meharg, 2003; Chen *et al.*, 2003; Hossain *et al.*, 2006). Some other higher classes of terrestrial and aquatic plant species have been reported for their potential towards As removal and remediation from soils and waters. Mediterranean aquatic plants such as *Apium nodiflorum* have widespread applications in removing As(V) from water, sediments and soils (Vlyssides *et al.*, 2005). In fact, separating As from soil is difficult because As is strongly retained by the soil, especially in oxidizing environments and at low pH. Even after its entry into the roots, As is not readily transported to the leaves of most plants (Pickering *et al.*, 2000). Therefore, to make the phytoextraction of As more effective, it is essential to find the means to enhance the transport of As from the root system to stems and leaves, where the metal can be easily harvested. In As-hyperaccumulating species, such as Chinese brake fern (*Pteris vittata*), As is rapidly transported as AsO_3^{3-} through the xylem to the fronds rather than being immobilized in the rhizoids (Su *et al.*, 2008). There are many reports on the potential use of *Pteris* spp. in remediating As-contaminated sites. Ma *et al.*, (2001) first reported the As-hyperaccumulator *P. vittata* that accumulated As in shoots up to 22,000 mg kg^{-1} (Huang *et al.*, 2004). Later, Salido *et al.*, (2003) observed that *P. vittata* could accumulate a huge amount of As in the above-ground plant tissue as much as

200-fold higher than most other plant species examined in As-contaminated soil. Hossain *et al.,* (2006) compared the ability of two Bangladeshi indigenous ferns, namely, *P. vittata* and *Nephrodium molle,* for their hyperaccumulation of As when grown in 0–100 mg As kg^{-1} soil. It was observed that *P. vittata* could remove more than 95% of the soil As, whereas the removal by *N. molle* was about 68% (Hossain *et al.,* 2006). Some ferns such as *Salvinia natans* (Mukherjee and Kumar, 2005) and *P. vittata* (Fitz *et al.,* 2003; Embrick *et al.,* 2005; Pickering *et al.,* 2006; Baldwin and Butcher, 2007; Wei *et al.,* 2007) showed enhanced capacity to accumulate As. Huang *et al.,* (2004) reported that *P. vittata* suspended in water with 20–500 μg l^{-1} of A(V) could remove 98.6% of 200 μg/l^{-1} of As within 24 h. Conversely, in a field study in Australia, Reichmann *et al.,* (2004) indicated that the ability of *P. vittata* to accumulate As from an As-contaminated soil decreased after subsequent frond harvests; however, fern species could not regrow well in the field which indicates their inefficiency for practical applications for the phytoremediation of As in Australian conditions. In a copper-chromium arsenate (CCA)-contaminated site of the United States, Kertulis–Tartar *et al.,* (2006) reported that *P. vittata* reduced the mean total As content in the sur-face (0–15 cm) soil from 190 to 140 mg kg^{-1} over 2 years and it was estimated that *P. vittata* would take 8 years to reduce the total As content in soil below 3.7 mg kg^{-1}. In China, a field survey was conducted by Wang *et al.,* (2006) investigating 24 fern species where fronds of four species (*Pteris vittata, P. multifida, P. cretica* var. *nervosa* and *P. oshimensis*) accumulated up to 9677 (range 57– 9677), 4056 (624–4056), 2363 (1162–2363) and 2142 (301–2142) mg As kg^{-1}, respectively. In their report, Sridokchan *et al.,* (2005) reported that As-tolerant ferns (*Adiantum capillus-veneris, Pteris cretica* var. albolineata, *Pteris cretica* var. wimsetti and *Pteris umbrosa*) were from the Pteridaceae family. *P. cretica* and *P. umbrosa* accumulated the majority of As in their fronds (up to 3090 mg As kg^{-1} dry weight) compared to the roots (up to 760 mg As kg^{-1}) and these ferns may be useful for phytoremediating As-contaminated sites because of their ability to hyperaccumulate and tolerate high As levels. Srivastava *et al.,* (2006) showed that *P. cretica, Pteris biaurita* L., *P. quadriaurita* Retz and *P. ryukyuensis Tagawa* could be used as new hyperaccumulators of As because the average As concentration ranged from 1770 to 3650 mg kg^{-1} dry weight in the fronds and 182–507 mg kg^{-1} dry weight in the roots of *P. cretica, P. biaurita, P. quadriaurita* and *P. ryukyuensis* when grown in soil with 100 mg As kg^{-1}. It is not always true that a species must be As-tolerant to be a hyperaccumulator. They first reported that ferns that are sensitive to As are As hyperaccumulators. For instance, *Asplenium australasicum* and *A. bulbiferum* could hyperaccumu-late As up to 1240 and 2630 mg As kg^{-1} dry weight, respectively, in their fronds after 7 days at 100 mg As l^{-1} (Sridokchan *et al.,* 2005). However, not all members of the *Pteris* genus are able to hyperaccumulate As. For example, Meharg (2003) found that *Pteris tremula* and *Pteris stramina* do not hyperaccumulate As. To date, the only non-*Pteris* fern to exhibit this ability is *P. calomelanos* (Francesconi *et al.*, 2002).

In Bangladesh, marigold (*Tagetes patula*) and ornamental arum (*Syngonuma* sp.) were also found to have the capacity to accumulate large amount of As which made them good candidates for phytoremediation of As-contaminated soil (Huq *et al.*, 2005). Japanese mustard spinach (*Brassica rapa* L. var. *pervirdis*) exposed to 67 μM As in a hydroponic system could accumulate 90.3 mg kg^{-1} As in shoots; however, in roots, the As concentration was much higher, that is, 4840 mg kg^{-1} without showing visible toxicity symptoms (Shaibur and Kawai, 2009). Khan *et al.*, (2009) exposed Indian mustard to 25 μM of As for 96 h and observed that root tissues accumulated 211 mg As kg^{-1} dry weight while As accumulation in the shoot was 322 mg As kg^{-1} dry weight. Alvarado *et al.*, (2008) monitored the removal of As by water hyacinth (*Eichhornia crassipes*) and lesser duckweed (*Lemna minor*) grown in a site having 0.15 mg l^{-1} As and with plant densities of 1 kg m^{-2} for lesser duckweed and 4 kg m^{-2} for water hyacinth (wet basis). Although no significant difference was observed in the bioaccumulation capability of these species, the removal rate of As was significant which accounted for 600 mg As ha^{-1} per day and 140 mg As ha^{-1} per day by *Eichhornia crassipes* and *L. minor*, respectively, with a removal recovery of 18 and 5%. Ozturk *et al.*, (2010) grew watercress (*Nasturtium officinale*) in 1, 3, 5, 10 and 50 μM AsO_3^{3-} and found that the leaves accumulated 1012 mg kg^{-1} dry weight of AsO_3^{3-} after 7 days of exposure. However, growth was negatively affected by higher doses of As. In another experiment conducted in a desert area, Vromman *et al.*, (2011) found that *Atriplex atacamensis* exposed to elevated As, could accumulate up to 400 mg kg^{-1} dry weight in the shoots and 3500 mg kg^{-1} dry weight in the roots which may act as a promising plant species that can be tested in field trials for its phytoremediation of As contamination. Islam *et al.*, (2013) investigated the phytoaccumulation potential of *E. crassipes* (water hyacinth), *Echinochloa crusgalli* (barnyard grass) and *Monochoria hastata* (water taro) in crop land soils contaminated by As naturally and artificially. In artificially As-contaminated soils, the highest As concentration was recorded in water hyacinth (68 and 47 mg kg^{-1} root and shoot, respectively) followed by water taro and barnyard grass at 100 mg As kg^{-1} treated soil. In naturally As-contaminated soils, the highest accumulation of As in barn-yard grass (57 and 27 mg kg^{-1} root and shoot, respectively) followed by water taro and water hyacinth in *Paranpur* soils (116 mg As kg^{-1} soil). Talukdar (2013a) investigated two *Leucaena* species for their As phytoaccumulation capacity in soil. They observed that between the two species, *Leucaena leucocephala* shoots accumulated significantly higher amounts of soil As compared to *L. esculenta*. *Leucaena leucocephala* grown in 100 mg kg^{-1} As accumulated 1.88, 67.88, 3.51, 45.99 and 2.17 mg kg^{-1} of As in their root, stem, leaf, pod and seed, respectively; while *L. esculenta* trapped most of the added As in their roots and could accumulate it in the above-ground parts.

This high bioaccumulation was due to efficient translocation of As from roots to above-ground parts (Talukdar, 2013b). The bioconcentration factors and translocation factors (TF) of plants are important for them to be potential candidates in phytoremediation, and these vary among the plant species (Dabrowska *et al.*, 2012). Bioconcentration is the ratio of the As concentration in plants to the concentration in soil, while the TF, also termed as shoot: root quotient is the ratio of the As concentration in roots to the concentration in shoots (Baker and Whiting, 2002; Mudhoo *et al.*, 2011) expressed as As concentration in the shoot in relation to As concentration in the root. Arsenic-tolerant plants translocate less than 2.8% As to the parts above-ground leading to low accumulation. For example, hyperaccumulators had values about two magnitudes higher, for example, 23.86 for *P. vittata* (Ma *et al.*, 2001), and 90.91 for *Pityrogramma calomelanos* (Franseconi *et al.*, 2002). The use of algae in bioremediation of As has been reported in a number of studies (Megharaja *et al.*, 2003; Shamsuddoha *et al.*, 2006). It has been observed that algae can hyperaccumulate As from water (Huq, *et al.*, 2005; Shamsuddoha *et al.*, 2006). Huq *et al.*, (2007) reported that the presence of algae in the growth medium reduces As accumulation in rice and the algae *Gloeotrichia, Oscillatoria, Chlamydomona, Lyngbya, Chlorella. Nitzschi* and *Navicula* were found to accumulate considerabe amounts of As in rice fields. Several research results suggested that some As-resistant bacteria may be applied to the bioremediation of As-contaminated sites. Interest in using soil bacteria in bioremediation of As has increased over the years, and the continuous advancements in molecular as well as biochemical techniques have helped to identify and characterize these microbes, to play a major role in understanding the underlying mechanisms of these processes (Bachate *et al.*, 2009; Hossain, 2012). Bachate *et al.*, (2009) isolated a total of 21 As-resistant bacteria in agricultural soils of Bangladesh and most of them were found to be capable of reducing As(V) to As(III) leading to the detoxification of As under anaerobic conditions. In recent years, the use of arbuscular mycorrhizal (AM) fungi to alleviate metal toxicity has come into focus (Long *et al.*, 2010). The role of mycor-rhiza in the growth of plants and in reducing As toxicity in plants has been demonstrated by Ahmed *et al.*, (2006). They examined the effects of As and inoculation with an AM fungus, *Glomus mosseae*, on *Lens culinaris* and it was observed that, besides improvements in growth and yield of the crop, *mycorrhizal inoculation* significantly reduced As concentration in roots and shoots. Jankong and Visoottiviseth (2008) reported that the effects of AM on reducing As toxicity vary with the host plant species. While studying the effects of AM fungi (*Glomus mosseae, G. intraradices* and *G. etunicatum*) on biomass production and As accumulation in *Pityrogramma calomelanos, Tagetes erecta* and *Melastomama labathricum*, they observed a great variability in the effects of AM fungi on phytoremediation of As by different plant species. For *P. calomelanos* and *T. erecta*, AM fungi reduced only As accumulation in plants, but had no significant effect on plant growth. In contrast, AM fungi improved growth and As accumulation in *M. malabathricum*. According to Cozzolino *et al.*, (2010), with phosphorus addition, inoculation with commercial inoculum of AM fungi reduced As toxicity which was due to the improvement of phosphorus nutrition and inhibiting As accumulation in plants. Christophersen *et al.*, (2009) revealed a strong interaction between As exposure and colonization of AM fungi retarded the As uptake which is lacking in non-mycorrhizal plants. An agricultural field is a complex system where a number of factors such as crop plants, weeds, microbes, management activities and environmental factors including climate interact with each other (Hossain, 2012). Success of the application of a biological agent for bioremediation will depend on the interactions of all these factors. Therefore, it is important to have a detailed knowledge of the effects of all these factors before starting a bioremediation program (Hossain, 2012). Although As is not a true metal, many studies revealed the vital role of PCs in both constitutive and adaptive tolerances to As. Schulz *et al.*, (2008) investigated six non-hyperaccumulating plant species (*Agropyron repens, Glechoma hederacea, Leonurus marrubiatrum, Lolium perenne, Urtica dio-ica* and *Zea mays*) and observed the role of PCs in the detoxification of As. They found that long-term (5-week) PC synthesis was positively, but non-linearly correlated with As, which proved that probably not all As is bound by PC. In the more tolerant grasses, *A. repens* and *L. perrenne*, it was chiefly the dithiol PCs which were observed. Conversly, the dominant PC species found in the less tolerant plants *V. dicica, G. herderaceae, L. marrubiastrum* and *Z. mays* was PCs, while PC2 and PC3 were detected as well (Schulz *et al.*, 2008). Tolerance to As is enhanced by increased thiol synthesis in transgenic plants overexpressing the genes of thiol (cysteine, GSH or PC) biosynthesis pathway (Tripathi *et al.*, 2007; Gasic and Korban 2007; Wojas *et al.*, 2008, 2010). An As-accumulating, hypertolerant *Brassica, Isatis cap-padocica* (Karimi *et al.*, 2009), collected from Iranian As-contaminated mine had PC-based tolerance (> 50% As complexed with PCs) rather than through suppression of high-affinity PO_4^{3-} / AsO_4^{3-} root transport. These findings provide conclusive evidence that thiols, particularly PCs, play a crucial role in As detoxification. Although the essentiality of PCs in both constitutive and adaptive tolerance to As is reported (Schat *et al.*, 2002), PCs do not contribute significantly towards As tolerance phenotype in hypertolerant (*H. lanatus* and *Silene paradoxa*) and hyperaccumulator plants (*P. vittata* and *P. cretica*) because of lower synthesis of PCs in these cases (Raab *et al.*, 2004; Arnetoli *et al.*, 2008). Schmöger *et al.*, (2000) reported that both As(III) and As(V) anions efficiently induce the biosynthesis of PC in vivo and in vitro. The rapid induction of the metal-binding PCs has been observed in cell suspension cultures of *Rau-volfia serpentina*, in seedlings of *Arabidopsis* and in enzyme preparations of *Silene vulgaris* upon challenge to arsenicals. Wojasa *et al.*, (2010) determined overexpression of either of two phytochelatin synthase genes, *AtPCS1* and *CePCS* in *Nicotiana tabacum* with respect to As tolerance and accumulation, and observed how responses relate to non-protein thiol metabolism. The expression of both genes resulted in an increase in As tolerance which was higher at *CePCS*. At the less toxic 50 μM As(V), *AtPCS1* and *CePCS* transformants accumulated more As in roots and leaves than wild type. An increase in PC production and the level of PC2 species were detected in leaves of *AtPCS1* and *CePCS* plants, which might explain their enhanced As accumulation and tolerance. Conversely, at the highly toxic 200 μM As(V), several disturbances in –SH metabolism of PCS-overexpressing plants were found, unexpectedly, including a decrease in PC levels both in roots and leaves of transgenic plants compared to wild type. Importantly, the plants overexpressing *AtPCS1* and *CePCS* showed increased tolerance to As, making these genes potential candidates for plant engineering for phytoremediation.

Role of Biotechnology in Remediation of Arsenic Toxicity

Biotechnology has changed our perception in almost every field of life. From food security to remediating hazardous elements from the environment, it has proved its mettle. Bioremediation, a cost effective and nature-friendly biotechnology that is powered by microbial enzymes, is effectively being used to remove hazardous materials from soil and water. Since heavy metals are ubiquitous in the environment, microorganisms have developed mechanisms to resist the toxic effects of these metals (White and Gadd, 1986). A large number of microorganisms are capable of growing in the presence of high concentrations of heavy metals including As (Anderson and Cook, 2004; Rehman *et al.*, 2007). Many strains of *Aeromonas, Exiguobacterium, Acinetobacter, Bacillus* and *Pseudomonas* can tolerate high concentrations of As species (up to 100 mM arsenate or up to 20 mM arsenit). Several Bacteria belonging to the genera *Acidithiobacillus, Bacillus, Deinococcus, Desulfitobacterium* and *Pseudomonas* (Suresh *et al.*, 2004; Ahmed and Rehman, 2009) have also been reported to be resistant to As. The information on the mechanisms of bioremediation-related enzymes such as oxido-reductases and hydrolases has been extensively studied.

Arsenic is also phytoremediated by genetically modified plants such as *Arabidopsis thaliana* which expresses two bacterial genes. One of these genes allows the plant to modify arsenate into arsenite, and the second one binds the modified arsenite and stores it in the vacuoles (Leung, 2004). Anawar (2006) reported that the plant species *Spergula arvensis, Phalasis caerulescens* and *Junsus effuses* can be used to partly remove the bioavailable toxic As, or transgenic plants may be transplanted via *Escherichia coli* genes for the phytoremediation of As-contaminated soils. These hyperaccumulating fern species available in the tropics may be commercially used in south-east Asia as a form of bioremediation technology.

Conclusion and Future Perspectives

There is growing apprehension regarding As toxicity because of its severe adverse effects on both plants and animals, including humans. Because of the entrance of As into the food chain from different routes, it has become a great conc. In recent years, considerable research has been carried out into understanding the physiological and molecular mechanisms of As uptake and transport in plants. However, the exact molecular basis of As hyperaccumulation by plants is still unknown. Therefore, future research should focus on the molecular approaches and biotechnological tools and, perhaps, transgenic plants with increased resistance and uptake. Adaption of multiple approaches is important for managing As toxicity. Phytoremediation can be considered as an effective technique to clean up soil by growing As-hyperaccumulating plants in As-toxic soil. Phytochelatin formation within the plants' cells is, thus, one of the basic mechanisms and is very important for the accumulation of As within the cell. Development of plant species having highe phytochelatin synthase activity or capacity to accumulate higher amounts of As by phytochelain formation, or development of plant species having thiol metabolism through transgenic or biotechnological approaches, might be good tools for reducing As toxicity. Polyomic approaches like proteomics, genomics, micromics, transcriptomics, metablomics, inomics, metallomics, etc. have emerged as powerful tools for understanding the mechanisms of plant responses under different stresses, and similar approaches might be considered in As stress. In relation to this, research on As transportation and safe sequestration in the cell are vital. Identification and characterization of microbes degrading As or its compounds in the soil is important. In fact, the aptitude of existing plant species or microbes, especially those grown in As-toxic environments, should be studied in detail; their metabolic profiles should be explored. Suitability of different agronomic practices should be studied, selected and applied considering soil, water and environmental status of a certain area where presence and types of biota including human, animal, plant and microbial, are important considerations. Planning on combined utilization of plants, microbes and agronomic practices with a view to remediating the dangerous As toxicity is vital, and cooperation among plant physiologists, microbiologists, agronomists and environmentalists is necessary, not to mention the importance of the involvement of government or non-government organizations in this combined project.

REFERENCES

Abercrombie, J.M., Halfhill, M.D., Ranjan, P., Rao, M.R., Saxton, A.M., Yuan, J.S., Stewart Jr, C.N., 2008. Transcriptional Responses of *Arabidopsis Thaliana* Plants to As(V) Stress. BMC Plant Biol. 8, 87.

Adriano, D.C., 2001. Trace Elements in Terrestrial Environments: Biogeochemistry, Bioavailability and Risks of Metals, Second edn. Springer, New York.

Afrous, A., Manshouri, M., Liaghat, A., Pazira, E., Sedghi, H., 2011. Mercury and Arsenic Accu-mulation by three Species of Aquatic Plants in Dezful, Iran. Afr. J. Agric. Res. 6, 5391–5397.

Ahmed, F.R.S., Killham, K., Alexander, I., 2006. Influences of Arbuscular Mycorrhizal Fungus *Glo-mus Mosseae* on Growth and Nutrition of Lentil Irrigated with Arsenic Contaminated Water. Plant Soil 258, 33–41.

Ahmed, A., Rehman, A., 2009. Isolation of Cr(VI) Reducing Bacteria from Industrial Effluents and their Potential use in Bioremediation of Chromium Containing Wastewater. J. Environ. Sci. 21, 814–820.

Ahsan, N., Lee, D.G., Alam, I., Kim, P.J., Lee, J.J., Ahn, Y.O., Kwak, S.S., Lee, I.J., Bahk, J.D., Kang, K.Y., Renaut, J., Komatsu, S., Lee, B.H., 2008. Comparative Proteomic Study of Arsenic-induced Differentially Expressed Proteins in Rice Roots Reveals Glutathione Plays a Central Role During As stress. Proteomics 8, 3561–3576.

Ahsan, N., Lee, D.G., Kim, K.H., Alam, I., Lee, S.H., Lee, K.W., Lee, H., Lee, B.H., 2010. Analysis of Arsenic Stress-induced Differentially Expressed Proteins in Rice Leaves by two-Dimensional Gel Electrophoresis Coupled with Mass Spectrometry. Chemosphere 78, 224–231.

Alam, M.B., Sattar, M.A., 2000. Assessment of Arsenic Contamination in Soils and Waters in Some Areas of Bangladesh. Water Sci. Technol. 42, 185–192.

Ali, M.A., Badruzzaman, A.B.M., Jalil, M.A., Hossain, M.D., Ahmed, M.F., Masud, A.A., Kamruzzaman, M., Rahman, M.A., 2003. Arsenic in Plant and Soil Environment of Bangladesh. In: Feroze, A.M., Ashraf, A.M., Adeel, Z. (Eds.), Fate of Arsenic in the Environment. Ban-gladesh University of Engineering and Technology, Dhaka, Bangladesh, and United Nations University, Tokyo, pp. 85–112.

Alvarado, S., Guedez, M., Lue-Meru, M.P., Nelson, G., Alvaro, A., Jesus, A.C., Gyula, Z., 2008. Arsenic Removal from Waters by Bioremediation with the Aquatic Plants water Hyacinth (*Eich-hornia Crassipes*) and Lesser Duckweed (*Lemna Minor*). Bioresour. Technol. 99, 8436–8440.

Anderson, C.R., Cook, G.M., 2004. Isolation and Characterization of Arsenate-Reducing Bacteria from Arsenic Contaminated Sites in New Zealand. Curr. Microbiol. 48, 341–347.

Anawar, H.M., 2006. Exposure and Bioavailability of Arsenic in Contaminated Soils from the La Parilla Mine, Spain. Environ. Geol. 50, 170–179.

Araújo, W.L., Tohge, T., Ishizaki, K., Leaver, C.J., Fernie, A.R., 2011. Protein Degradation—An Alternative Respiratory Substrate for Stressed Plants. Trends Plant Sci. 16, 489–498.

Arnetoli, M., Vooijs, R., ten Bookum, W., Galardi, F., Gonnelli, C., Gabbrielli, R., Schat, H., Verkleij, J.A.C., 2008. Arsenate Tolerance in *Silene Paradoxa* does not Rely on Phytochelatin-dependent Sequestration. Environ. Pollut. 152, 585–591.

Ashraf, M., 2009. Biotechnological Approach of Improving Plant Salt Tolerance Using Antioxidants as Markers. Biotechnol. Adv. 27, 84–93.

Avron, M., Jagendorf, A., 1959. Evidence Concerning The Mechanism of Adenosine Triphosphate Formation by Spinach Chloroplasts. J. Biol. Chem. 234, 967–972.

Azad, M.A.K., Mondal, A.H.M.F.K., Hossain, M.I., Moniruzzaman, M., 2012. Effect of Arsenic Amended Irrigation Water on Growth and Yield of BR-11 Rice (*Oryza sativa* L.) Grown in Open Field Gangetic Soil Condition in Rajshahi. J. Environ. Sci. Nat. Resour. 5, 55–59.

Bachate, S.P., Cavalca, L., Andreoni, V., 2009. Arsenic Resistant Bacteria Isolated from Agricultural Soils of Bangladesh and Characterization of Arsenate-reducing Strains. J. Appl. Microbiol. 107, 145–156.

Baker, A.J.M., Whiting, S.N., 2002. In Search of the Holy Grail—A Further Step in Understanding Metal Hyperaccumulation? New Phytol. 155, 1–7.

Baldwin, P.R., Butcher, D.J., 2007. Phytoremediation of Arsenic by Two Hyperaccumulators in a Hydroponic Environment. Microchem. J. 85, 297–300.

Banglapedia, 2013. Arsenic. In: Banglapedia – The National Encyclopedia of Bangladesh. Asiatic Society of Bangladesh, Dhaka.

Ben Hassine, A., Ghanem, M.E., Bouzid, S., Lutts, S., 2008. An Inland and a Coastal Population of the Mediterranean Xero-Halophyte Species *Atriplex halimus* L. Differ in their Ability to Accumulate Proline and Glycinebetaine in Response to Salinity and Water Stress. J. Exp. Bot. 59, 1315–1326.

Benbrahim-Tallaa, L., Waalkes, M.P., 2008. Inorganic Arsenic and Human Prostate Cancer. Envi-ron. Health Perspect. 116, 158–164.

BGS, 1999. British Geological Survey. Groundwater Studies for Arsenic Contamination in Bangladesh: Final Report. V. I. Summary. Department of Public Health Engineering, Govern-ment of Bangladesh, Dhaka. p. 21.

BGS / DPHE (British Geological Survey / Department of Public Health Engineering [Bangladesh]), 2001. In: Kinniburgh, D.G., Smedley, P.L. (Eds.), Arsenic Contamination of Groundwater in Bangladesh. Report WC/00/19, British Geological Survey, Keyworth.

Bock, R., 2007. Structure, Function, and Inheritance of Plastid Genomes. In: Bock, R. (Ed.), Cell and Molecular Biology of Plastids, Topics in Current Genetics, Vol. 19. Springer, Berlin, pp. 29–62.

Bolan, N.S., Thiyagarajan, S., 2001. Retention and Plant Availability of Chromium in Soils as Affected by Lime and Organic Amendments. Aust. J. Soil Res. 39, 1091–1103.

Bondada, B.R., Tu, S., Ma, L.Q., 2004. Absorption of Foliar-applied Arsenic by the Arsenic Hyperac-cumulating fern (*Pteris vittata* L.). Sci. Total Environ. 332, 61–70.

Brammer, H., 2007. Arsenic Accumulation in Irrigated Paddy Soils and Possible Mitigation Meth-ods. Proceedings of a Symposium: Arsenic—The Geography of a Global problem, Royal Geo-graphical Society (RGS) in London.

Brammer, H., 2009. Mitigation of Arsenic Contamination in Irrigated Paddy Soils in South and South-east Asia. Environ. Int. 35, 856–863.

Brammer, H., Ravenscroft, P., 2009. Arsenic in Groundwater: A Threat to Sustainable Agriculture in South and South-east Asia. Environ. Int. 35, 647–654.

Bravin, M.N., Travassac, F., Le Floch, M., Hinsinger, P., Garnier, J.M., 2008. Oxygen Input Controls the Spatial and Temporal Dynamics of Arsenic at the Surface of a Flooded Paddy Soil and in the Rhizosphere of Lowland rice (*Oryza sativa* L.): A Microcosm Study. Plant Soil 312, 207–218.

Briat, J.F., 2010. Arsenic Tolerance in Plants: "Pas De Deux" Between Phytochelatin Synthesis and ABCC Vacuolar Transporters. Proc. Natl. Acad. Sci. USA. 107, 20853–20854.

BRRI, 2013. Bangladesh Rice Research Institute. www.brri.gov.bd.

Callender, E., 2003. Heavy Metals in The Environment—Historical Tends. Treat. Geochem. 9, 67–105.

Carbonell, A.A., Aarabi, M.A., Delaune, R.D., Gambrell, R.P., Patrick Jr., W.H., 1998. Arsenic in Wetland Vegetation: Availability, Phytotoxicity, Uptake and Effects on Plant Growth and Nutri-tion. Sci. Total. Environ. 217, 189.

Chakrabarty, D., Trivedi, P.K., Misra, P., Tiwari, M., Shri, M., Shukla, D., Kumar, S., Rai, A., Pandey, A., Nigam, D., Tripathi, R.D., Tuli, R., 2009. Comparative Transcriptome Analysis of Arsenate and Arsenite Stresses in Rice Seedlings. Chemosphere 74, 688–702.

Chaney, R.L., Malik, M., Li, Y.M., Brown, S.L., Brewer, E.P., Angle, J.S., Baker, A.J., 1997. Phy-toremediation of Metals. Curr. Opin. Biotechnol. 8, 279–284.

Chatterjee, A., Mukherjee, A., 1999. Hydrogeological Investigation of Ground Water Arsenic Contamination in South Calcutta. Sci. Total Environ. 225, 249–262.

Chen, T., Yan, X., Liao, X., Xiao, X., Huang, Z., Xie, H., Zhai, L., 2005. Subcellular Distribution and Compartmentalization of Arsenic in *Pteris vittata* L. Chin. Sci. Bull. 50, 2843–2849.

Chen, T.B., Huang, Z.C., Huang, Y.Y., Xie, H., Liao, X.Y., 2003. Cellular Distribution of Arsenic and other Elements in Hyperaccumulator *Pteris Nervosa* and their Relations to Arsenic Accumulation. Chin. Sci. Bull. 48, 1586–1591.

Choudhury, Q.R.M.D., Islam, T.S., Alam, R., Sen, R., Hasan, J.G.M., Chowdhury, I.A.M.D., 2009. Effect of Arsenic Contaminated Irrigation Water on the Cultivation of red Amaranth. Am-Eur J. Sci. Res. 4, 14–19.

Christophersen, H.M., Smith, F.A., Smith, S.E., 2009. Arbuscularmycorrhizal Colonization Reduces Arsenate Uptake in Barley Via Downregulation of Transporters in the Direct Epidermal Phosphate Uptake Pathway. New Phytol. 184, 962–974.

Chun-xi, L., Shu-li, F., Yun, S., Li-na, J., Xu-yang, L., Xiao-li, H., 2007. Effects of Arsenic on Seed Germination and Physiological Activities of Wheat Seedlings. J. Environ. Sci. 19, 725–732.

Collins, A., 2001. Carotenoids and Genomic Stability. Mutat. Res. 475, 1–28.

Cozzolino, V., Pigna, M., Di Meo, V., Caporale, A.G., Violante, A., 2010. Effects of Arbuscular Mycorrhizal Inoculation and Phosphorus Supply on the Growth of *Lactuca sativa* L. and Arsenic and Phosphorus Availability in an Arsenic Polluted Soil under Nonsterile Conditions. Appl. Soil Ecol. 45, 262–268.

Cullen, W.R., 2008. Is Arsenic an Aphrodisiac? The Sociochemistry of an Element. Royal Society of Chemistry, Cambridge, U.K.

Czech, V., Czovek, P., Fodor, J., Boka, K., Fodor, F., Cseh, E., 2008. Investigation of Arsenate Phy-totoxicity in Cucumber Plants. Acta Biol. Szeged 52, 79–80.

Dabrowska, B.B., Vithanage, M., Gunaratna, K.R., Mukherjee, A.B., Bhattacharya, P., 2012. Bio-remediation of Arsenic in Contaminated Terrestrial and Aquatic Environments. In: Lichtfouse, E., Schwarzbauer, J., Robert, D. (Eds.). Environmental Chemistry for a Sustainable World: Reme-diation of Air and Water Pollution, vol. 2. Springer, New York, pp. 475–509.

Dahal, B.M., Fuerhacker, M., Mentler, A., Karki, K.B., Shrestha, R.R., Blum, W.E.H., 2008. Arse-nic Contamination of Soils and Agricultural Plants through Irrigation Water in Nepal. Environ. Pollut. 155, 157–163.

Das, H.K., Mitra, A.K., Sengupta, P.K., Hossain, A., Islam, F., Rabbani, G.H., 2004. Arsenic Con-centrations in rice, Vegetables, and Fish in Bangladesh: A Preliminary Study. Environ. Int. 30, 383–387.

Dave, R., Tripathi, R.D., Dwivedi, S., Tripathi, P., Dixit, G., Sharma, Y.K., Trivedi, P.K., Corpas, F.J., Barroso, J.B., Chakrabarty, D., 2012. Arsenate and Arsenite Exposure Modulate Antioxi-dants and Amino Acids in Contrasting Arsenic Accumulating Rice (*Oryza Sativa* L.) Genotypes. J. Hazard. Mater. http://dx.doi.org/10.1016/j.jhazmat.

Delgado, M., Bigeriego, M., Guardiola, E., 1993. Uptake of Zn, Cr and Cd by Water Hyacinth. Water Res. 27, 269–272.

Del-Toro-Sánchez, C.L., Zurita, F., Gutiérrez-Lomelí, M., Solis-Sánchez, B., Wence-Chávez, L., Rodríguez-Sahagún, A., Castellanos-Hernández, O.A., Vázquez-Armenta, G., Siller-López, F., 2013. Modulation of Antioxidant Defense System after Long Term Arsenic

Exposure in *Zantede-schia Aethiopica* and *Anemopsis Californica*. Ecotoxicol. Environ. Saf. 94, 67–72.

DPHE, 2013. Department of Public Health and Engineering, Government of the People's Republic of Bangladesh. www.dphe.gov.bd.

Duman, F., Ozturk, F., Aydin, Z., 2010. Biological Responses of Duckweed (*Lemna Minor* L.) Exposed to the Inorganic Arsenic Species As(III) and As(V): Effects of Concentration and Duration of Exposure. Ecotoxicol. 19, 983–993.

Duquesnoy, I., Champeau, G.M., Evray, G., Ledoigt, G., Piquet-Pissaloux, A., 2010. Enzymatic Adaptations to Arsenic-induced Oxidative Stress in *Zea Mays* and Genotoxic Effect of Arsenic in Root Tips of *Vicia Faba* and *Zea Mays*. C. R. Biol. 333, 814–824.

Duxbury, J.M., Zavala, Y.Z., 2005. What are Safe Levels of Arsenic in Food and Soils? In Behavior of Arsenic in Aquifers, Soils and Plants: Implications for Management. International Symposium Held in Dhaka, Bangladesh. Jan. 16–18, 2005. Organized by CIMMYT, CU, TAMU, USGS, and GSB.

Duxbury, J.M., Mayer, A.B., Lauren, J.G., Hassan, N., 2003. Food Chain Aspects of Arsenic Contamination in Bangladesh: Effects on Quality and Productivity of rice. J. Environ. Sci. Health 38, 61–69.

Eisler, R., 2004. Arsenic Hazards to Humans, Plants, and Animals from Gold Mining. Rev. Environ. Contam. Toxicol. 180, 133–165.

Embrick, L.L., Porter, K.M., Pendergrass, A., Butcher, D.J., 2005. Characterization of Lead and Arsenic Contamination at Barber Orchard, Haywood County, NC. Microchem. J. 81, 117–121.

Faisal, M., Hasnain, 2005. Chromate Resistant *Bacillus Cereus* Aguments Sunflower Growth by Reducing Toxicity of Cr(VI). J Plant Biol. 48, 187–194.

FAO (Food and Agriculture Organization), 2006. Arsenic Contamination of Irrigation Water, Soil and Crops in Bangladesh: Risk Implications for Sustainable Agriculture and Food Safety in Asia. RAP Publication 2006/20. FAO Regional Office for Asia and the Pacific, Bangkok, Thailand. 38 pp.

Fayiga, A.O., Ma, L.Q., Santoa, J., Rathinasabapathi, B., Stamps, B., Littell, R.C., 2005. Effects of Arsenic Species and Concentrations on Arsenic Accumulation by Different Fern Species in a Hydroponic System. Int. J. Phytoremed. 7, 231–240.

Fazal, M.A., Kawachi, T., Ichion, E., 2001a. Validity of the Latest Research Findings on Causes of Groundwater Arsenic Contamination in Bangladesh. Water Int. 26, 380–389.

Fazal, M.A., Kawachi, T., Ichion, E., 2001b. Extent and Severity of Groundwater Arsenic Contamination in Bangladesh. Water Int. 26, 370–379.

Finnegan, P.M., Chen, W., 2012. Arsenic Toxicity: The Effects on Plant Metabolism. Front Physiol. 182, 1–18.

Fitz, W.J., Wenzel, W.W., Zhang, H., et al., 2003. Rhizosphere Characteristics of the Arsenic Hyper-accumulator *Pteris Vittata* L. and Monitoring of Phytoremoval Efficiency. Environ. Sci. Technol. 37 (21), 5008–5014.

Franseconi, K., Visootiviseth, P., Sridokchan, W., Goessler, W., 2002. Arsenic Species in an Arsenic Hyperaccumulating Fern, *Pityrogramma Calomonanos*: A Potential Phytoremediator of Arsenic-contaminated Soils. Sci. Total Environ. 284, 27–35.

Gani Molla, M.O., Islam, M.A., Hasanuzzaman, M., 2010. Identification of Arsenic Hyperaccumu-lating Plants for the Development of Phytomitigation Technology. J. Phytol. 2, 41–48.

Garbisu, C., Hernandez-Allica, J., Barrutia, O., Alkorta, I., Becerril, J.M., 2002. Phytoremediation: A Technology using Green Plants to Remove Contaminants from Polluted Areas. Rev. Environ. Health 17, 75–90.

Garg, N., Singla, P., 2011. Arsenic Toxicity in Crop Plants: Physiological Effects and Tolerance Mechanisms. Environ. Chem. Lett., 9, 303–321.

Garg, N., Singla, P., 2012. The Role of *Glomus Mosseae* on Key Physiological and Biochemical Parameters of Pea Plants Grown in Arsenic Contaminated Soil. Sci. Hortic. 143, 92–101.

Gasic, K., Korban, S.S., 2007. Transgenic Indian Mustard (*Brassica Juncea*) Plants Expressing an *Arabidopsis* Phytochelatin Synthase (*AtPCS1*) Exhibit Enhanced As and Cd Tolerance. Plant Mol. Biol. 64, 361–369.

Geng, C.N., Zhu, Y.G., Tong, Y.P., Smith, S.E., Smith, F.A., 2006. Arsenate (As) Uptake by and Distribution in two Cultivars of Winter Wheat (*Triticum Aestivum* L.). Chemosphere, 62, 608– 615.

Ghanem, M.E., van Elteren, J., Albacete, A., Quinet, M., Martinéz-Andújar, C., Kinet, J.M., Perez-Alfocea, F., Lutts, S., 2009. Impact of Salinity on Early Reproductive Physiology of Tomato (*Solanum Lycopersicum*) in Relation to a Heterogeneous Distribution of Toxic Ions in Flowers Organs. Funct. Plant Biol. 36, 125–136.

Gill, S.S., Tuteja, N., 2010. Reactive Oxygen Species and Antioxidant Machinery in Abiotic Stress Tolerance in Crop Plants. Plant Physiol. Biochem. 48, 909–930.

Goessler, W., Kuehnelt, D., 2002. Analytical Methods for the Determination of Arsenic and Arsenic Compounds in the Environment. In: Frankenberger Jr., W.T. (Ed.), "Environmental Chemistry of Arsenic". Marcel Dekker, New York, USA, pp. 27–50.

Gumaelius, L., Lahner, B., Salt, D.E., Banks, J.A., 2004. Arsenic Hyperaccumulation in Gametophytes of *Pteris Vittata*. A New Model System for Analysis of Arsenic Hyperaccumulation. Plant Physiol. 136, 3198–3208.

Gunes, A., Pilbeam, D.J., Inal, A., 2009. Effect of Arsenic–phosphorus Interaction on Arsenic-Induced Oxidative Stress in Chickpea Plants. Plant Soil 314, 211–220.

Guo, W., Zhang, J., Teng, M., Li, H., Wang, J., 2009. Arsenic Uptake is Suppressed in a rice Mutant Defective in Silicon Uptake. J. Plant Nutr. Soil Sci. 172, 867–874.

Gupta, D.K., Inouhe, M., Rodríguez-Serrano, M., Romero-Puertas, M.C., Sandalio, L.M., 2013. Oxidative Stress and Arsenic Toxicity: Role of NADPH Oxidases. Chemosphere 90, 1987–1996.

Gupta, M., Sharma, P., Sarin, N.B., Sinha, A.K., 2009. Differential Response of Arsenic Stress in two Varieties of *Brassica Juncea* L. Chemosphere 74, 1201–1208.

Gusman, G.S., Oliveira, J.A., Farnese, F.S., Cambraia, J., 2013. Arsenate and Arsenite: The Toxic Effects on Photosynthesis and Growth of Lettuce Plants. Acta Physiol. Plant 35, 1201–1209.

Harvey, C.F., Swartz, C.H., Badruzzaman, A.B.M., Et Al., 2005. Groundwater Arsenic Contamination on the Ganges Delta: Biogeochemistry, Hydrology, Human Perturbations, and Human Suffering on a Large Scale. C.R. Geosci. 337, 285–296.

Hasanuzzaman, M., Fujita, M., 2012. Heavy Metals in the Environment: Current Status, Toxic Effects on Plants and Possible Phytoremediation. In: Anjum, N.A., Pereira, M.A., Ahmad, I., Duarte, A.C., Umar, S., Khan, N.A. (Eds.), Phytotechnologies: Remediation of Environmental Contaminants. Taylor and Francis/CRC Press, USA, pp. 7–73.

Hasanuzzaman, M., Fujita, M., 2013. Exogenous Sodium Nitroprusside Alleviates Arsenic-Induced Oxidative Stress in Wheat (*Triticum Aestivum* L.) Seedlings by Enhancing Antioxidant Defense and Glyoxalase System. Ecotoxicol. 22, 584–596.

Hasanuzzaman, M., Nahar, K., Fujita, M., Ahmad, P., Chandna, R., Prasad, M.N.V., Ozturk, M., 2013. Enhancing Plant Productivity under Salt Stress: Relevance of Polyomics. In: Ahmad, P., Azooz, M., Prasad, M.N.V. (Eds.), Salt Stress in Plants. Signalling, Omics and Adaptations, Springer, New York, pp. 113–156.

Health, M.R., 2013. Maine Rural Health Association 2013 Outstanding Service Award. Available at http://www.maineruralhealth.org/award.htm (Accessed 10.22.13).

Hironaka, H., Ahmad, S.A., 2003. Arsenic Concentration of Rice in Bangladesh. In: Ahmed, M.F. (Ed.), International Symposium on Fate of Arsenic in The Environment. BUET, Dhaka, Bangladesh, pp. 123–130.

Hossain, A., Joardar, J.C., Imamul Huq, S.M., 2006. Comparison of Arsenic Accumulation by two Ferns: *Pteris Vittata* and *Nephrodium Molle*. Dhaka Univ. J. Biol. Sci. 15, 95–103.

Hossain, M.Z., 2012. Bioremediation of Arsenic: Prospects and Limitations in the Agriculture of Bangladesh. Int. J. Econ. Env. Geol. 3, 6–14.

Huang, J.W., Poynton, C.Y., Kochian, L.V., Elless, M.P., 2004. Phytofiltration of Arsenic from Drinking Water using Arsenic-Hyperaccumulating Ferns. Environ. Sci. Technol. 38, 3412–3417.

Hughes, M.F., Beck, B.D., Chen, Y., Lewis, A.S., Thomas, D.J., 2011. Arsenic Exposure and Toxicology: A Historical Perspective. Toxicol. Sci. 123, 305–332.

Huq, S.M.I., 2008. Fate of Arsenic in Irrigation Water and its Potential Impact on The Food Chain. In: Ahuja, S. (Ed.), Arsenic Contamination of Groundwater: Mechanism, Analysis, and Remediation. Wiley, New Jersey, pp. 23–49.

Huq, S.M.I., Naidu, R., 2003. Arsenic in Groundwater of Bangladesh: Contamination in The Food Chain. In: Ahmed, M.F. (Ed.), Arsenic Contamination: Bangladesh Perspective. ITN-Bangladesh, Bangla-desh University of Engineering and Technology, Dhaka, Bangladesh, pp. 203–226.

Huq, S.M.I., Abdullah, M.B., Joardar, J.C., 2007. Bioremediation of Arsenic Toxicity by Algae in Rice Culture. Land Contam. Reclam. 15, 327–333.

Huq, S.M.I., Shila, U.K., Joardar, J.C., 2006. Arsenic Mitigation Strategy for Rice, using Water Regime Management. Land Contam. Reclam. 14, 805–814.

Huq, S.M.I., Rahman, A., Sultana, S., Naidu, R., 2003. Extent and Severity of Arsenic Contamination in Soils of Bangladesh. In: Ahmed, F., Ali, M.A., Adeal, Z. (Eds.), Fate of Arsenic in the Environment. Preprints of BUET-UNU International Symposium, Dhaka, Bangladesh, pp. 69–84.

Huq, S.M.I., Bulbul, A., Choudhury, M.S., Alam, S., Kawai, S., 2005. Arsenic Bioaccumulation in a Green Alga and its Subsequent Recycling in Soil of Bangladesh. In: Bundschuh, J., Bhattacharya, P. (Eds.), Proceeding of Natural Arsenic in Groundwater: Occurrence, Remediation and Management. Balkema, New York, USA, pp. 119–124.

Irgolic, K.J., Greschonig, H., Howard, A.G., 1995. Arsenic. In: Townshend, A. (Ed.), The Encyclopedia of Analytical Science, 1995. Academic Press, pp. 168–184.

Islam, M.R., Jahiruddin, M., 2010. Effects of Arsenic and its Interaction with Phosphorus on Yield and Arsenic Accumulation in Rice. 19th World Congress of Soil Science, Soil Solutions for a Changing World. 1–6 August 2010. Brisbane, Australia. Published on DVD.

Islam, M.R., Jahiruddin, M., Rahman, G.K.M.M., Miah, M.A.M., Farid, A.T.M., Panaullah, G.M., Loeppert, R.H., Duxbury, J.M., Meisner, C.A., 2005. Arsenic in Paddy Soils of Bangladesh: Levels, Distribution and Contribution of Irrigation and Sediments. In: Behavior of Arsenic in Aquifers, Soils and Plants (Conference Proceedings). Dhaka.

Islam, M.S., Wahid-Uz-Zaman, M., Rahman, M., 2013. Phytoaccumulation of Arsenic from Arsenic Contaminated Soils by *Eichhornia Crassipes* L., *Echinochloa Crus-galli* L. and *Monochoria Has-tata* L. Bangladesh. Int. J. Environ. Protec. 3, 17–27.

Islam, S.M.A., Fukushi, K., Yamamoto, K., 2004. Severity of Arsenic Concentration in Soil and Arsenic-rich Sludge of Bangladesh and Potential of their Biological Removal: A Novel Approach for Tropical Region. Proc. Second Intl. Symp. Southeast Asian Water Environ. Hanoi, Vietnam.

Jain, M., Gadre, R.P., 2004. Inhibition of 5-amino Levulinic Acid Dehydratase Activity by Arsenic in Excised Etiolated Maize Leaf Segments during Greening. J. Plant Physiol. 161, 251–255.

Jankong, P., Visoottiviseth, P., 2008. Effects of Arbuscular Mycorrhizal Inoculation on Plants Growing on Arsenic Contaminated Soil. Chemosphere 72, 1092–1097.

Jin, J.W., Xu, Y.F., Huang, Y.F., 2010. Protective Effect of Nitric Oxide Against Arsenic-induced Oxidative Damage in Tall Fescue Leaves. Afr. J. Biotechnol. 9, 1619–1627.

Juzl, M., Stefl, M., 2002. The Effect of Leaf Area Index on Potatoes in Soils Contaminated by Some Heavy Metals. Rostlinna Vyroba 48, 298–306.

Kachenko, A.G., Bhatia, N.P., Singh, B., Siegele, R., 2007. Arsenic Hyperaccumulation and Local-ization in the Pinnule and Stipe Tissues of the Gold-dust Fern (*Pityrogramma Calomelanos*) (L.) Link Var. Austroamericana (Domin) Farw. using Quantitative Micro-PIXE Spectroscopy. Plant and Soil 300, 207–219.

Kachout, S.S., Mansoura, A.B., Leclerc, J.C., Mechergui, R., Rejeb, M.N., Ouerghi, Z., 2010. Effects of Heavy Metals on Antioxidant Activities of: *Atriplex Hortensis* and *A. Rosea*. EJEAFChe 9, 444–457.

Karimi, N., Ghaderian, S.M., Raab, A., Feldmann, J., Meharg, A.A., 2009. An Arsenic Accumulating, Hyper Tolerant Brassica, Isatis Cappadocica. New Phytol. 184, 41–47.

Kertulis-Tartar, G.M., Rathinasabapathi, B., Maa, L.Q., 2009. Characterization of Glutathione Reductase and Catalase in the Fronds of two *Pteris Ferns* upon Arsenic Exposure. Plant Physiol. Biochem. 47, 960–965.

Kertulis-Tartar, G.M., Ma, L.Q., Tu, C., Chirenje, T., 2006. Phytoremediation of an Arsenic Contaminated Site using *Pteris Vittata* L.: A two-year Study. Int. J. Phytorem. 8, 311–322.

Khan, I., Ahmad, A., Iqbal, M., 2009. Modulation of Antioxidant Defence System for Arsenic Detoxification in Indian Mustard. Ecotoxicol. Environ. Saf. 72, 626–634.

Klump, S., Kipfer, R., Cirpka, O.A., et al., 2006. Groundwater Dynamics and Arsenic Mobilization in Bangladesh Assessed using Noble Gases and Tritium. Environ. Sci. Technol. 40, 243–250.

Knudson, J.A., Meikle, T., DeLuca, T.H., 2003. Role of Mycorrhizal Fungi and Phosphorus in the Arsenic Tolerance of Basin Wildrye. J. Environ. Qual. 32, 2001–2006.

Krämer, U., 2005. Phytoremediation: Novel Approaches to Cleaning up Polluted Soils. Curr. Opin. Biotechnol. 16, 133–141.

Kvesitadze, G., Khatisashvili, G., Sadunishvili, T., Ramsden, J.J. (Eds.), 2006. Biochemical Mechanisms of Detoxification in Higher Plants. Springer, Berlin.

Laizu, J., 2007. Speciation of Arsenic in Vegetables and their Correlation with Inorganic Phosphate Level. Bangladesh. J. Pharmacol. 2, 88–94.

Lal, N., 2010. Molecular Mechanisms and Genetic Basis of Heavy Metal Toxicity and Tolerance in Plants. In: Ashraf, M., Ozturk, M., Ahmad, M.S.A. (Eds.), Plant Adaptation and Phytoremedia-tion. Springer, Dordrecht, pp. 35–58.

Lei, M., Wan, X.M., Huang, Z.C., Chen, T.B., Li, X.W., Liu, Y.R., 2012. First Evidence on Different Transportation Modes of Arsenic and Phosphorus in Arsenic Hyperaccumulator. *Pteris Vittata*. Environ. Pollut. 161, 1–7.

Leterrier, M., Airaki, M., Palma, J.M., Chaki, M., Barroso, J.B., Corpas, F.J., 2012. Arsenic Triggers the Nitric Oxide (NO) and S-nitrosoglutathione (GSNO) Metabolism in *Arabidopsis*. Environ. Pollut. 166, 136–143.

Li, C., Feng, S., Shao, Y., Jiang, L., Lu, X., Hou, X., 2007. Effect of Arsenic on Seed Germination and Physiological Activities of Wheat Seedlings. J. Environ. Sci. 19, 725–732.

Li, X.W., Lei, M., Chen, T.B., Wan, X.M., 2009. Roles of Sulfur in the Arsenic Tolerant Plant *Adiantum Capillus-Veneris* and The Hyperaccumulator *Pteris Vittata*. J. Korean Soc. Appl. Biol. Chem. 52, 498–502.

Liao, X.Y., Chen, T.B., Xie, H., Liu, Y.R., 2005. Soil As Contamination and its Risk Assessment in Areas Near the Industrial Districts of Chenzhou City, Southern China. Environ. Intl. 31, 791–798.

Liu, Q.J., Zheng, C.N., Hu, C.X., Tan, Q.L., Sun, X.C., Su, J.J., 2012. Effects of High Concentrations of Soil Arsenic on the Growth of Winter Wheat (*Triticum Aestivum* L) and Rape (*Brassica Napus*). Plant Soil Environ. 58, 22–27.

Long, L.K., Yao, Q., Guo, J., Yang, R.H., Huang, Y.H., Zhu, H.H., 2010. Molecular Community Analysis of Arbuscular Mycorrhizal Fungi Associated with five Selectged Plant Species form Heavy Metal Polluted Soils. Eur. J. Soil Biol. 46, 288–294.

Low, K.S., Lee, C.K., Tai, C.H., 1994. Biosorption of Copper by Water Hyacinth Roots. J. Environ. Sci. Health 29, 171.

Leung, M., 2004. Bioremediation: Techniques for Cleaning up a Mess. J. Biotech. 2, 18–22.

Luongo, T., Ma, L.Q., 2005. Characteristics of Arsenic Accumulation by *Pteris* and Non-*Pteris Ferns*. Plant Soil 277, 117–126.

Lyubenova, L., Schröder, P., 2010. Uptake and Effect of Heavy Metals on the Plant Detoxification Cascade in the Presence and Absence of Organic Pollutants. In: Sherameti, I., Varma, A. (Eds.), Soil Heavy Metals. Soil Biol, 9. Springer, Berlin Heidelberg, pp. 65–85.

Ma, L.Q., Komar, K.M.M., Tu, C., Zhang, W., Cai, Y., Kenence, E.D., 2001. A Fern that Hyperaccumulates As. Nature Lond 409, 579.

Ma, J.F., Yamaji, N., Mitani, N., Xu, X.Y., Su, Y.H., McGrath, S.P., Zhao, F.J., 2008. Transporters of Arsenite in Rice and their Role in Arsenic Accumulation in rice Grain. Proc. Natl. Acad. Sci. USA 105, 9931–9935.

Mahimairaja, S., Bolan, N.S., Adriano, D.C., Robinson, B., 2005. Arsenic Contamination and its Risk Management in Complex Environmental Settings. Adv. Agron. 86, 1–82.

Mahmud, R., Inoue, N., Kasajima, S., Shaheen, R., 2007. Effect of Soil Arsenic on Yield and As and P Distribution Pattern Among Plant Organs of Buckwheat and Castor Oil Plant. Proceedings of the 10th International Symposium on Buckwheat. Section D Physiology and Cultivation.

Malik, J.A., Goel, S., Kaur, N., Sharma, S., Singh, I., Nayyar, H., 2012. Selenium Antagonises the Ttoxic Effects of Arsenic on Mungbean (*Phaseolus Aureus* Roxb.) Plants by Restricting its Uptake and Enhancing the Antioxidative and Detoxification Mechanisms. Environ. Exp. Bot. 77, 242–248.

Mallick, S., Sinam, G., Sinha, S., 2011. Study on Arsenate Tolerant and Sensitive Cultivars of *Zea Mays* L. Differential Detoxification Mechanism and Effect on Nutrients Status. Ecotoxicol. Environ. Saf. 74, 1316–1324.

Mandal, B.K., Suzuki, K.T., 2002. Arsenic Round the World: A review. Talanta 58, 201–235.

Marques, I.A., Anderson, L.E., 1986. Effects of Arsenite, Sulfite, and Sulfate on Photosynthetic Carbon Metabolism in Isolated Pea (*Pisum Sativum* L., cv Little Marvel) Chloroplasts. Plant Physiol. 82, 488–493.

Mateos-Naranjo, E., Andrades-Moreno, L., Redondo-Gómez, S., 2012. Tolerance to and Accu-Mulation of Arsenic in the Cordgrass *Spartina Densiflora* Brongn. Bioresour. Technol. 104, 187–194.

Matschullat, J., Perobelli Borba, R., Deschamps, E., Figueiredo, B.R., Gabrio, T., Schwenk, M., 2000. Human and Environmental Contamination in The Iron Quadrangle, Brazil. Appl. Geo-chem. 15, 181–190.

Mazej, Z., Germ, M., 2009. Trace Element Accumulation and Distribution in four Aquatic Macrophytes. Chemosphere 74, 642–647.

Megharaja, M., Ragusa, S.R., Naidu, R., 2003. Metal–algae Interactions: Implication of Bioavail-ability. In: Naidu, R., Gupta, V.V.V.S.R., Rogers, S., Kookana, R.S., Bolan, N.S., Adriano, D.C. (Eds.), Bioavailability, Toxicity and Risk Relationships in Ecosystems. Science Publishers, Enfield, New Hampshire, UK, pp. 109–144.

Meharg, A., Jardine, L., 2003. Arsenite Transport into Paddy Rice (*Oryza Sativa*) Roots. New Phytol. 157, 39–44.

Meharg, A.A., Hartley-Whitaker, J., 2002. Arsenic Uptake and Metabolism in Arsenic Resistant and Non-resistant Plant Species. Tansley Rev. New Phytol. 154, 29–43.

Meharg, A.A., Macnair, M.R., 1992. Suppression of the High Affinity Phosphate Uptake System a Mechanism of Arsenate Tolerance in *Holcus Lanatus* L. J. Exp. Bot. 43, 519–524.

Meharg, A.A., Rahman, M.M., 2003. Arsenic Contamination of Bangladesh Paddy Field Soils: Implications for Rice Contribution to Arsenic Consumption. Environ. Sci. Technol. 37, 229–234.

Mishra, S., Srivastava, S., Tripathi, R.D., Dwivedi, S., Trivedi, P.K., 2008. Thiol Metabolism and Antioxidant Systems Complement Each Other During Arsenate Detoxification in *Ceratophyllum Demersum* L. Aquat. Toxicol. 86, 205–215.

Miteva, E., Peycheva, S., 1999. Arsenic Accumulation and Effect on Peroxidase Activity in Green Bean and Tomatoes. Bulg. J. Agric. Sci. 5, 737–740.

Mittler, R., Vanderauwera, S., Gollery, M., Van Breusegem, F., 2004. Reactive Oxygen Gene Network of Plants. Trends Plant Sci. 9, 490–498.

Mkandawire, M., Dudel, G., 2005. Accumulation of Arsenic in *Lemna Gibba* (Duckweed) in Tailing Waters of two Abandoned Uranium Mining Sites in Saxony, Germany. Sci. Total Environ. 336, 81–89.

Soil Environment and Conservation **Pages 187-197**
Edited by: Dr. Ashok K. Rathoure; Dr. Pawan Kumar 'Bharti' and Dr. Alka Chauhan
ISBN: 978-93-88854-10-8
Edition: 2019
Published by: Discovery Publishing House Pvt. Ltd., New Delhi (India)

10

Soil Sampling, Analysis and Rock Phosphate Amendments

[1]Dr. Ashok K. Rathoure

ABSTRACT

Soil plays a vital role in supporting the growth of crops and other vegetation maintaining the environment clean and act as source and sink for atmospheric gases. Soils are natural bodies on which plant grow. The increasing population, industrialization and changing life style have negative effect on soil and responsible for soil pollution. Good soil and climate for more crop production are valuable things for any nation. Soil amendments can be used to cost-effectively reduce the bioavailability and mobility of toxic metals in contaminated soils. Organic amendments considerably affect nutrient balance and interaction mobility of nutrients by influencing the chemical, physical, and biological environment in soils. Here in this chapter, we have discussed the soil, its profile & type, analysis, benefits on rock phosphate amendments.

Keywords: Amelioration, Fertility Index, Soil, Rock Phosphate.

Introduction

Soil is the summation of natural bodies in the earth's surface, which contain living matter and supports or capable of supporting plants out-of-doors. To sum it up, it can be understood as a layer of earth crust that is thin and serves as a natural nutrient medium for the plant growth. One should study soil as it is being used as a rich medium responsible for the growth of plants and trees that provides a niche for biotic as well as abiotic interaction. Such study of soil profile from silvi-culture and crop husbandry point of view is important as, it reveals the characteristics of surface and sub-surface as also different qualities of soil namely, depth, texture, structure, drainage conditions and soil moisture relationship directly affecting the plant growth. Soil is also an unconsolidated mineral matter that is inveigled by genetic and environmental factors like- parent material, climate, organisms and topography all acting over a period of time. Soil properties differ in various ways such as physical, chemical, biological and morphological properties from the parent material. Based on

[1] Independent Researcher, Eco Chem Sales & Services, Surat (GJ) India

the differences in genetic and environmental factors, there are different types of modified soils present such as red, black, deep shallow, coarse textured and fine textured. Soil provides water as well as a reservoir of nutrients in variety of crops, which are helpful in providing mechanical anchorage and favorable tilt. The different components of soils such as matrix of mineral, water, organic matter and air, vary in proportions for the growth of plant.

Soil Profile and Classification

Soil profile can be studied vertically through the soil area. It is normally regarded as a plane at right angles to the surface. In practice, a description of a soil profile comprises soil properties that can be determined only by examining volumes of soil. A description of a pedon is normally based on examination of a profile, and the properties of the pedon are expected from the properties of the profile. The width of a profile ranges from a few decimeters to several meters or more. It shall be adequate to include the largest structural units. A soil horizon is a parallel layer to the soil surface which can be distinguished by the adjacent layers through a characteristic set of properties, which is produced by the processes of soil formation.

Soil texture act as an important part in management of nutrients because it impacts retention of nutrient, for example, soils with fine texture tend to have greater ability to store soil nutrients. The simplest method of determining the type of soil is by simply feeling it to determine texture and predicting about primary makeup of the soil is. To perform the task, a baseball size portion of the soil is grabbed in hands and wetted with water, while working the moist soil with hands. The stickier it is, the more clay there is. The soapier the soil feels, the higher the silt content. Grittiness is representative of sand. Particle size distribution has an important impact on permeability of soil or water intake rate, water storage capacity ability to aggregate, crushing and the chemical makeup of the soil. The value of land, land use capability and soil management practices are largely determined by the texture.

Salinity and alkalinity in soil happens in arid and semi-arid regions, where precipitation is inadequate to meet evapo-transpiration needs of plants, and the salts move up to the surface. Salt affected soils are present inside irrigated lands. Salt accumulation happens through irrigation water and over-irrigation. The salt content in soil is measured in terms of electrical conductivity.

The classification of soil as per colour and texture is as follows:

Red Soil: Red colour is due to presence of various oxides of iron. The soils are poor in nitrogen, phosphorus and potassium and with pH of 7 to 7.5. The red color is due to the diffusion of iron in soil profile. These soils are light textured with porous structure. Lime is absent with low soluble salts *e.g. alfisol, inceptisol* and *ultisol.*

Lateritic Soil: This type of soil is seen in those areas which have high rainfall. Under high rainfall conditions silica is released and leached downwards and the upper horizons of soils become rich in oxides of iron and aluminum. It is comprised of a mixture of hydrated oxides of aluminum and iron with small amounts of manganese oxide. The texture is light with free drainage structure. Clay is predominant and lime is deficient. The pH ranges from 5 to 6 with low in base exchange capacity, contained more humus and are well drained *e.g. alfisol, ultisol* and *oxisol.*

Black Soil: Black soil is characterized by dark grey to black colour with high clay content; the soils are neutral to slightly alkaline in reaction. It has a high proportion of calcium and magnesium carbonates and has a high degree of fertility. There are occurrences of deep cracks, which are developed during summer; the depth of the soil varies from less than a meter to several meters. This type of soil is rich in lime and potash and hence has high pH, examples are *vertisol, inceptisol* and *entisol.*

Alluvial Soil: This type of soil is considered as the most important soil from the agriculture point of view. The soils range from sandy loam to clay loam with light grey colour to dark colour; structure is loose and more fertile. But the soils are low in Nitrogen, Phosphorus, Potassium and Humus. Alluvial soil is considered as the largest and the most important group of soils. The soil is well supplied with lime and pH ranges from 7 to 8, examples include *entesol, inceptisol* and *alfisol.*

Desert Soil: The soils are mostly sandy to loamy fine sand with brown to yellow colour; it contains large amounts of soluble salts and lime with pH ranging 8.0 to 8.5. Nitrogen content is very low. The presence of Phosphate and Nitrate make the desert soils fertile and productive under supply of water. They occur mostly in dry areas and their important content is quartz *e.g.* entisol and aridisol.

Forest and Hill Soils: Soils are dark brown with more sub-soil humus content. They are more acidic. It has high organic matter *e.g.* alfisol.

Problem Soils: The soils which owe characteristics that they cannot be economically used for the cultivation of crops without adopting proper reclamation measures are known as problem soils.

Sampling Techniques

The soil sampling techniques of soil would vary depending on the soil type and their characteristics. Proper location of sampling points and auxiliary equipment is thus very important. Sampling strategies are developed by the project team to satisfy project-specific data needs that are identified in the technical planning process. Sampling strategies may also be significantly influenced by factors such as matrix and contaminant characteristics, physical site constraints, safety, and cost. Soil sampling poses a variety of challenges due to the natural variability of the media, and the logistical problems of sampling at increased depths. Additionally, the particle size distribution of the soils must be evaluated. The technical planning process that results in the development of the sampling strategy is critical because of difficulties in acquiring representative samples, the reduction of action levels, and the problems associated with trace level cross-contamination. Development of a sampling scheme to characterize a study area should follow the successful sampling scheme. It requires a logical design to allow an evaluation of potential constituents in relation to background conditions, vertical extent, horizontal extent, and mobility in various media.

Sampling procedures for soil has different methods as follows:

Collection of Soil Samples with Trier

(*i*) The Trier should edge into the material to be sampled at a 0 to 45 angle from horizontal. This coordination reduces the spillage of sample.

(*ii*) The Trier should be rotate once or twice to cut a core of material.

(*iii*) The Trier is gradually removed such that the slot is facing upward.

(*iv*) When there is a requirement of Volatile Organic analyses, the sample is transferred into a suitable, labeled sample container with a stainless steel lab spoon or equivalent and tightly secures the cap. The remainder of the sample is placed into a stainless steel, plastic, or other appropriate homogenization container, and mixed thoroughly to obtain a homogenous sample representative of the entire sampling interval. Then, the sample are placed into appropriate, labeled containers and the caps are tightly secured; or, if composite samples are to be accumulated then a sample is placed from another sampling interval into the homogenization container and mixed thoroughly. When compositing is complete, the sample is placed into appropriate, labeled containers and the caps are tightly secured.

Collection of Samples with Auger

(*i*) The auger must be attached to a drill rod extension, and the T handle to the drill rod.

(*ii*) The area to be sampled is first cleaned and made free from surface debris such as twigs, rocks, and litter.

(*iii*) It is recommended to remove the surface soil for an area around six inches in radius around the drilling location.

(*iv*) The auguring is started, and then intermittently removed and accumulated soils are deposited on top of plastic sheet spread near the hole. This avoids accidental brushing of loose material back down the borehole when removing the auger or adding drill rods.

(*v*) The Auger is removed with care from the hole after achieving desired depth. When sampled directly from the auger, the sample is collected after the auger is removed from the hole.

(*vi*) The auger tip is then taken away and replaced with a pre-cleaned thin wall tube sampler. Proper cutting tip is installed.

(*vii*) It is then lowered into the tube sampler and progressively forced into the soil. The scrapping of borehole sides must be avoided. Hammering threads are avoided as the vibrations may cause the boring walls to collapse.

(*viii*) The tube sampler is then removed and the drill rods unscrewed.

(*ix*) The cutting tip and also the core are removed from the device.

(*x*) The top of the core (~ 1 inch) is discarded as this represents material collected before penetration of the concerned layer. The rest of the core is placed into the appropriate labeled sample container. Sample homogenization is not necessary here.

(*xi*) If volatile organic analysis is to be performed, the sample is transferred into an appropriate, labeled sample container with a stainless steel lab spoon or equivalent and the cap is tightly secured. The rest of the sample is placed into a stainless steel, plastic, or another appropriate homogenization container and mixed thoroughly to gain a homogenous sample representative of the entire sampling interval. The sample is then placed into appropriate, labeled containers and the caps tightly secured.

(*xii*) The hole is refilled depending upon its depth. Generally, shallow holes can simply be backfilled with the removed soil material.

Collection of Samples with Scoops and Shovels

(*i*) Vegetation and the top layer of soil can be removed by using pre-cleaned stainless steel scoop or trowel.

The soil is further loosened to the required volume.

(*ii*) The distinct grab sample is then transferred into container.

(*iii*) For composite sample, sole stainless steel or glass mixing or any other appropriate container must be used and tools such as stainless steel spoon, trowel, or pestle must be used for collection.

(*iv*) The sample containers must be marked while soil sample data sheets mentioning depth, location, color other observations, are filled up.

(*v*) The glass sample containers must be placed in sealed plastic bags and packed into an iced shipping container. Samples must be compulsorily cooled and maintained at 4°C as soon as possible.

(*vi*) The cycle of custody and shipping must be finish as fast as possible to reduce its holding time. When the sample arrives at laboratory, it should be within the holding time.

Collection of Samples with Split Spoon (Barrel) Sampler

(*i*) The sampler is assembled by aligning both the sides of barrel and screwing the drive shoe to the bottom and the head piece on top.

(*ii*) The sampler is then placed in a perpendicular position to the sample material.

(*iii*) The well ring should be good to drive the tube. However, it should not drive past the bottom of the head piece; otherwise it may result in compression of the sample.

(*iv*) The length of the tube is then penetrated into the material to be sampled, and the number of blows recorded to get to this depth.

(*v*) The sampler is then withdrawn and opened by unscrewing the bit and head and splitting the barrel. The amount of recovery and soil type is recorded on the boring log. In case a split sample is required, cleaned, stainless steel knife is used to divide the tube contents in half, longitudinally.

(*vi*) The core is transferred without disturbing to an appropriate labeled sample container(s) and sealed tightly.

Sampling at Depth with Augers and Thin Wall Tube Samplers

(*i*) It employs use of an auger, or a thin-wall tube sampler, a series of extensions, and "T" handles. The auger is used to bore a hole to a desired sampling depth, and then withdrawn. The sample can be collected directly from the auger.

(*ii*) The core of sample can be collected by replacing the auger tip with a thin wall tube sampler. It is then lowered down the system into the borehole, and driven into the soil to the completion depth.

(*iii*) There are several types of augers available; which includes bucket type, continuous flight (screw), and post-hole augers. Bucket type augers are better for direct sample recovery as they provide a large volume of sample in lesser time.

(*iv*) The continuous flight augers are useful in collecting the sample directly from the flights. Their use is satisfactory when a composite of the complete soil column is required. Post-hole augers have limited utility for sample collection as they are designed to cut through fibrous, rooted, swampy soil and cannot be used below a depth of approximately three feet.

Sampling Pattern

The sampling pattern should be selected to best represent the field, accounting for known sources of variability such as major soil type changes, past cropping patterns, etc. A grid pattern is usually the best way to be sure the entire field is represented, but with the possibility of patterns developing from past nutrient applications, cropping effects and other uniform patterns, it is advisable to use a sampling scheme that avoids arranging sampling points in a straight line. For conventional sampling, a common approach is to divide the field into cells of about 2 ½ to 5 acres, and collect 5 cores in a zigzag pattern within each cell to make up the sample. This area sampling method provides for fairly complete sampling of the field and a good estimate of the needs for a single uniform application rate to be applied to the entire field.

Sediment Collection Procedure

Grab samplers/Dredges are used for the collection of bottom sediment deposits, which are designed to recover sediment material from the top few centimeters of the lake/river bed. Grab samplers consist of either a set of jaws which are lowered to the surface of the bottom sediment or contain a bucket which rotates into the sediment upon reaching the bottom. The dredges usually have bevelled lips to scrap upper layers of the sediments. For special cases, the dredges may have teeth to plough the bottom and stir out burrowing molluscs, worms etc. The fine-grained bottom sediments are collected with Van Veen type of the sediment sampler. This device consists of two bowl-clamp shaped sections, which are held open by a catch. When the sampler touches the sediment, the catch is released and the bowl shape sections close together, trapping sediment from a penetration depth of about 20 cm. For general operational suitability of Grab samplers, there are some properties needed for it, such as stability and capability to prevent sample loss from washout. Also sample volume must be considered while choosing a surface sediment sampler. The bottom sediment sampler devices are widely used variety which is designed for biological and geological studies mainly in marine environment. Other than this, they can also be used in pollution studies in the marine and freshwater environment.

Soil Analysis

Parameters for Soil Analysis

Primary Nutrients: The primary nutrients, Nitrogen (N), Phosphorous (P) and Potassium (K) are essential elements for crop growth. The application of commercial N, P and K fertilizers has contributed to a tremendous increase in yields of agricultural crops that feed the world's population. However, excessive use of these fertilizers has been cited as a source of contamination of surface and ground water. Ideally, application rates should be adjusted based on estimates of the requirements for optimum production at each location because there is high spatial variability of N, P and K within individual agricultural fields. A healthy soil produces healthy crops. Maintaining a healthy soil demands care and effort from farmers. Nitrogen is an important for a growth because it is a major part of all amino acids, which are the building blocks of all proteins, including the enzymes which control virtually all biological processes. A good supply of nitrogen stimulates root growth and development, as well as the uptake of other nutrients. Phosphorous enhances many aspects of plant physiology, including the fundamental processes of photosynthesis, nitrogen fixation, flowering, fruiting and maturation. In plant, it is present mainly as a structural component of the nucleic acid, deoxyribonucleic acid (DNA) and ribose nucleic acid (RNA). It is present in both organic and inorganic forms, both of which are readily translocated within the plant. All energy transfers in the cell are critically dependent on phosphorous. Phosphorous is concentrated at the most actively growing points of a plant and stored within seeds in anticipation of their germination. Phosphorous is available to plants in limited quantities in most soils because it is released very slowly from insoluble phosphates and is rapidly fixed once again. Potassium occurs in all parts of plants in substantial amounts. Potassium is important in leaves and at growing points. It is outstanding among the nutrient elements for its mobility and solubility within plant tissue. Potassium regulates the opening and closing of the stomata by a potassium ion pump.

Secondary Nutrients: Secondary and micronutrients are important in enhancing crop productivity. Calcium (Ca), Magnesium (Mg) and Sulphur (S) are secondary macro nutrients. The measure source for supplementing the soil with calcium is dolometic lime (aglime). Calcium is also available from variety of fertilizer source *i.e.* Gypsum (Calcium Sulphate$CaSO_4$, 22.5 %Ca). It is used as secondary nutrients. Calcium is component of plant cell wall and regulates the cell wall construction. Calcium deficiency is uncommon in monotona and Wyoming areas due to presence of Calcium carbonate and gypsum in most agriculture soil. In sufficient Ca cause young leaves to become distorted and turn abnormally dark green. Leaf tips often become dry or brittle and will eventually wither and die. Stems are weak and germination is poor. The predominant role of Mg is as a major constituent of the chlorophyll molecule and it is therefore actively involved in photosynthesis and it also assists the movement of sugars within a plant. Sulphur is the secondary nutrients it requires in the smaller amount than the primary nutrient. It is essential constituents of certain amino acids and proteins. It is available in fertilizers such as potassium and magnesium sulphate, Gypsum (Calcium sulphate) and elemental sulphur. The deficiency symptoms initially occur in younger leaves, causing them to turn light green to yellow (chlorosis). In later growth the entire plant may be pale green. Characteristic spot or strips are generally not displayed. Additionally plant deficient in sulphur tends to be spindly, small and stems are often thin.

Micro Nutrients: The micro nutrients are Boron (B), Chlorine (Cl), Copper(Cu), Iron(Fe), Molybdenum and Zinc (Zn).These plant food elements are used in very small amounts, but they are just as important to plant development. Boron is essential for the movement and metabolism of sugar in the plant and synthesis of plant harmonic and nucleic acids. It also functions in the lignin formation of cell walls. Chlorine is necessary for osmosis and ionic balance; it also plays a role in photosynthesis. Copper is a formation of cell walls involved in the photosynthesis respiration and processes within the plant involving nitrogen. Iron is involved in photosynthesis, respiration and chlorophyll formation and many enzymatic reactions. Molybdenum is involved in nitrogen fixation and nitrification. Zinc is a component of organic complexes and DNA proteins. It is an important enzyme for protein synthesis. Zinc is evolved in the growth of harmonic production and seed development. Manganese is a component of enzymes and is also involved in photosynthesis and root growth. It is also involved in nitrogen fixation (Ashvini *et al.,* 2016).

Rock Phosphate Amendments

Rock phosphate, a naturally occurring mineral source of phosphate, could serve as an alternative source of phosphorus in developing countries. It has been found to be much less expensive than soluble phosphorus fertilizers (Lorion, 2004). However, rock phosphate material has poor solubility when used as a fertilizer in soils. The rock phosphate can be finding in three forms viz. colloidal phosphate, soft rock phosphate and hard rock phosphate. These minerals release a small percentage of their phosphorus each year, the colloidal phosphate a bit faster than the others. These rocks also contain micronutrients. Treating rock phosphate with organic materials is found to be a technique for enhancing the solubility and the subsequent availability to plants of phosphorus (Zapata and Roy, 2004). Several studies have been conducted on amending rock phosphates to enhance their rate of dissolution after application to soils. The incorporation of agricultural wastes like poultry manure and cow dung with rock phosphate significantly improved the release of P and performance of crops (Singh and Amberger, 1990; Akande et.al. 2005; Akande et.al. 2008).

Compositing of rock phosphates with agricultural wastes is known to increase solubility of rock phosphates (Bangar *et al.,* 1985; Mey *et al.,* 1986; Mishra *et al.,* 1984; Mishra and Bangar, 1986; Kothandaraman, 1987; Singh and Amberger, 1990; Akande *et al.,* 1998). The content of P solubility of a given rock phosphate varies with the kind of organic material and the rate of decomposition (Banger *et al.,* 1985). Akande *et al.,* (2003) reported that okra growth and yield were significantly increased by the combined used of rock phosphate with either poultry manure and to a lesser degree urea compared to sole used of the materials. They also reported an increase in soil available P of between 112 and 115%, and 144 and 153%, respectively for a two year field trials(Morra *et al.*, 1991; Ben-Dor and Banin, 1995; Brunet *et al.*, 2007).

The immediate or short term effects of applied fertilizers are often emphasized to the neglect of residual effects. Yet when farming is continued on the same site for several years, residual effects of fertilizer treatments may considerably affect the soil chemical properties and consequently crop yield (Enwezor *et al.*, 1989). Reviewing residual effect of rock phosphates, Khasawneh and Doll (1978) did not confirm the common assumption that rock phosphates have greater residual effect than soluble phosphorus fertilizer. On the contrary, it appeared that the residual effects of soluble phosphorus fertilizer were greater than those of rock phosphate in the first 3 or 4 years after application.

Phosphorus-containing amendments were greatly concerned amendments on in situ remediation of metal contaminated soils. Rock phosphate can remove Pb, Zn, Cu and other heavy metalsfrom aqueous solutions (Xu *et al.*, 1994; Brown *et al.*, 2005; Ma *et al.*, 1997; Hettiarachchi and Pierzynski, 2002; Cao *et al.*, 2004; Ownby *et al.*, 2005; Chen *et al.*, 2006; 2007; 2009).

Conclusion

Growing concern about environmental pollution by excessive use of fertilizers lead to increases in needs to monitor soil nutrients required for crop growth. The sensor network technology will help the farmers to know the soil requirements which will help them take better decisions and preventive measures at the right time. To maintain the soil sustainability, it is urgently needed to popularize the amelioration techniques for soil amendments.

REFERENCES

Akande, M.O., Adediran, J. A., Oluwatoyinbo, F. I., 2005. Effect of Rock Phosphate Amended with Poultry Manure on Soil Available P and Yield of Maize and Cowpea. *African Journal of Biotechnology* 4: 444-448.

Akande, M.O., Oluwatoyinbo, F. I., Kayode, C. O., Olowookere, F. A., 2008. Response of Maize (*Zea mays*) and Okra (*Abelmoschusesculentus*) Intercrop Relayed with Cowpea (Vignaunguiculata) to Different Levels of Cow Dung Amended Phosphate Rock. *African Journal of Biotechnology* 7 (17): 3039-3043.

Ashwini A. Chitragar, Sneha M. Vasi, SujataNaduvinamani, Akshata J. Katigar and Taradevi I. Hulasogi (2016). Nutrients Detection in the Soil: Review Paper, *In*: International Journal on Emerging Technologies (Special Issue on ICRIET-2016) 7(2): 257-260.

Ben-Dor, E., Banin, A. (1995). Near-infrared Analysis as a Rapid Method to Simultaneously Evaluate Several Soil Properties. Soil Science of American Journal 59, 364–372.

Brunet, D., Barthes, B.G., Chotte, J.L., Feller, C. (2007). Determination of Carbon and Nitrogen Contents in Alfisols, Oxisols and Ultisols from Africa and Brazil using NIRS Analysis: Effects of Sample Grinding and Set Heterogeneity. Geoderma 139, 106–117.

Cao, X.D., Wahbic, A., Ma, L., Li , B., Yang, Y.L. (2009). Immobilization of Zn, Cu, and Pb in Contaminated Soils Using Phosphate Rock and Phosphoric Acid. Journal of Hazardous Materials. 164, 555-564.

Chen, S., Xu, M., Ma, Y., Yang, J. (2007). Evaluation of Different Phosphate Amendments on Availability of Metals in Contaminated Soil. Ecotoxicology and Environmental Safety. 67:278-285.

Chen, S.B., Chen, L., Ma, Y.B. (2009). Huang YZ. Can Phosphate Compounds be Used to Reduce the Plant Uptake of Pb and Resist the Pb Stress in Pb contaminated Soils? Journal of Environmental Sciences. 21:360-365.

Chen, S.B., Zhu, Y.G., Ma, Y.B. (2006). The Effect of Grain Size of Rock Phosphate Amendment on Metal Immobilization in Contaminated Soils. Journal of Hazardous Materials. 134:74-79.

Hettiarachchi, G.M., Pierzynski, G.M. (2002). In situ Stabilization of Soil Lead Using Phosphorus and Lorion, R.M., 2004. Rock Phosphate, Manure and Compost Use in Garlic and Potato Systems in a High Intermontane Valley in Bolivia. Available at: http://www.dissertations.wsu.edu/thesis/summer2004/r_lorion_071404.pdf.

Ma, L.Q., Rao, G.N. (1997). Effects of Phosphate Rock on Sequential Chemical Extraction of Lead in Contaminated Soils. Journal of Environmental Quality. 26, 788-796.

Manganese oxide: Influence of Plant Growth. Journal of Environmental Quality. 31, 564-572.

Morra, M.J., Hall, M.H., Freeborn, L.L. (1991). Carbon and Nitrogen Analysis of Soil Fractions Using Near-infrared Reflectance Spectroscopy. Soil Science Society of America Journal 55, 288–291.

Ownby, D.R., Belden, J.B., Lotufo, G.R., Lydy, M.J. (2005). Accumulation of Trinitrotoluene (TNT) in Aquatic Organisms: Part 1—Bioconcentration and Distribution in Channel Catfish (Ictaluruspunctatus).Chemosphere. 58, 1153-1159.

Singh, C.P., Amberger, A., 1990. Solubilization and Availability of Phosphorus During Decomposition of Rock Phosphate Enriched Straw and Urine. Biological Agriculture & Horticulture: An International Journal for Sustainable Production Systems 7: 261-269.

Soil Survey Staff (1993). Soil Survey Manual. Soil Conservation Service. U.S. Department of Agriculture Handbook 18. Archived from the Original on 2006-02-14. Retrieved 2006-07-02.

US EPA (2012). Environmental Response Team Soil Sampling Standard Operating Procedures.

Zapata F., Roy R.N., (2004). Use of Phosphate Rocks for Sustainable Agriculture. FAO Fertilizer and Plant Nutrition Bulletin 13, Rome.

Index